Religion and American Life:
Resources

Religion and American Life

Resources

Edited by
Anne T. Fraker

University of Illinois Press
Urbana and Chicago

© 1989 by the Board of Trustees of the University of Illinois
Manufactured in the United States of America
C 5 4 3 2 1

This book is printed on acid-free paper.

Library of Congress Cataloging-in-Publication Data

Religion and American life : resources / edited by Anne T. Fraker.
    p. cm.
    Includes indexes.
    ISBN 0–252–01588–6 (alk. paper)
    1. United States—Religion—Bibliography. 2. Bibliography—
Bibliography—Religion. I. Fraker, Anne T., 1946–
Z7757.U5R45 1989
[BL2525]
016.2'00973—dc19   88–19933
                                                        CIP

Contents

Introduction

Religion is important to people in all parts of the world. Practices and beliefs may vary, but most people possess some system of ritual and beliefs that binds them together, giving them a sense of meaning and purpose in life. The ways in which religion, certain brands of Christianity in particular, has been so readily integrated into the fabric of American society are especially notable. How ironic this is in view of the intent with which the founding fathers moved to assure a separation between church and state. Because this separation continues to be blurred and because religion continues to influence American life, scholars, clergy, and lay people have an ongoing interest in examining those influences and in discerning possible trends and implications for future days. If someone is interested in beginning to study religion and its impact on American culture, or if one wishes to refresh the mind about books and articles on this broad topic, where does the search begin?

Several bibliographies with the words *religion* and *America* in their titles already exist on library reference shelves. They cover a wide variety of subjects from specific topics such as politics or literature to all-inclusive, multivolume works presenting resources relevant to any number of perspectives on religion and America. In addition, there are other reference works that cover religion in all parts of the world with sections designated for America or North America. But when the question arises as to where one can go to find relevant literature about religion's influence on American life, there is no easy answer. One has had to search through the card catalogues and extant reference works to glean information about books and articles that contribute to the reader's understanding of religion's place in America. In order to fill this gap, this book includes annotations for a selection of books and articles that are central to any survey of questions regarding the significance of American religion, past and present.

This bibliography is intended to serve as the first tool in a student's search for answers to questions about America's religious underpinnings. The selections in this volume cover various topics from history to literature to philosophy. Although not exhaustive, the list of cited works is special because it includes outstanding pieces from numerous disciplines plus those that present diverse ways of looking at America, its place in the world, and the varied expressions of religion in assorted realms of the nation's life.

This collection of summaries and comments about significant books and articles represents the combined efforts of scholars and clergy from numerous institutions across the country. These people were participants in a two-year project at Indiana University-Purdue University at Indianapolis for which the main goal was to facilitate critical discussion about religion's role in American life with special attention given to the changing understandings of America's special place in the world. Four major themes guided the discussions: the depth and dynamism of religion in American public and private experience; the role and importance of personal and corporate expressions of the religious dimension in American self-definition; the place and significance of religion, past and present, in altering American self-understanding; and the character and continuity of America as a field for religious reimagination and renewal. Guided by these major themes, the discussants examined the manner in which religion's past influences are related to current perceptions, problems, and issues, and to the role they could play in the nation's future vision of itself. The participants also speculated about new ways in which history of religion in American life could be studied that in turn might bring about new understandings of the nation.

Based on these discussions, a search for relevant readings was initiated. This search began in the university library reference room and resulted in a list of several bibliographies to assist in the study of religion in America. However, a great degree of persistence is required to pick out from these bibliographies the works relevant to attaining an understanding of religion's place in American life. Although still useful, some of the resources are dated and do not meet the need for more contemporary information. For instance, the bibliography on religion and America listed in the valuable volume *A Religious History of the American People* by Sydney Ahlstrom (see p. 3), includes only eight relevant titles, some of them dating from the late 1800s up through the 1960s. More current resource books are available, but the older volumes are still heavily used as research tools. These volumes usually present short descriptions of the works mentioned, leaving the researcher with little idea about the relative merits of any reference cited. This bibliography addresses the task of presenting these materials in an evaluative context by presenting lengthier descriptions of and critical comments on each title as a means of offering the researcher helpful information for compiling a list of works for further study.

Two of the bibliographies covering the range of subjects related to religion and America are given detailed attention in the text of this volume. This is because these works possess special value for the researcher. *Religion in American Life* by Nelson Burr (see p. 18) includes important works with particular emphasis on social aspects of religion in the twentieth century. Each work is given one line of description. An earlier resource by Burr in collaboration with James W. Smith and A. Leland Jamison, entitled *A Critical Bibliography of Religion in America* (see p. 19), is a two-volume work of bibliographical essays on resources in all fields related to religion and America, such as historiography, general histories and surveys, sociology, religion and law, politics, education, social reform, and American theology.

Among the other bibliographies examined, a large volume with the title *Religion and Society in North America: An Annotated Bibliography*, edited by Robert deV. Brunkow, includes resources not only for the United States but also for Canada. It covers areas such as the arts, government and politics, missionaries, the occult, revivalism, social and economic reform, war, peace, and traditional and lesser-known religious groups. The annotations are reproduced abstracts of articles on religion printed between 1973 and 1980 drawn from a database of resources entitled *America: History and Life* (volumes 11--18).

Religious Books 1876–1982 is a massive work that requires a great deal of time to study. This multivolume work published by the R. R. Bowker Company includes three subject volumes supplemented with an author/title volume. Over 130,000 entries are included in this resource tool. The materials selected for these volumes were drawn from publication records of R. R. Bowker Company and reflect publishing in religious writing.

As noted earlier, the scope of the bibliographical volumes uncovered during the project's search reflects the diversity of the field of American religious studies. For instance, a bibliography with the broad title of *The Religious Heritage of America* by Albert M. Shulman is a resource book on religion, cults, and sects in America. A few works with general titles do include materials relevant to the study of religion and American life. For instance, *A Bibliography of Bibliographies in Religion* by John Graves Barrow lists all separately published bibliographies in religion for Europe and America under one cover. This work was published in 1955, however, and as a result lacks more recent research tools available to students. Another general bibliography, *The Religious Life of Man: A Guide to Basic Literature* by Leszek M. Karpinski, covers all types of religious traditions worldwide with short, descriptive entries for each resource. Volume two of *Bibliography of New Religious Movements in Primal Societies* by Harold W. Turner focuses on North America. In this volume, particular emphasis is given to Indians of the United States as well as to those of other North American countries.

In addition to bibliographies that cover diverse topics or focus on one topic in several areas of the world, our library search uncovered bibliographies that devote their attention to one topic as it relates to America. George N. Boyde and Lois A. Boyd have compiled a bibliography called *Religion in Contemporary Fiction: Criticism from 1945 to the Present.* Although not limited to America, this bibliography lists numerous resources pertinent to the study of religion and literature and their intersection in the United States. Many contemporary American authors receive attention in this resource. *Freethought in the United States: A Descriptive Bibliography* by Marshall G. Brown and Gordon Stein is a small book that includes short descriptions of resources focusing on American ideas that diverge from orthodoxies. A helpful, but dated volume published by the National Council of Churches of Christ is *A Bibliography of Doctoral Dissertations Undertaken in American and Canadian Universities, 1940–1962 on Religion and Politics.* George R. LaNoue produced this work, which simply lists dissertations about religion and politics. These lists appear under various categories: American national, regional, state, and local Constitutional and Legal Philosophy and Theory; anthropology; education; history; law; philosophy; political science; sociology; and religion. John F. Wilson has edited a book of bibliographical essays called *Church and State in America: A Bibliographical Guide: The Colonial and Early National Periods.* The contributions in this resource examine the literature from the colonial period to the early republic era plus material on five specific themes: reform; new religions; education; law; and women. A companion volume covering the period from the Civil War to the present is planned. Another bibliography focuses on the southern United States and its people; *Bibliography of Religion in the South* by Charles

H. Lippy contains several bibliographical essays supplemented by an extensive listing of books and articles on southern religion.

Among the bibliographies with a specific focus, Albert J. Menedez has compiled a resource entitled *Religious Conflict in America: A Bibliography*. This resource covers religious conflict from 1565–1983 in areas such as religious repression, civil religion, cults, public school controversies, political campaigns, and the Ku Klux Klan. There are no individual annotations; however, certain works receive attention in short introductory paragraphs that precede each section of the book. In *American Religion and Philosophy: A Guide to Information Sources*, Ernest R. Sandeen and Frederick Hale present a chronological arrangement of reference works and general studies of historical movements that have occurred in the United States. There are sections on transplanted European churches, the First Great Awakening, denominationalism, philosophy, and theology with all their changing ramifications down to the last quarter of the twentieth century. Each entry includes a short one- or two-sentence description.

Another tool, intended to assist librarians, is a guide to major reference works entitled *Religious Bibliography in Serial Literature: A Guide*. This work was done by Michael J. Walsh with the assistance of John V. Howard, Graham P. Cornish, and Robert J. Duckett.

Two additional bibliographies devote their attentions to only one church—the Catholic church in America. John Tracy Ellis and Robert Trisco compiled *A Guide to American Catholic History* in 1959. In 1982 the original edition was revised and expanded to give wider coverage to the topic. Another bibliography about the Catholic church is *The Catholic Church in America: An Historical Bibliography* by Edward R. Vollmer, S. J.

The selection of books and articles for which annotations are included in this reference work took several stages. Our initial search through indexes, card catalogues, and extant bibliographies yielded a bibliography with about 1,200 entries. This list was sent to the project participants for their study and determination as to which books and articles would be appropriate to include in a research tool intended to provide a solid orientation to students in American religion. In addition to selecting appropriate works, these people also made suggestions that increased the bibliography to about 1,400 entries. Enough unanimous selections emerged from that expanded collection to draw up the list of 116 books and 121 articles included in this volume. These works represent high-quality scholarly works that reflect the best current material about the interaction between religion and American life, in the view of the project participants.

Some selections raise the question of whether there is a national (civil) religion. They examine avenues through which that civil religion interacts with denominational religion and how each reinforces or reduces support for the other. There are also representative pieces reflecting the notion of a pluralistic rather than a "melting pot" society as the voices of blacks, women, Hispanics, and native Americans, among others, are heard and the implications of their words are pondered. More specific areas such as law, sociology, literature, anthropology, education, and political science are represented in the selected books and articles. Other works focus on special religious movements that have had particular importance in the history of religion in America (Mormons, Moonies, etc.) and on particular groups such as Roman Catholics and Jews who have been an integral part of the rich religious heritage of this country. Some of the entries may appear to be very narrow in their content, but they represent seldom-mentioned areas of study or present new perspectives that add to a student's understandings.

The entries in this volume are somewhat long compared to other bibliographies to provide room for more description and critical discussion of the source. Each work is described briefly, but there is also some suggestion as to the work's usefulness for additional study. Because forty contributors have written these annotations, there are an equivalent number of writing styles. Thus the stories are told in differing forms; but all of them include materials to guide persons as they begin the challenging task of doing research about religion in America.

The entries are arranged alphabetically by author in two sections—books and articles. Such an arrangement was decided upon rather than a "by subject" classification because many of the works span several historical periods or several areas, making it difficult to pinpoint a specific theme or time period under which to classify the work. The bibliographical information for books makes note of various editions, with the number of pages of the latest edition cited. Cross-references to works in this bibliography have the format "(see p. 00)." Direct quotes from the works omit the word "see." At the end of each entry, the reader will find initials to indicate the author of the piece. The key to the authors' initials and their current professional affiliations follows the introduction.

Because of the lapse in time between the selection process and the publication of this volume, there are inevitable omissions, as deserving new books and articles are being published all the time. Information about some of the newer book resources is included in the afterword. All of the people involved in producing this reference work hope that it will prove to be a useful tool for students of religion and American life.

Bibliographies cited

Barrow, James Graves. *A Bibliography in Religion*. Ann Arbor: Edwards Brothers, 1955.

Boyde, George N., and Lois A. Boyd. *Religion in Contemporary Fiction: Criticism from 1945 to the Present*. San Antonio: Trinity University Press, 1973.

Brown, Marshall G., and Gordon Stein. *Freethought in the United States: A Descriptive Bibliography*. Westport: Greenwood Press, 1978.

Burr, Nelson R. *Religion in American Life*. New York: Appleton-Crofts, 1971.

———, James W. Smith, and A. Leland Jamison. *A Critical Bibliography of Religion in America*. Princeton: Princeton University Press, 1961.

de V. Brunkow, Robert, ed. *Religion and Society in North America: An Annotated Bibliography*. Santa Barbara: ABC-Clio Information Services, 1983.

Ellis, John Tracy, and Robert Trisco. *A Guide to American Catholic History*. Santa Barbara: ABC-Clio Information Services, 1982.

Karpinski, Leszek M. *The Religious Life of Man: A Guide to Basic Literature*. Metuchen, NJ: Scarecrow Press, 1978.

LaNoue, George R., ed. *A Bibliography of Doctoral Dissertations Undertaken in American and Canadian Universities, 1940–1962 on Religion and Politics*. New York: National Council of Churches of Christ, 1963.

Lippy, Charles. *Bibliography of Religion in the South*. Macon: Mercer University Press, 1985.

Menendez, Albert J. *Religious Conflict in America: A Bibliography*. New York: Garland, 1985.

Religious Books, 1876–1982. New York: R. R. Bowker, 1983.

Sandeen, Ernest R., and Frederick Hale. *American Religion and Philosophy: A Guide to Information Sources*. Detroit: Gale Research Company, 1978.

Shulman, Albert M. *The Religious Heritage of America*. San Diego: A. S. Barnes, 1981.

Turner, Harold W. *Bibliography of New Religious Movements in Primal Societies*. Vol. 2, *North America*. Boston: G. K. Hall, 1978.

Vollmer, Edward R., S. J. *The Catholic Church in America: An Historical Bibliography*. New York: Scarecrow Press, 1963.

Walsh, Michael J., John V. Howard, Graham P. Cornish, and Robert J. Duckett. *Religious Bibliography in Serial Literature: A Guide*. Westport: Greenwood Press, 1981.

Wilson, John F. *Church and State in America: A Bibliographical Guide. The Colonial and Early National Periods*. Westport: Greenwood Press, 1986.

Key to Contributors

T.A.   Thomas Alexander, Professor of History; Director, Charles Redd Center for Western Studies, Brigham Young University, Provo, Utah.

V.T.A.   Valeen T. Avery, Assistant Professor of History, Department of History; Director, Center for Colorado Plateau Studies, Northern Arizona University, Flagstaff.

S.C.B.   Spencer C. Bennett, Associate Professor of History/Religious Studies, Department of Humanities, Siena Heights College, Adrian, Michigan.

R.G.B.   Roger G. Betsworth, Professor, Department of Religion, Simpson College, Indianola, Iowa.

H.W.B.   Henry Warner Bowden, Professor of Religion, Department of Religion, Douglass College, Rutgers University, New Brunswick, New Jersey.

J.M.C.   Julia M. Corbett, Associate Professor of Religious Studies, Department of Philosophy, Ball State University, Muncie, Indiana.

P.J.C.   Paul Jerome Croce, Assistant Professor of History, Department of History, Rollins College, Winter Park, Florida.

R.A.D.   Roland A. Delattre, Professor of American Studies, Program in American Studies, University of Minnesota, Minneapolis.

W.D.D.   William D. Dinges, Assistant Professor, Department of Religion and Religious Education, Catholic University of America, Washington, D.C.

A.T.F.   Anne T. Fraker, Project Coordinator, Project on Religion and the Life of the Nation, Indiana University-Purdue University at Indianapolis.

G.G.   Giles Gunn, Professor of English and Religious Studies, Department of English, University of California at Santa Barbara.

R.W.H.   Robert W. Hattery, Professor of Political Science, Department of Political Science, Indiana University, Bloomington.

J.K.H.   Joyce K. Hendrixson, Associate Faculty in Anthropology, Department of Anthropology, Indiana University-Purdue University at Indianapolis.

J.S.H.   Janet S. Huettner, Bibliographer, Indiana University Center on Philanthropy, Indiana University-Purdue University at Indianapolis.

R.T.H.   Richard T. Hughes, Professor, Religion Division, Pepperdine University, Malibu, California.

L.A.H.   Lloyd A. Hunter, Roger D. Branigan Professor of History, Associate Professor of History and Religion, Department of History, Franklin College, Franklin, Indiana.

C.J.   Carol Jablonski, Associate Professor of Communication, Department of Communication, University of South Florida, Tampa.

L.S.J.   L. Shannon Jung, Associate Professor of Rural Ministry and Christian Ethics; Director of Rural Ministry Program/ Center for Theology and Land, University of Dubuque Theological Seminary, Dubuque, Iowa.

E.T.L.   Edward Tabor Linenthal, Associate Professor of Religious Studies, Department of Religious Studies, University of Wisconsin at Oshkosh.

M.H.L.   Monroe H. Little, Jr., Assistant Professor of History and Director of the Afro-American Studies Program, Indiana University-Purdue University at Indianapolis.

H.M.   Herbert Mather, Associate General Secretary, The General Board of Discipleship, The United Methodist Church, Nashville, Tennessee.

J.G.M.-n J. Gordon Melton, Director, The Institute for the Study of American Religion, Santa Barbara, California.

J.G.M.-y James G. Moseley, Vice-President of Academic Affairs, Chapman College, Orange, California.

W.C.O. Wayne C. Olson, Director, Metropolitan Indianapolis Campus Ministry, Indianapolis, Indiana.

N.P. Nicholas Piediscalzi, Professor of Religion, Department of Religion; Director, Master of Humanities Degree Program, Wright State University, Dayton, Ohio.

A.P. Amanda Porterfield, Associate Professor, Department of Religion, Syracuse University, Syracuse, New York.

L.K.P. Linda K. Pritchard, Assistant Professor of History, Division of Behavioral and Cultural Sciences, University of Texas at San Antonio.

B.A.R. Bruce A. Ronda, Boulder, Colorado.

J.K.R. John K. Roth, Russell K. Pitzer Professor of Philosophy, Department of Philosophy, Claremont McKenna College, Claremont, California.

J.D.S. Jonathan D. Sarna, Associate Professor of American Jewish History, Department of History; Director, Center for the Study of the American Jewish Experience, Hebrew Union College-Jewish Institute of Religion, Cincinnati, Ohio.

M.L.S. Mary L. Schneider, Professor of Religious Studies, Department of Religious Studies, Michigan State University, East Lansing.

R.A.S. Rowland A. Sherrill, Professor of Religious Studies, Department of Religious Studies, Indiana University-Purdue University at Indianapolis.

J.S. Jan Shipps, Professor of History, Department of History; Director, Center for American Studies, Indiana University-Purdue University at Indianapolis.

G.H.S. Gregory Holmes Singleton, Professor of History, Department of History, Northeastern Illinois University, Chicago.

W.U.S. Winton U. Solberg, Professor of History, Department of History, University of Illinois, Urbana.

D.S. Douglas Sturm, Professor, Departments of Religion and Political Science, Bucknell University, Lewisburg, Pennsylvania.

M.K.T. Marian K. Towne, Associate Faculty in Speech Communication, Department of Communication and Theatre, Indiana University-Purdue University at Indianapolis.

E.A.W. Edward A. Warner, Associate Professor of Humanities and Religion, Department of Humanities, Indiana State University, Terre Haute.

L.W. Lewis Wilkins, Associate Executive, Synod of Lincoln Trails, Presbyterian Church, Indianapolis, Indiana.

C.R.W. Charles Reagan Wilson, Associate Professor of History and Southern Studies, Departments of History and Southern Studies, University of Mississippi, University.

Acknowledgments

Many people have contributed to the successful completion of this work. It goes without saying that the cooperation of the Religion and American Life project group members has been extraordinary. Most of them have been willing to assist at all levels as the project has developed and have been very tolerant of appeals for assistance. Also, some of these persons have been amenable to suggestions for revising their writing in order to make the entries in this volume exhibit some consistency. Without them, this undertaking would not have been possible.

Jan Shipps and Rowland "Tony" Sherrill, project codirectors, were available for consultations about the bibliography and offered helpful suggestions for work as the project grew. One of the participants in this endeavor, Henry Warner Bowden, provided invaluable advice and offered much-appreciated support. K. Amy Phillips, the project assistant for two years, was very conscientious in typing out the initial massive bibliographical list and in taking care of correspondence and mailings related to this project. Grace Whittemore assumed her duties as project assistant late in the process and contributed by continuing mailings and typing some of the entries. Karl Illig, computer consultant for the Indiana University-Purdue University School of Liberal Arts, developed the guidelines by which the entries were to be written and by which they were entered on computers. Joy Sherrill contributed her expert computer skills to produce the final manuscript copy—without her expertise, this undertaking would have been slowed in its completion. Numerous persons at the reference desk at the Indiana University library in Bloomington were always willing to assist in the search for elusive documents. Of course, gratitude must go to the Lilly Endowment, Inc., and to the Indiana Committee for the Humanities for providing the funding to support the two-plus year project and this bibliography.

BOOKS

Ahlstrom, Sydney E. *A Religious History of the American People*. New Haven: Yale University Press, 1972; Reprint. Garden City, NY: Image Books, 1975. xvi + 1158 pp.

Before publishing this book, the author had already acquired a reputation for interest in theology and the history of ideas. Here, too, he includes standard considerations of intellectual categories that ranged from systems to vague impulses. But, this work goes far beyond doctrinal developments to incorporate social history, cultural trends, and statistical evidence. It draws on specialized studies of Jews, Catholics, Eastern Orthodox, blacks, and nonecclesiastical religion in American life. It is a triumph of comprehensive topical coverage and interdisciplinary synthesis. Its utilization of sophisticated studies in American religion, coupled with its own interpretive appreciation of religious variables in national experience, make it one of the most important historiographical landmarks to appear since midcentury.

Material collected for decades produced a book of magisterial sweep with rich and varied contents. It also tended to make the narrative complex and convoluted. One suggestion for managing its themes is to consider Ahlstrom's work as though it is three volumes instead of one. On a primary level, the study concentrates on religious activities associated with European roots and contemporary voices tied to tangible structures. The thoughts and actions of people who worked through organized religious groups have been identifiable for centuries, and on that simple level of historical focus, this volume gives full analysis to sociologically defined religious activity. It provides a straightforward account of multiple denominations and of the polarities arising within those associative bodies. Beyond institutional history, Ahlstrom deals with religions not confined to structured patterns. Although more difficult to define and pinpoint, this second level of inquiry shows that many forms of religion in America have flourished alongside traditional channels. The third book in this single volume emphasizes the reciprocal connections between religion and American social life. Religion has made an impact in contexts wider than churches, and culturally conditioned values have modified religious teachings. In this overview, Ahlstrom shows not only how components of our religious heritage can be studied in temporary isolation, but also he insists that each feature be understood ultimately within a larger framework that blends the various parts and gives each greater perspective.   [H.W.B.]

Albanese, Catherine L. *Corresponding Motion: Transcendental Religion and the New America.* **Philadelphia: Temple University Press, 1977. xxiii + 210 pp.**

A study of the Transcendentalist movement as a religious phenomenon, *Corresponding Motion* seeks to place the thought of Ralph Waldo Emerson and his circle in a tradition that emphasizes the spiritual understanding of relationship, correspondence, and harmony. Albanese suggests that using a phenomenological approach—what did these New England rebels believe and how did they express it—and a "comparative religions" approach may lead to better understanding of the distinctive religious insights of American Transcendentalists.

Relying on an impressive array of examples drawn from ancient Near Eastern, Asian, and native American religions, Albanese describes a spirituality that differs dramatically from the Judeo-Christian one. This spirituality of "association" proposes that life in the small scale (microcosmos) mirrors life on the grand scale (macrocosmos) and that all creation is an endless series of analogues and reflections. In such a spirituality, one is both an insignificant speck in a vast cosmos that throbs with life and a being whose divinity matches that of all creation. In contrast to the Judeo-Christian stress on sin, fall, punishment, alienation, and the need for supernatural redemption, this alternative tradition teaches "correspondence," the sense that all things are natively caught up in a vast and intricate interrelationship. The essential and universal truth for this tradition is harmony, not alienation.

Albanese shows how the two mythos of history and science replaced the old Christian understanding of a providential God, but that for the old faith and the new, beliefs in progress toward lofty goals and in the triumph of human potential were similar. In the neighborhood of Boston, these beliefs in progress and the mastery of human intellect were paramount in the early nineteenth century.

Against what they perceived as intellectual and spiritual aridity, Emerson and his circle launched their revolution. Focusing on the six founding members of the Transcendental Club—Emerson, James Freeman Clarke, Frederic Hedge, Convers Francis, George Ripley, and Bronson Alcott—Albanese demonstrates how American Transcendentalists derived their own version of the alternative spirituality she earlier describes. In addition to beliefs in correspondence and in the essential harmony of the universe, these Americans stressed motion. Rather than a static cosmos of mirrored realities, American Transcendentalists offered one of fluidity and change. Rather than the circle as the central symbol of faith, they offered the spiral.

How relevant was this "gnostic spirituality" to the restless antebellum America in which the Transcendentalists lived? Albanese wishes to show that there was a connection between their version of correspondence, which stressed motion, and the constant change and turmoil of the larger society. She demonstrates that the Emerson circle was reasonably knowledgeable about practical matters and tried to bring their emerging spirituality to bear on the circumstances of American life. But the expansive nature of American society had little in common with the insights of the Transcendentalist or of any alternative religion, and everything to do with revivalism and sectarianism. As Albanese admits at the conclusion, "the Transcendentalists were instructed by the new America, but the new America had still to be instructed by the corresponding motion of Transcendental religion" (p. 173). [B.A.R.]

Albanese, Catherine L. *Sons of the Fathers: The Civil Religion of the American Revolution.* Philadelphia: Temple University Press, 1976. xiv + 274 pp.

The first really successful attempt at an extended interpretation of American civil religion during a particular period, *Sons Of The Fathers* relies heavily upon the work of anthropologists for its framework. Using the concepts of Lévi-Strauss, Albanese analyzes the myths and symbols of the American Revolution in their "reinternalization as objective realities after they have been projected onto the world as word and action" (p. 7). The colonists found new religious symbols to represent their strengths in their emergence from colony to nation. There were, of course, the covenant relationship with the great Jehovah and the myth of themselves as the "New Israel." But there were also other symbols more expressive of the "natural" generation of the Republic including the Liberty Tree (which the author compares to the sacred axis uniting the human to the divine realm) and the secret society of Freemasons, to which a great number of the founding fathers belonged. Thus the sources of enlightenment philosophy and natural theology become as important as those of Christianity for the public identity.

Although the colonists were not self-conscious about moving between the images of the Jehovah of Battles and the God of nature and design to justify their cause, Albanese posits that they used the deistic God to sustain the postwar vision. In this interpretation, the victors in their new prosperity were less dependent upon God's grace and more on their forefather's natural inheritance. As natural theology became natural law, the citizens of the new nation saw themselves as both the generators and the product of their destiny.

The strengths of this book are many. It sustains the civil religion argument through a skillful interpretation of religious myths. It offers new insights about the minds of the colonists in their self-understanding. It develops a new thesis about the secularizing effects of a civil religion theology as the colonists attributed their success more as the product of their own endeavors than of God's favor. However, the strengths of Albanese's arguments pose the civil religion dilemma. She believes that civil religion flourished under different sets of symbols in the postwar period. But the tenor of her judgment is that the sacred component in early American civil religion is increasingly diluted until it becomes indistinguishable from a purely humanistic rationale. If so, American civil religion died in the eighteenth century rather than, as critics suggest, in the twentieth century. [S.C.B.]

Baird, Robert. *Religion in America*. A critical abridgement with introduction by Henry Warner Bowden. New York: Harper and Row, 1970. xxxvii + 314 pp.

One of the advantages that those of us in American religious history had in getting into the field two or more decades ago is that we could still obtain out-of-print copies of major works going well back into the nineteenth century that really formed the foundation of this field of study. Now many of those same works, if available, are terribly expensive, whereas others are becoming very scarce or virtually nonexistent.

Probably the earliest self-conscious survey of American religious history was Robert Baird's *Religion in America*, in both its 1844 and 1856 versions. It was actually first published in Scotland in 1843 and then reprinted in America in 1844. The 1856 edition, which is the one Bowden edited, is a revised and enlarged version with added comments that are directed much more at an American than at a European audience and with a considerable amount of new data included. Bowden makes available to us approximately one-third of the 1856 edition of *Religion in America* supplemented with an insightful, helpful, critical introduction.

The era in which the configuration of American religious commitment and denominational membership changed most dramatically was during the early National period, roughly 1790 to 1850 or so. It is precisely at the height of this era that Baird collected his data and offered us his formative interpretations of that information, providing us one of the very few accessible primary sources on American religious activity in the first half of the nineteenth century. Not only does Baird precede Philip Schaff's work by a few years, but he offers us both a far greater amount of factual data collected in that very era and a wider range of interpretive themes with which to make sense of that data.

Bowden is right in pointing out that Baird had no formal ecclesiology and no precise clarification of his theological principles. Although Baird had a Princeton education and a Presbyterian background that probably led him to contend that "creeds are unavoidable," no specific creed was presented or defended. But time and again, in various ways, Baird makes it clear to his readers that he takes a stance in favor of mainline Protestant principles and denominations, which he often refers to as "evangelical Christianity."

Bowden's edition is capably and discriminatingly done. All of Baird's major categories and contentions are included; and the student reading only this selection will come away with a very fair and reliable profile of the early American religious historian. Students will miss the opportunity to read some of Baird's critical quips about the sects, which reveal some of the charm, quaintness, and ethnocentricity of his perspective; otherwise, Bowden's selection is a solid and balanced one. The American religious enterprise profits from this fine contribution.   [E.A.W.]

Baltzell, E. Digby. *The Protestant Establishment: Aristocracy and Caste in America.* **New York: Random House, 1964. xviii + 429 pp.**

Written at the time of John F. Kennedy's election to the presidency, this sociological study reflects on the traditions that have provided American leadership, on the changes that must take place if America is to retain its role as the leader of the Western world and, at the same time, share the fruits of its development with the rest of humankind, and on what the author perceives to be a crisis in the nation's leadership. He states that "a crisis in moral authority has developed in modern America largely because of the White-Anglo-Saxon-Protestant establishment's unwillingness, or inability, to share and improve its upper-class traditions by continuously absorbing talented and distinguished members of minority groups into its privileged ranks" (p. x). Thus, in essence, this book is concerned with the issues of exclusion and prejudice extant in the white community and their impact on the ability of *all* to share in the American dream.

Baltzell traces the development of aristocracy and caste in America and illustrates, with incidents from the Jewish community, how the exclusion of these persons, which he believes is applicable to the exclusion of other minority groups, led to the development of a caste system in America. He says that the creation of a caste is detrimental to the continuous provision of adequate leaders, while he uses the term *aristocracy* in a positive sense by defining it as the system that assimilates *all* persons into its ranks, regardless of ethnic or racial factors. Based on these uses of the terms, the author illustrates how caste and aristocracy have developed from Lincoln's day through 1963. It is the author's hope that those who study his work reject the caste ideas of such associations as the country club in favor of ideals that inspired such leaders as Woodrow Wilson, Theodore and Franklin Roosevelt, and John F. Kennedy.

This book, which is the continuation of an earlier study entitled *Philadelphia Gentlemen, The Making of a National Upper Class* (Glencoe, IL: The Free Press; reprinted in paperback as *An American Business Aristocracy*, New York: Collier Books, 1962), was followed by a reflection on the Protestant Establishment revisited in 1976 (see p. 144). This particular book and the subsequent essay lament the state of leadership, but present intriguing notions for improving this situation. Even though this book is dated, it gives readers insights for understanding why we are where we are in terms of leadership, and there are ideas to consider that are relevant when examining America's leadership role in a constantly changing world. [A.T.F.]

Bellah, Robert N. *The Broken Covenant: American Civil Religion in a Time of Trial.* New York: Seabury Press, 1975. xvi + 172 pp.

An attempt at the cultural interpretation of the religious themes in American intellectual history, *The Broken Covenant* is less successful as a focused analysis of civil religion than it is in pointing out the inconsistencies in the original premise of a covenanted nation. Bellah picks out three natural times of trial in the nation's history: the Revolution, the Civil War, and the disruptive years of the late 1960s through Watergate. Each period is marked by dialectical tensions between the call of individual liberties and the claim of social obligations. John Winthrop represents the model for individual wealth while speaking in metaphoric terms of the covenanted community in the Old Testament sense. Our forefathers spoke of the liberty inherent in revolution, but moved quickly toward the acts of institution and establishment in the Constitution. W. L. Garrison decried the Constitution as a covenant with hell for its silence on slavery, while abolitionist Theodore Weld advocated working within a system of government that produced the Thirteenth, Fourteenth, and Fifteenth amendments.

It is in the delicate balance between individual conversion and the claims of the larger society that the issue of a covenanted nationhood becomes oblique. Was there ever a time when the holistic sense of community in America was not confounded to the point of distraction by a larger sense of cultural and social pluralism? Bellah argues that the Anglo-Saxon traditions of Biblical prophesy and social justice are concepts that apply equally to all minorities. Yet he admits that the problem of social exclusion of racial minorities in clubs, intermarriage, and neighborhood residence patterns is a real one. If so, then differences of understanding about what Bellah believes to be common cultural assumptions about the meaning of covenant must be very diffuse and complicate his definition.

Perhaps the escape from traditional religious moral values to what Bellah deplores as a materially individualistic world is really a reaction to the complexities of cultural pluralism. Middle-class Americans faced with social and economic claims from contending minorities find solace in the simplicity of values in corporate capitalism however much they distort the issues inherent in cultural pluralism. In that case, the task is a more careful analysis of civil religions among minorities in American history. Until we examine the prior covenants and work toward a typology of civil religions, a national covenant is too abstract and distant a concept to have much common meaning.   [S.C.B.]

Bellah, Robert N., with Richard Madsen, William M. Sullivan, Ann Swidler, and Steven M. Tipton. *Habits of the Heart: Individualism and Commitment in American Life.* Berkeley: University of California Press, 1985. xiii + 355 pp.

Alexis de Tocqueville would be pleased. The beliefs and practices that he saw shaping the American character a century and a half ago, what he called "habits of the heart," have now been freshly examined and reinterpreted for the 1980s. In perhaps the most penetrating study of American culture in three decades, Bellah and four younger scholars probe the lives of over two hundred Americans and find that deep within them was a profound struggle with the effects of our culture's stress on the individual. The authors seek to "transform this inner moral debate . . . into public discourse" (p. vii), and in so doing they demonstrate that, as Tocqueville warned, our intense individualism also undercuts our capacity for commitment to each other.

Readers may quarrel with the sources selected by Bellah and his associates and with the methodology employed in interpreting their findings. Stressing the central role of the middle classes in the success of free institutions, the research team consciously chose to interview white, middle-class Americans, predominantly from California and areas around Boston and Philadelphia. Although one may wonder how representative such subjects may be, there is no denying that the researchers have unveiled the honest self-perceptions of Americans as individuals and as a people.

As those interviewed discuss the ways in which they understand themselves and their relation to society, it is evident that they employ a "common moral vocabulary"—what Bellah describes as "the first language of individualism" (p. 20). This shared discourse, grounded in a fierce belief in personal autonomy, makes it difficult for them to comprehend and define the "common good." Consequently, they display the symptoms of excessive individualism in both their private and public lives. As the only individuals in the world expected to leave home and church "to become one's own person, almost to give birth to oneself" (p. 82), Americans create "lifestyle enclaves"—alternatives to genuine community that are centered on shared private concerns. For example, love and marriage have become enclaves serving as mere settings for expressive individualism. Religion also has become dangerously privatized. Furthermore, therapy has become the basic mode of human interaction, and "getting involved" has come to mean "love thy lifestyle enclave" while eschewing politics.

If this sounds ominous, Bellah's solution seems nostalgic—and yet powerfully attractive. Hidden beneath their "first language" of individualism, Americans harbor the remnants of a "second language," one that might transcend their radical self-orientation. Rooted in the biblical and republican strands of our cultural heritage, this new— or, more accurately, "renewed"—moral discourse could take flesh in social movements devoted to the creation of a new "social ecology" (p. 183). As in the civil rights movement of the 1960s, Bellah contends, religion would play a major role in this transformation. Consequently, his chapter on religion as "public church" is essential reading for all analysts of the nation's spiritual life and constitutes yet another reason to take seriously this cogent study of American culture.   [L.A.H.]

Bercovitch, Sacvan. *The American Jeremiad.* Madison: University of Wisconsin Press, 1978. xvi + 239 pp.

The jeremiad is a political sermon, so named after the Hebrew prophet Jeremiah. Prior to the great migration to New England early in the seventeenth century, it had the form of a lament over unfaithfulness of God's people to his covenant, a call to repentance, and a threat of divine punishment, and even destruction, if the people did not return to God's ways. In contrast to Perry Miller's stress upon this dark side of the jeremiad, Bercovitch stresses the "unshakeable optimism" of the American Puritans whose jeremiad "inverted the doctrine of vengeance into a promise of ultimate success" (p. 7) and directed an imperiled people not to a recovery of past integrity but forward toward the fulfillment of their destiny, identifying that destiny with God's promises. That forward movement, whether understood as holy errand or American mission or unending progress, is what America was all about. At least so went the "myth of America" that acquired cultural hegemony in the colonies and the new nation. The myth was partly fashioned and very largely energized by the ritual power of the American jeremiad.

Bercovitch's achievement in this book is to demonstrate the distinctive character of the American jeremiad and to show, by a detailed analysis of a wider range of literature and texts than just the political sermons that carefully distinguishes between intention and effect in the rhetoric, just how crucial the jeremiad as ritual has been to the cultural hegemony of the "myth of America." Bercovitch traces the modulations by which the ritual retained and even gained cultural power as a vehicle of personal identity and socialization, and as an instrument of both social control and motivation.

Bercovitch sheds fresh light on the Puritan jeremiad, but what is most striking is his analysis of the ritual power of the jeremiad to survive the decline of Puritanism and serve beyond New England. It became a national ritual during the Revolution and an instrument of cultural consolidation through the nineteenth century, first "confining the concept of revolution to American progress" (p. 154) and then ritually celebrating middle-class culture and the free-enterprise capitalist system as the real meaning of "America." If there was—as indeed there was—a discrepancy between assertion and fact, between rhetoric and experience, it only underlined the need to press forward and the rhetoric of the jeremiad helped the process to succeed.

In a characteristic passage about the "ritual of consensus" in the nineteenth century, Bercovitch concludes: "In virtually every area of life, the jeremiad became the official ritual form of continuing revolution. Mediating between religion and ideology, the jeremiad gave contract the sanctity of covenant, free enterprise the halo of grace, progress the assurance of the chiliad, the nationalism the grandeur of typology. In short, it wed self-interest to social perfection, and conferred on both the unique blessings of American destiny" (p. 141). Claims of this breadth are supported by Bercovitch's bold reading of the relevant rhetoric evidence, keeping his focus upon ways in which the symbol of America was ritually invested with attributes of divinity.   [R.A.D.]

Bercovitch, Sacvan. *The Puritan Origins of the American Self*. New Haven: Yale University Press, 1975. x + 250 pp.

To explore the meaning of American identity, Bercovitch examines the Puritans themselves and also those who subsequently kept the Puritan sense of selfhood alive. When examining the doctrinal developments that expressed the ambivalence inherent in the Puritans' understanding of themselves, Bercovitch observes that their "pietistic voluntarism . . . raised personal choice to the central position it held in humanist theology—without, however, losing sight of man's inability to choose correctly" (p. 21). Later, when looking forward toward "a long procession of solitary keepers of the dream," he argues that each of "the leading figures in our cultural tradition . . . in his own way, responded to the problems of his time by recourse to . . . the genre of auto-American biography: the celebration of the representative self as America, and of the American self as the embodiment of a prophetic universal design" (p. 136).

Between these two insights Bercovitch traces how the Puritans and their cultural descendants willfully read their own secular story as providential history instead of interpreting their own experience in the light of biblical models. By virtue of this inversion of hermeneutics, American events were invested with the ultimate importance that would traditionally have been seen only in the sacred story. Thus the act of imagining America became terribly important, even to the extent of providing the content for one's own sense of spiritual identity. Telling one's own story as the story of America became a way of securing a place in the history of redemption, a way of merging one's individual and social identities and of viewing their fusion as the fulfillment of prophecy.

Bercovitch closely analyzes Cotton Mather's portrayal of John Winthrop as "Nehemias Americanus" as a classic example of the creation of this new American selfhood, and he speculates toward the end that Emerson and Thoreau also wrote of themselves in this manner. Mather's life of Winthrop, included as an appendix, provides a focus for Bercovitch's wide-ranging reflections about American culture. Mather's rhetoric bears such heavy analysis because, Bercovitch contends, even after the failure of the Puritan theocracy, recurrent crises of corporate self-definition called for continuing restatements of the Puritan myth, linking self and society in ways that supported the American way of life and national destiny. America was thus imagined and experienced as delivering salvation from the unsettling ambiguities of early Puritanism.

The book is difficult because the subject is complex, and important because the rhetorical tradition it interprets continues to provide terms for achieving identity in America. It shows brilliantly how historical scholarship can uncover a continuity of symbolic strategy within the diversity of American literary, religious, and social experience. The American self has Puritan origins, finally, because the rhetoric of "auto-American biography" has been compelling enough in content and flexible enough in form to invite adaptation. Thus Bercovitch discloses resources for recovering America and the self in the same imaginative act. By both recounting and interpreting the central story of our culture, Bercovitch provides a model of—and a model for—revisioning America.   [J.G.M.-y]

Berger, Peter L. *The Noise of Solemn Assemblies: Christian Commitment and the Religious Establishment in America.* **Garden City, NY: Doubleday, 1961. 189 pp.**

Professor, sociologist, and Lutheran layman Peter Berger has written an impassioned polemic on the American church. The first half of the book is an interpretation of the religious scene as viewed from the close of the 1950s. Berger aims his heavy artillery on white middle-class Protestantism. The civil rights struggles of the 1950s provide most of his examples.

Similar issues are around in the 1980s, but the battle lines have shifted dramatically. Still, Berger's analysis has clear enough parallels for today that anyone involved in the contemporary church establishment will squirm uncomfortably when reading this man's work.

American Protestantism is described as "highly functional" in society. That is, a socially stratified cultural religion is blessed through the churches. Religion in America is closely allied to the state in that it helps persons adjust to the status quo. The author protests that the church is not called to help persons adjust, but to witness to the biblical demand for justice and righteousness.

Two biblical passages become the texts for this book. The title comes from Amos 5:21–24 ("I take no delight in your solemn assemblies"). The New Testament text is Matthew 7:21, "Not everyone who says to me, 'Lord, Lord,' shall enter the kingdom of heaven, but he who does the will of my Father who is in heaven." Within the church, the proper words are used but there is little evidence, in Berger's analysis, of obedience in faith and action. Although functional in society, the church is irrelevant.

Norman Vincent Peale is the paradigm of religious establishment coming under the blistering attack by Berger. More than anyone else, Peale turns the gospel into a program for psychological well-being. The author's theological bias is clear when he says, "The Christian faith is about history—not psychology" (p. 115).

In the last half of his book, Berger moves from analysis to an appeal to the church to live up to its nature as a prophetic witness in society. He calls this the churches' "task of disestablishment" (p. 113). By this, he means that the task of the church is set by the witness of the Scriptures rather than the usefulness to society as defined by the state. There is more to being a Christian than simply to be a good citizen.

Berger provides a four-pronged outline for Christian engagement with society. His prolegomenon for obedience consists of: (1) Christian diaconate—aid to individuals in distress; (2) Christian action—attempts to modify social structures; (3) Christian presence—models of Christian community in the world; and (4) Christian dialogue—talking *with* instead of *to* the secular world.

The book is written with passion. In making his plea, Berger chooses facts to buttress his case but could be accused of ignoring facts that might challenge his position. Still, the reader is captivated by this Christian rebel appealing to others to be Christian rebels. The rebellion is centered on calling the church to its intended mission in the world.   [H.M.]

Blau, Joseph L. *Judaism in America: From Curiosity to Third Faith.* Chicago History of American Religion Series. Chicago: University of Chicago Press, 1976. xiv + 156 pp.

Yet another volume in the prestigious Chicago History of American Religion series edited by Martin E. Marty, Joseph Blau's analysis of American Judaism meets the rigorous standards one has come to expect from that series. Blau describes the course of American Judaism using an approach that is characteristically "history of religions": he analyzes the interplay of the traditions of historic Judaism with their cultural setting in the United States. Such analysis clearly demonstrates the development of a Judaism that is both traditional and in continuity with Judaism in all times and places and at the same time uniquely American.

There are four features of American culture that play a central role in the development of a uniquely American Judaism: "Protestantization" as applied generally means "that movement in religion . . .

which allows of a multiplicity of conclusions." "Pluralism," on the other hand, is defined as "the religious manifestation of the view that all starting points are equally valid." Thus religion in America is marked by openness on either end. "Moralism," a positive or at least value-neutral term as used in the book, is the persistent tendency to put more emphasis on living an upright, socially responsible life than on attendance at ritual and other directly "religious" functions. "Voluntaryism" indicates the option for both voluntary association with a religious group and the equal opportunity for voluntary nonaffiliation (pp. 8–11). This list indicates one of the strongest points of Blau's work. The thoughtful reader will have a better understanding not only of American Judaism but of the factors at work in American religion as a whole.

The analysis used works best when applied to the three main Jewish "denominations"—Orthodoxy, Conservatism, and Reform—and to Reconstructionism, as well as in the final chapter on the "Americanization of American Judaism." It is also informative in Blau's rather complex chapter on the interplay of individual and community in Judaism; however, it appears less directly relevant to his discussion of Zionism. These analytic chapters are preceded by a brief but cogent historical sketch of American Judaism.

Judaism has prospered in the United States, according to the author. It has ceased to be a mere curiosity and has become an "alternative religious interpretation of the fundamental spiritual qualities" (p. 131) of American life. Official nondiscrimination (in the main) has provided a climate in which Judaism could grow and become truly creative, despite unofficial discrimination. There are, however, no guarantees. Blau's concluding assessment is sobering, not only for Judaism, but for religion in America as a whole: "Voluntaryism can mean a voluntary return to the rigidities of the past or a voluntary facing of the future with courage, confidence, and creative originality. Pluralism can lead to a self-segregating insistence on the right of Judaism to be seclusive, anachronistic, and irrelevant, just as it can lead to a vital interplay with other varieties of American religious culture and a creative interchange of symbols and ideas" (p. 138). [J.M.C.]

Bowden, Henry Warner. *American Indians and Christian Missions: Studies in Cultural Conflict.* Chicago History of American Religion Series. Chicago: University of Chicago Press, 1981. xix + 255 pp.

One of the many areas needing scholarly attention and fresh interpretation to fill in gaping holes in American religious and cultural history is in the domain of American aboriginal religio-cultural systems as well as the interrelations and confrontations between "Indians" and Europeans, whites, and Christians. Bowden's book is a valuable contribution to meet this need and is in the same genre as other similarly well done studies.

The work, a volume in the Chicago History of American Religion series, begins with a pithy foreword by Professor Martin E. Marty setting it in a useful historiographical context. As a single-volume treatment, it simply cannot hope to chronicle the entire history of all white Christian missions to the American natives; neither can it attempt to survey the whole variety and array of aboriginal religio-cultural systems from clan to tribe to empire. But what it does accomplish is to present three minivolumes in one: a brief history of major Christian missions among the aborigines; a selective overview of American Indian religion(s); and a scenario of representative contacts and conflicts integrated with the other two dimensions in a religious context.

Bowden writes with admirable objectivity and evenness of concern. He neither gives into a "shaming" of the whites for their treatment of the redskin in a former era, nor does he resort to the glorification of Indians as mistreated noble naturalists who never wronged their own kind. Bowden tries to understand and accurately present the mind-set and outlook of the Christian missionary without agreeing with, condoning, or arguing against it. He points out very effectively the incongruity between the missionary's attempt to religiously "save" the native American and what was actually the beginning of the cultural condemnation of the "savage." White evangelists "believed they were doing the natives a favor by offering them hope of a better afterlife even as they and their colleagues were trampling on Indian hopes in this one" (p. xii).

Although many such studies grossly overemphasize the late eighteenth and, certainly, the nineteenth centuries, Bowden provides measured and balanced attention across each of the seven areas of his study: pre-Columbian; southwestern-Spanish missions; northeastern-French missions; northeastern-English missions; eighteenth-century missions; nineteenth-century missions; and twentieth-century missions.

This type of sweeping historical overview is properly accomplished only by a discriminating and selective reliance on a host of other sources that are noted succinctly and openly. The work concludes with a briefly annotated set of suggestions for further reading. If the reader wants and needs further help than this, he ought to consult the superb historiographical essay on this subject, with references, by Robert S. Michaelsen entitled "Red Man's Religion/White Man's Religious History" (see p. 195). [E.A.W.]

Bromley, David G., and Anson D. Shupe, Jr. *Moonies in America: Cult, Church and Crusade*. Sage Library of Social Research, vol. 92. Beverly Hills: Sage Publications, 1979. 269 pp.

This work is a sociological examination of the growth, spread, organizational structure, and societal response to Sun Myung Moon's Unification church in America. Through two years of interviews with rank-and-file members, perusal of Unification church documents, and observation of both the church and its opponents, Bromley and Shupe provide an insightful account of the early history and formation of the church in Korea and its growth in the United States. In so doing, they also demythologize both the Unification church movement and its anti-cult opposition. Although focused specifically on the Unification church, this study addresses conceptual and theoretical issues pertinent to the sociological study of other new religious movements. Each chapter is followed by a discussion (in the form of several propositions) of the sociological implications of the research findings derived from examination of the Unification church.

The Unification movement has been shaped by the demands of mobilization to achieve its goals and by the societal reaction to the consequences of that mobilization. Classical studies of marginal or outside-the-mainstream religious movements ("sects" and "cults") have been characterized by a pervasive psychological reductionism. Participation in such movements has been interpreted as a form of "compensation" for alleged "deprivations" of a socioeconomic or psychological nature. *Moonies in America* is part of the growing body of literature on marginal religious movements that employs resource mobilization theory as an alternative analytical framework. In this approach, emphasis is focused on the "how" of movement growth, on the conduciveness of sociocultural environments, on the dynamics of the commitment and recruitment process, and away from motivational explanations based on assumptions of "psychological maladjustment." The main objectives of the Unification church have been to increase membership, to gain legitimacy and visibility, and to establish the foundation for restoring humans to God. As a type of "world transforming movement," the Unification church's objectives are aimed at a total structural change in the world order. Achievement of these goals, however, has been tempered by the imperatives of sociocultural adaptation.

Moonies in America sheds light on the reaction (often negative) of institutions (religion, government, media, science) to the growth of the Unification church. Those interested in the anti-cult movement and the bitter "deprogramming" controversy will find this work particularly helpful. The generally negative response to the growth of the Unification church is a good illustration of what can happen when a movement's proselytizing strategies are characterized by zealous high pressure tactics that are perceived as being underhanded and manipulative. Like many other religious movements that have animated the American religious saga, once the Unification church moved beyond the stage of cult, it began to implement bureaucratic principles intrinsic to the organizational quest for power and stability. As a result, predictable shifts have occurred in the goals of the movement. These shifts, in turn, often contradict the reasons for the movement's existence. This book is a valuable work for those interested in social theory, the sociology of religion, and religion in America. [W.D.D.]

Burr, Nelson R., comp. *Religion in American Life.* New York: Appleton-Century-Crofts, 1971. xix + 171 pp.

This comprehensive bibliography of American religion, compiled by historian Nelson R. Burr, was published as one of the influential Goldentree Bibliographies in American History during the 1970s. Each of its approximately twenty-five volumes was devoted to a major period or topic in American history. A well-known scholar in the field selected the most important monographs, journal articles, and dissertations, organized them by thematic and chronological categories, and wrote brief descriptions of each entry. According to the editor of the series, historian Arthur S. Link, this format offered "a middle course between the brief list of references provided in the average textbook and the long bibliography in which significant items are often lost in the sheer number of titles listed" (p. v).

Nelson Burr's volume provides an excellent overview of American religion through the 1960s. His selections reflect the important scholarship of the major historiographic traditions in the field. Burr's description of each entry is lively and informative and his organization is thoughtful. Over 1,600 entries are distributed among twenty-two categories: bibliographic guides, American church history, the classic denominational pattern, Roman Catholic church, Eastern Orthodox churches, sects and cults, German sects, southern religion, liberal religion, Judaism, Oriental religions, Indian religion, Negro religion, ecumenical movements, religion and politics, sociology of religion, special ministries, religion and education, theology and religious philosophy, science and religion, art and religion, and religion and literature.

This volume is useful not only for reference purposes, but for assessing the state of religious history at midcentury as well. Scholarship about dominant culture religion, for example, clearly pervaded the field. The religion of white, northern European Protestants was more than five times as likely to be studied as the religion of anyone else, based on the number of publications compiled by Burr. By the time this bibliography appeared, however, research into minority culture religion had begun. Some of the language is now dated, especially in the category called "Negro religion," but Burr included the first contemporary work on black, Indian, Roman Catholic, Jewish, Asian, and Mormon religion. Also of note is that the general church histories listed by Burr are the same ones currently used, with the addition of Sydney Ahlstrom's more recent volume (see p. 3).

Yet several important changes in American religious history have occurred since this compilation was published. Perhaps the most important is the recent interest in women and religion. No entry in Burr's bibliography addressed the current issues of women's spirituality, the impact of religion on women's social position, nor the comparative roles of men and women in American religion. Further research on minority religion has occurred as well, with significant new work on Hispanic, immigrant, and southern religion. Evangelical religion, which Burr subsumed in a category called "special ministries," also has become a flourishing field in its own right. Finally, anthropological concepts of symbol and myth have largely replaced sociological ones for the purpose of analyzing the relationship between religion and society. Despite these limitations, this bibliography remains a valuable resource for the study of American religion.   [L.K.P.]

Burr, Nelson, with James Ward Smith and A. Leland Jamison. *A Critical Bibliography of Religion in America.* **2 vols. Princeton, NJ: Princeton University Press, 1961. xx + 541 pp.; xv + 1210 pp.**

Between 1948 and 1958 Princeton University sponsored a Special Program in American Civilization. Three times that decade faculty members concentrated on "Religion in American Life" and published the results in four volumes with that general title. The bibliography under review is volume 4 of that series, published in two separate books, initiated by campus faculty but completed by a staff member of the Library of Congress. Choosing Burr as author of the finished product was fortuitous, and his accomplishment is remarkable for both breadth of coverage and depth of analysis. This massive overview is more than a list of books with occasional comments. It is a synthetic condensation of scholarship on religion in this country, eminently readable as a continuous text and dependable for both accuracy and thorough coverage of inclusive categories. Besides providing a general orientation to major publications in every field, it illustrates the manifold influences of religion in American life and thought.

Burr's work summarizes coverage of many themes up to his day, and his remarks afford a state-of-the-art commentary on the status of current research. He begins with previous bibliographies and surveys, covering more generally the question of historiographical changes and perspectives that have informed previous generations of scholarship. Then he addresses the evolution of American religion from state churches to disestablishment and the rise of classic denominations. He incorporates sectarian movements, black churches, ecumenical consciousness, missions, religious education, and immigration as separate themes. Burr also surveys studies of Roman Catholicism, Eastern Orthodoxy, Judaism, and Oriental religions in America. Turning to larger social questions, he mentions pertinent studies of religion and law, politics, education, and social reform. He rounds out this panorama with works related to architecture, liturgical art, music, fiction, poetry, drama, and sermons. This monumental survey is essential for beginning students and specialists alike.   [H.W.B.]

Bushman, Richard L. *From Puritan to Yankee: Character and Social Order in Connecticut, 1690–1765*. Cambridge: Harvard University Press, 1967. xiv + 343 pp.

Bushman writes history by telling the story of a society's character in evolution. This book offers a convincing explanation of how Connecticut society evolved "From Puritan to Yankee" during the three-quarters of a century from the late 1600s to the eve of the American Revolution. Because changes in the nature and role of freedom are central to this history, it is appropriately part of a series sponsored by the Center for the Study of the History of Liberty in America. Where that freedom came from, how it was accepted, and what it did to Connecticut's social order make the stuff and drama of Bushman's story.

Bushman's book is compellingly written and persuasive because it conveys a narrative of events that culminates in a powerful account of how Connecticut lost its Puritan strictures and became a Yankee dominion. In the seventeenth century, Connecticut's social order had served the zealous demands of Puritan piety. Members of the Puritan elect ruled and expected and received deference and submission from the mass of Connecticut's residents.

From Puritan to Yankee chronicles the way in which economic, social, and geographic changes conspired and accumulated, especially after 1690, to overturn the traditional Puritan leadership and its pattern of social authority. The first changes that Bushman notes came in the expansion of settlement that naturally took people further afield from their towns as "outlivers" from the Puritan "circle of virtue and order" (p. 56). As Connecticut towns grew in number and size, the traditional order was further strained. Economic success bred a speculative and acquisitive spirit that undermined traditional Puritan admonitions to live in the world but be not of it. Opportunities on the land and in trade prompted formerly humble citizens to challenge traditional authority figures in politics and religion. Amid these changes, Puritan ideas did not disappear; instead they reared up in the consciences of many of the most successful in the form of profound guilt. In this context, religious revivalists found fertile ground. The Great Awakening peaked in the 1740s but left a lasting impact not only on countless individuals, but also on the character of Connecticut's social order. The "New Lights" who were ignited by the revivalists' message were less likely to show deference for established authority than were their Puritan ancestors. After the Awakening, respect for authority would come "voluntarily or not at all."

Bushman's volume makes the argument that the New Lights of the Great Awakening contributed to colonial support for the "secular New Lights" of the American Revolution because in both "defiance of eminent men in government had become almost habitual" (p. 256). But Bushman's greatest contribution is his study of the origin and effects of America's chaotic freedom. He demonstrates that the roots of Yankee practicality and initiative lie in Puritan moral and religious values once transformed by Connecticut's socioeconomic changes in the early eighteenth century. [P.J.C.]

Carter, Paul Allen. *The Spiritual Crisis of the Gilded Age.* DeKalb: Northern Illinois University Press, 1971. xiii + 295 pp.

This book focuses on the post–Civil War generation of Americans and the cultural confrontation in that era between faith and doubt. The author sees American developments as part of a broad Anglo-American Victorian cultural pattern, and he shows how revolutionary the new Darwinian scientific doctrines were. It is primarily intellectual history, dealing with the years from 1865 to 1895 and stressing the paradox of some Americans agonizing over their loss of faith while the evangelical churches were at the same time marching on triumphantly.

Carter points out that the spiritual crisis of the era was most pronounced among urban Protestants from denominations of British background, Jews of German-speaking origins, and American-born Jews. Catholics, Lutherans, and rural Protestants were not as affected, but the author questions whether even they escaped the questioning of religious values. The spiritual crisis was part of a changing American society that was grappling with industrial growth, the triumph of scientific and technological influences, and the impact of mass education. The crisis took on special meaning as a symbol for the decline of New England culture; the Yankee WASP certainly saw it in those terms, as Carter shows that religious doubts even affected the pulpit itself in that region.

The attitude of those with a scientific outlook was confident. Many religious leaders were eager for "peaceful coexistence" with scientists, but most individuals on both sides had a crusading spirit of commitment to scientific or religious ideas, which had to be aggressively defended. By the end of the century, a mounting scientific consensus favored evolution. Carter sketches the initial trauma to the collective human psyche of Darwin's challenge to human uniqueness, especially fears of the effects of scientific naturalism on moral principles. Darwinism seemed to many people a new version of atheism, and this feeling increased after the publication of *The Descent of Man* (1871), which extended the debate over evolution to its particular meaning for the nature of the human.

Carter discusses the attitudes of a variety of denominations, including the Lutherans, the Anglicans, the Jehovah's Witnesses, and the Christian Science movement. Theosophy appears prominently, but there is little specific discussion of how the southern and midwestern churches escaped the worst of the religious skepticism. Chapters deal with literary reflections of the spiritual crisis; its impact on residual Calvinism in American culture; the concern for life after death; and the religious fears of growing materialistic American values. Carter ends the book with a discussion of the appearance in the United States of mystical religions, which made a dramatic appearance during the World's Parliament of Religions at the 1893 Chicago World's Fair. Carter's frequent references to events and opinions in the 1960s suggest his belief that Americans then were still living with a spiritual crisis. [C.R.W.]

Cauthen, Kenneth. *The Impact of American Religious Liberalism.* New York: Harper and Row, 1962; 2d ed. Lanham, MD: University Press of America, 1983. 308 pp.

When this book first appeared in 1962 it met a real need because few remembered the vibrancy of liberal Protestant thought as it had flourished in earlier times, and critical studies of American religious ideas were just beginning to emerge. As a revised doctoral dissertation, the book contributed significantly to a renewed appreciation of liberalism and its nurturing context. It was superseded in 1976 by William R. Hutchison's *The Modernist Impulse in American Protestantism* (see p. 64), but the work survives as a valuable reference work and responsible example of theological interpretation for historical purposes.

Cauthen bases his analysis on a thorough knowledge of the literature that forms the bulk of his report. He places those formulations against their social and intellectual background and explains their emergence at least in part by reference to environmental setting. In fair and balanced terms he displays the diverse interests of liberal spokesmen who sought to make Christianity relevant to contemporary life at the turn of this century. Cauthen is neither blindly admiring nor uniformly critical of these professors and preachers during their subsequent decades of activity. Probably the most important contribution is Cauthen's use of types to provide a classification system of an intellectual map for understanding different emphases in liberal thought. He uses "evangelical liberalism" as a category for discussing W. A. Brown, H. E. Fosdick, W. Rauschenbusch, A. C. Knudson, and E. W. Lyman. A more extreme group called "modernistic liberalism" includes expositions of S. Mathews, D. C. Macintosh, and H. N. Wieman. These categories and their carefully expounded contents remain the chief virtue of this perennially useful text. Beyond that, the author offers more debatable suggestions about which aspects of liberal thinking survived into later decades when neo-orthodox categories became dominant. Whether or not conservative theologians incorporated liberal perspectives, Cauthen's period piece is a study of lasting merit. [H.W.B.]

Cherry, Conrad, ed. *God's New Israel: Religious Interpretations of American Destiny.* Englewood Cliffs, NJ: Prentice-Hall, 1971. xii + 381 pp.

This is a sourcebook of primary documents for students of American civil religion. It is selective but fairly comprehensive beginning with the colonial period and extending through the civil rights movement of the 1960s. The sermons, speeches, addresses, poetry, and policy statements have been selected for either their sense of providential calling of America as a light to other nations or for their indications of judgment upon the United States for having failed in that calling. The parallels with ancient Israel are present throughout, but sometimes they are used to single out the theme of "chosenness." At other times, they point out national sins as jeremiads against pride and self-aggrandizement. Such parallels make it convenient for Cherry to span the centuries.

Jonathan Edwards in "The Latter-Day Glory Is Probably To Begin in America" and John F. Kennedy in "The Doctrine of National Independence" share an upbeat vision of the country as an example of ordained purified idealism to a war-torn and ethically tattered Europe. On the other hand, Nicholas Street preaching in hard days of the early Revolution and J. William Fulbright writing in the bleak twilight of Vietnam are forthright about the arrogance of power in national deceit posing as the righteousness of God.

Other selections include: Lyman Beecher's "Plea for the West" as typical of manifest destiny, Horace Bushnell's theory of national atonement in his post–Civil War sermon "Our Obligations to the Dead," the thrust of the Social Gospel in a wedding of the secular and the spiritual in Washington Gladden's "The Nation and the Kingdom," and Martin Luther King's Pauline epistle on faith and civil reasoning in "Letter from Birmingham Jail." In addition, Cherry provides some fieldwork of his own on civil religion and death and analysis of where civil religion stands vis à vis the spectrum of American religion.

Taken as a whole, *God's New Israel* moves from the explicit language of religious transcendence to a much more ambiguous and complex level of national symbolism as the decades pass. In part, this is due to the lessening influence of the ministry in shaping public speech, in part due to the rise of science and progress as public concepts, and in part due to ever increasing cultural pluralism. A case could be made for changes in the text that include stronger exponents of civil religion in our time. Kennedy's first inaugural would have made a better choice than the article cited. It is a more forceful statement and one that is important in light of Robert Bellah's classic exegesis. Protests against Anglo-American exclusion of minority history in constructing an American civil religion are, with two exceptions, missing from the book. These need to be there as examples of the call for an inclusive public faith that Cherry discusses in his introduction. These shortcomings can easily be corrected in a revised edition. Given Cherry's relevant commentary and the continuing importance of most of the selections, *God's New Israel* maintains its place as the historical casebook for an introduction to American civil religion. [S.C.B.]

Clebsch, William A. *American Religious Thought: A History.* Chicago: University of Chicago Press, 1973. xxi + 212 pp.

Clebsch's review of the history of American religious thought rests upon three explicit methodological assumptions. First, he distinguishes between theology and religious thought and concentrates upon the latter, which, rather than expounding, defending, or interpreting Christian doctrine, develops a distinctive American spirituality. Second, he argues that American religious thought has consistently moved beyond moralism toward an aesthetic sense of human religiousness, toward "a consciousness of the beauty of living in harmony with divine things—in a word, being at home in the universe" (p. xvi). Third, he uses eponyms—founders and bearers rather than clergymen, per se—to suggest how the aesthetic focus of American religious thought actually informs a definable tradition.

Thus his major chapters are on "the sensible spirituality of Jonathan Edwards," "the hospitable universe of Ralph Waldo Emerson," and "the human religiousness of William James." As Clebsch summarizes, "Edwards found divine things lovely in themselves for persons whose lives were made works of divine art. Emerson found nature welcoming persons to the indivisible act of reliance on God and on the self. James found in humanity itself a companionship open to men and women of strenuous mood and serious mind." All three found the universe "an eminently hospitable home for the human spirit" (p. 7). Brief interchapters outline the historical context of these ideas, relating Edwards, Emerson, and James to one another and to others (the Puritans, Channing, Bushnell, Rauschenbusch, Dewey, and the Niebuhrs) in the tradition as a whole.

In Clebsch's view, the heritage he examines offers a corrective to the misdirection of current American spiritual options, for "in this heritage our relations to nature and to humanity and to God are inseparable" (p. 9). This is a large order for the historian to fill; yet Clebsch offers a promising beginning, for he knows that Americanness is "not an inherent quality unfolding itself through time but something the historian sees in retrospect" (p. 3). This knowledge allows him *as a historian* to issue invitations at the ends of the chapters on his eponyms for contemporary Americans to embrace a new awareness of the essentially still possible hospitality of the world that is disclosed by a review of the spirituality of Edwards, Emerson, and James. The study of history is thus shown to have spiritual implications of its own—one may recover the past and one's self in the same imaginative act. So Clebsch's work shows that there is a distinctively American mode of religious thought and also suggests that interpretation locates the student within that heritage—keeping the tradition alive by making it new. [J.G.M.-y]

Clebsch, William A. *From Sacred to Profane America: The Role of Religion in American History.* **New York: Harper and Row, 1968. xi + 242 pp.**

Clebsch's thesis is that "the chief features of the American dream were formed by people's religious concerns and they came into realization outside the temple" (p. ix). He presents his methodology (phenomenology) and theoretical assumptions (a kind of dialectical idealism) in an introductory chapter. In general, his argument is that those elements most important to American secular life emerged initially from concerns within American religion, and through a process of implementation became shorn of their religious content. In the sweep of American history during its European phase, he argues, one can see this dialectic clearly in the evolution of education, pluralism, welfare and morality, the participatory tradition, the fascination with novelty, and concepts of nationality. In six essay-chapters, Clebsch deals in detail with each of these elements and suggests how they are intertwined. In "Ahead of History," the author explores the peculiarly American fascination with teleology and eschatology. "Equals—And Some More Equal" explores the contradictory tendencies in American religion that have led to both exclusion and inclusion of women, children, and minorities in and from American life. The most ironic and paradoxical example of secularity arising from religious concerns is found in "A Little Learning," a treatment of the labyrinthine history of American education. "Let Men Be Good" analyzes the Calvinistic origins and perfectionist development of American concepts of welfare and mortality. In "This Nation Under God," Clebsch speculates on the Hebraic concept of nationhood prevalent in American thought. "Apolypolitan Culture" explores a theory of radical pluralism.

Using an interesting variation of historical dialectic, Clebsch suggests that the relationship between religion and American culture began with a dynamic role of religion. As the goals of religion were transformed into secular success, the role of religion became static. Will some new crisis, Clebsch wonders, lead to a dynamic role again?

Clebsch pulls together a fair number of secondary and primary sources as the documentation for his suggestive essay. [G.H.S.]

Cone, James H. *Black Theology and Black Power*. New York: Seabury Press, 1969. x + 165 pp.

This book was the first written solely from the perspective of the black Christian community, interpreting the message of salvation from the black experience of oppression. Its themes parallel those of Latin American liberation theology, but are not directly related to it. It is a precursor of the special-interest theological writings that have arisen, such as feminist theology. Although reflecting the beginnings of black consciousness in theological writing, the radicalism in tone and themes and its link to the Black Power movement date it as a historical classic.

Cone addresses the dilemma of the black people in white America, recognizing their black history and the absurdity of a situation in which persons are oppressed solely because of color. Two choices are offered: to accept this situation or to be courageous enough to challenge it and to work for change. Cone sees the latter as the only viable and Christian alternative.

To accomplish the transformation of the social order, Cone links the Christian gospel to the tenets of the Black Power movement. Politicizing the gospel by interpreting it in and through black power categories and ideology does not distort it since politics, social realities, attitudes, and world views are always intertwined with it. Whites have used the gospel to justify their racism based upon their willful misreading and misappropriation of the message.

But, Cone says, the gospel has a true predilection for the poor and oppressed; God, through Jesus, works as liberator of persons in *this* world, not simply in the next. Liberation not only includes a spiritual liberation from sin, but a concrete liberation from oppressive historical realities. The Christian church in America—whether black or white—has failed to live its commitment to its goals; failed to be a liberating force.

The post–Civil War black churches have failed as they avoided the pre–Civil War churches' emphasis on freedom and equality in history while stressing the afterlife. Cone feels the Black Power movement is needed to reorient the black church to its true mission and to confront the white churches with their sinful complicity in the underlying violence of American society. Linking this movement to black theological analysis of the gospel will liberate theology from its "whiteness" and will create a new community, a new black church.

Black theology does not intend to make the experience of Christ secondary to the experience of black oppression. Rather, God's reconciling act in Christ will ultimately make possible an affirmation of blackness as a positive good and this self-affirmation will lay a foundation for a dialogue with whites, enabling them to see a humanity beyond their "whiteness." [M.L.S.]

Cone, James H. *God of the Oppressed*. New York: Seabury Press, 1975. viii + 280 pp.

Based on the success of the three earlier publications (*Black Theology and Black Power* in 1969 [see p. 27], *A Black Theology of Liberation* in 1970, and *The Spiritual and the Blues* in 1972), many articles in various journals, numerous lectures, and a secure professorship at prestigious Union Theological Seminary (New York), Cone has come to be regarded as one of the most articulate spokespersons for modern black religion and theology.

In his previous books and articles, Cone explored the intellectual foundations of his "black theology" and sought to make it theologically and analytically respectable. In *God of the Oppressed* Cone does not depart from the former venture but turns it in another direction—a more personal and autobiographical one, in harmony with the introspective and genealogical interests of the current mood. He contends that more often than not "it is a theologian's *personal* history, in a particular sociopolitical setting, that serves as the most important factor shaping the methodology and content of his or her theological perspective" (p. vi). The distinction of this volume is that in it Cone aims at and succeeds in being more honest and informative about the nonintellectual and existential roots of his faith and black theological enterprise—which are to be discovered in the black community and black experience itself. Specifically, his pilgrimage begins and is planted in the Macedonia African Methodist Episcopal Church in Bearden, Arkansas; and, for Cone, God's important early visits were there—not at Sinai or Goshen, Bethlehem or New York!

Although the clarity of his thought and writing makes Cone's earlier works comparatively easy to grasp, the life experiences discussed so openly in this spiritual autobiography make it even more enjoyable reading than Cone's previous writings. He peppers this text generously with quotes from hymns, spirituals, sermons, stories, black oral history, favorite Scriptures, songs, prayers, popular black liturgies, folklore, and black sayings, expressions, and euphemisms. It is a feast of cultural wit, anecdote, remembrance, and testimony done with compelling charm, vivacity, and integrity. All this is integrated into and interspersed with some of the more sophisticated theological insights and reflections of our time. It not only succeeds at explicating black American theology, but also serves as an excellent model for the personalized theology of a member of any ethnic, national, or religious community. Its thoroughly experiential character makes it compatible with other autobiographical material that is not just black or religious per se. It is a volume that will prompt spiritual uplift and not just impart intellectual illumination.   [E.A.W.]

Cox, Harvey G. *Religion in the Secular City: Toward a Postmodern Theology.* New York: Simon and Schuster, 1984. 304 pp.

Those who predicted the demise of religion in the industrial world, claims Harvey Cox, were in error. In most recent times, he points out, there has been a dramatic rebirth of "traditional religions." Many who are involved in this "revival" link their religious and political commitments. From among these groups, Cox selects two movements as representative case studies—"political fundamentalism" in the United States of America as embodied in the ministry of Jerry Falwell, and a Christian-base community of liberation in Latin America. Both emerge from grass-roots situations; reject "liberal" theology albeit for different reasons; are in the process of establishing new forms of religious communal relationships; stress the need for political involvement; and prefer the leadership of charismatic leaders. In his final analysis Cox favors the Latin American base communities because they, unlike "the political fundamentalists," support a universal and pluralistic approach to theology and politics. They propound a theology of corporate salvation that seeks to prevent religious fervor from turning into a narrow, narcissistic, and destructive henotheism.

Cox's concluding section seeks out sources for a viable postmodern theology. It must take into consideration the needs of our new world community, reject the weaknesses of "liberal" theology without discarding its strengths, and utilize "global" sources. North Americans who seek to develop such a theology will need to develop their own liberation theology and their own base communities that draw upon their own "evangelical-conservative" traditions while avoiding "being engulfed and deformed by the fundamentalists" and, at the same time, absorbing "the liberation currents into a form of popular religion that is characteristically North American" (p. 267). [N.P.].

Cox, Harvey. *The Secular City: Secularization and Urbanization in Theological Perspective.* New York: Macmillan, 1965; rev. ed. New York: Macmillan, 1966. viii + 276 pp.

Cox sees secularization as a liberation, not as an enemy to religion or, in particular, to Christianity. The more influential Christianity can be, the more effective its ethical and moral precepts become in society, the less need there is for the organized church per se. The ordering of society becomes a human task; we can no longer pass it on to some religious power.

This, of course, is viewed as a compliment to the creature whom God turns loose now, in our Eden become global, to nurture it and make it fit for human habitation. The mythic and cultic meanings always associated with our origins and histories are past. Now it is our time to do with it what we must and will.

It is in his chapter on "The Church and the Secular University" that Cox is at his prophetic and academic best. He traces the early history of higher education in its philosophic and religious origins, showing how the university has always been a problem child for the church. As the university has grown, it has become more and more irrelevant to the purposes and mission of the church, although the "church tradition" still survives in its midst.

The need for money has pretty much destroyed the eliteness of the university setting, especially as the demand for more and more graduate students in technological and specialized fields increases. And as the church struggles with its own issues of relevance and survival, it has less and less motivation or resources to be involved in higher education. But Cox does outline the three ways that the church has attempted to be effective on campuses.

Cox's praise, muted though it be, for the para-church groups, Inter-Varsity, and the YMCA is truly prophetic. For it is the para-church that is making the most inroads on the university campus today. The work of the so-called mainline denominations is failing for precisely the reasons Cox offered, and the unaffiliated groups are filling that void.

So "God" is now evident in the sociological, political, and cultural life of the world. It is not a term reserved for use by theologians alone. Or, to reverse it, theologians who wish to speak about God must now do so in sociological and political, as well as cultural arenas in addition to or in place of the more traditional theological loci of the past. Cox believes this wider understanding of the Deity explains why "the religious compulsion of man, whether in its mythological or in its metaphysical form, has never been too happy with Jesus" (p. 226). Such incarnational theology is too limited, too exclusive, to be effective in the larger secularization of the human scene. It is time now for a new name for this being we have called God, even if we must do without a name for a while.   [W.C.O.]

Cross, Robert D. *The Emergence of Liberal Catholicism in America.* Cambridge: Harvard University Press, 1958. 328 pp.

This historical monograph describes the late nineteenth-century conflict within the Roman Catholic church over its relationship to the dominant American culture. Until this time, the Catholic church in the United States was isolated from mainstream culture because of Protestant persecution and a desire to protect itself from the secular society. According to Cross, by the 1880s "a coherent challenge was being made to traditional Catholic folkways by a group of clergy and laity anxious to promote a friendly interaction between their religion and American life" (p. vii). Catholic liberals pushed for more religious accommodation with American society, while Catholic conservatives fought against any dilution of orthodox beliefs.

Cross traced the emerging differences between these Catholic factions in postbellum periodicals. The debate centered around the proper relationship of American Catholics to a non-Catholic state and the dominant Protestant culture, political democracy, social and economic problems, education, "revealed truth" and science, and American individualism. Although Cross acknowledged "the great extent of beliefs and practices shared by all American Catholics" (p. vii), he demonstrated that liberals were more willing than conservatives to embrace the distinctive American values of religious voluntarism, human effort, and public education.

When it was published in 1958, this volume was a welcome addition to a growing body of Catholic scholarship. More important, it offered an innovative approach to the study of religion and social change. Earlier work had focused primarily on the differences between Catholic and Protestant America, finding Roman Catholicism either a blasphemous threat to the Protestant establishment or a hapless victim of Protestant prejudice and discrimination. Cross explored the Roman Catholic adaptation to American society as an internal process of denominational realignment initiated by a diversifying

Catholic constituency. Competing subcultures produced contrary strategies for improving the position of Catholics in the United States. This approach is especially valuable because it facilitates a comparison of American Catholics with other religious groups in terms of their response to social change.

Subsequent historians have refined many of this study's conclusions about late nineteenth-century Catholicism. Cross claimed that the liberal-conservative conflict permeated this denomination, yet he presented evidence only for an ideological rift among the clergy. The new immigration history has identified the conservative laity as primarily immigrants who used religious traditionalism to anchor their culture in the United States. Cross also alluded to a rapidly changing American society, but he did not clarify the implications of continued industrialization for the Catholic church. Recent scholars have shown that most religious movements responded to the modernizing American society with similar internal divisions. His concluding chapter is especially dated. Cross suggested that the mid-twentieth-century success of Catholic political candidates demonstrated the successful reconciliation of Catholicism and American society. The ensuing Catholic discord over Vatican II, feminism, and "liberation theology" ended this speculation and underscores the need for continued attention to the study of religion and society in tension.   [L.K.P.]

Cross, Whitney R. *The Burned-over District: The Social and Intellectual History of Enthusiastic Religion in Western New York.* Ithaca: Cornell University Press, 1950; 2d ed. New York: Harper and Row, 1965. xiii + 383 pp.

This historical monograph is a portrait of the Second Great Awakening in New York State west of the Appalachian Mountain ranges. Between 1800 and 1850, repeated revivals, theological and ritualistic innovations, and bitter disputes over the nature of Christianity gave this area the appellation "the burned-over district." With evangelist Charles Finney as the catalyst, the religious fire began, but could not be contained, within the mainline Protestant denominations. Each successive religious variant spawned still another, so that a continuum of religious groups, ranging from ultratraditional to those outside the boundaries of Christianity, coexisted within the same religion. This same western New York arena engendered the highly evangelical New School wing of the Presbyterian, U.S.A. denomination as well as the Mormons, the Adventists, the Spiritualists, and an array of quasi-religious utopian groups such as the Oneida Community.

Yet the importance of this volume extends well beyond western

New York. It has become an American religious history classic because of the author's analytical imagination and comprehensiveness. Whitney Cross believed that a "microcosmic study" of a particular location over several decades fostered an "integrated treatment of cultural, social, economic, political, and ideological causations" (p. viii) of religious change. Cross's efforts yielded a volume more sensitive to the larger social context of religious change than those that had come before. Social historians who would come later have embraced this approach.

This study was also one of the first to document a relationship between evangelicalism, religious pluralism, and economic modernization. Although Whitney Cross owed his primary intellectual debt to Frederick Jackson Turner, his major findings significantly revised the belief that only frontier environments fueled antebellum religious change and the rise of evangelicalism. Cross argued that the dislocations of accelerating social and economic development, not early settlement conditions, sparked the religious conflagration. He pointed specifically to the successful western New York revivals and new religious movements in the commercial towns surrounded by burgeoning agricultural hinterlands that the opening of the Erie Canal had stimulated in 1825. Cross further challenged the frontier thesis by arguing that the cultural predisposition of western New York gave the area a special proclivity for ecstatic and bizarre religiosity. He suggested that the Yankee ethnic heritage of most New Yorkers, rooted as it was in Puritan millennialism and the experience of the First Great Awakening, provided the tinder for the religious excitement in western New York.

Subsequent scholars have continued to explore the relationship between the religious changes wrought by the Second Great Awakening and the general process of modernization in the antebellum United States. As it turns out, western New York probably was not unique in its religious transformation, nor was the region wholly dependent on its New England cultural heritage for religious enthusiasm. Still, *The Burned-over District* provides a comprehensive study of religious change in one of the Second Great Awakening's most vital centers. [L.K.P]

Dolan, Jay P. *Catholic Revivalism: The American Experience, 1830–1900.* Notre Dame: University of Notre Dame Press, 1978. xx + 248 pp.

Predated by Dolan's article in *Horizons* (vol. 3, Spring 1976), this is the first book to focus historical attention on an important wellspring of nineteenth-century American Catholic spiritual vitality—the revival-oriented parish mission. Its European beginnings, in a generic sense, can be traced back centuries, particularly to the post-Reformation use of the Ignatian *Spiritual Exercises* for group retreats. In its distinctive American form, the parish mission grew rapidly and evolved into a set pattern of activities and preaching content from the 1850s until the 1890s. It became a very popular religious experience for Catholic Americans.

Referred to as "sacramental evangelicalism," the missions featured some characteristics common to Protestant revivalism: emphasis on emotional preaching designed to achieve conversion; a stress on disciplined morality, especially chastity and temperance and other individualistically oriented behaviors; a heavy eschatological stress on themes of death, judgment, heaven and hell, and a corresponding emphasis on the availability of God's grace for those willing to repent.

Dolan analyzes the content of the sermons of representative preachers, who were mainly members of religious orders. These itinerant preachers aimed to renew and fortify the faith of the believer and to revitalize the sacramental life of the congregation, especially the sacramental reception of Penance and Holy Communion. The success of the days given over to the mission was measured by the immediate increase in confession and reception of communion—distinguishing features not found in Protestant revivalism. More lasting effects on the quality of faith and practice in the parish are difficult to find and verify.

The mission brought new forms of popular piety to the immigrant church, strengthened ties to Rome, and solidified clerical leadership as well as afforded a uniformity of devotional experience among the diverse ethnic parishes. This devotional experience also contributed to the acceptance of a low economic status through its "otherworldly" stress, even while it stabilized a Catholic community in its New World existence. By the end of the nineteenth century, the mission had become a routinized affair with a stylized pattern that persisted into the 1950s and still exists, to some extent, today.

Dolan does relate the contemporary Catholic charismatic movement to both Protestant revivalism and the "sacramental evangelicalism" of the old mission experience, arguing that the movement has more in common with the former. Revivalism in American culture was not a totally Protestant phenomenon; the Catholic tradition had its own version and history of "enthusiastic" religious activity.   [M.L.S.]

Ellis, John Tracy. *American Catholicism.* **Chicago History of American Civilization Series. Chicago: University of Chicago Press,**

1956; rev ed. Chicago: University of Chicago Press, 1969. xviii + 322 pp.

American Catholic historical scholarship came of age in this author who is the foremost contemporary scholar in his field. A long list of earlier publications had already established Ellis's reputation as an authority on Catholic life in North America, so it was natural for him to deliver the Walgreen Lectures in 1955 on this inclusive topic. The following year these essays were printed as part of the Chicago History of American Civilization Series, and in a second edition, they feature another chapter that surveys developments down to 1968.

This superlative overview flows with the graceful style for which Ellis has always been admired, and it affords him another opportunity to make balanced judgments about how his ecclesiastical tradition fits the larger contours of American life. He uses institutional history and the Catholic hierarchy as a skeleton for church history. Moving beyond that familiar outline, Ellis probes religious awareness among the laity at various epochs and incorporates sociological studies of parish life. These interior focal points acquire additional meaning when discussed against changes in international politics and amid the American context of republican values.

Ellis helps both beginning and advanced students by supplying fresh perspectives and periodization. He avoids common Anglo distortions by recounting Spanish and French colonial experiences as well as early English activities in the New World. This early period of planting churches among native Americans and European arrivals ended with the Revolutionary War. The early national period for Catholics extended to 1852 when the church held its First Plenary Council. A third phase witnessed the Civil War and massive immigration of new peoples up to 1908 when the American church was released from care of the Congregation de Propoganda Fide. After that the church experienced changes to an arbitrary date, and subsequently it underwent more transformation related to the Second Vatican Council. This masterful summary is the best short introduction to a large field anyone could wish to have.   [H.W.B.]

Ellwood, Robert S. Jr. *Alternative Altars: Unconventional and Eastern Spirituality in America*. Chicago History of American Religion Series. Chicago: University of Chicago Press, 1979. xiii + 192 pp.

This book is divided into perspectives on the problem and case histories of representative alternative religions. In the first section are three chapters. "Temple and Cave in America," a discussion of various typologies of established and emerging religions, draws upon Solomon's Temple and Plato's Cave analogies for paradigms of two constantly coexisting forms of religious orientation in American culture. Ellwood presents a model of occult conversion to demonstrate the similarities and points of conflict and contradiction between established and emerging religion.

"Excursus Religion" begins with a summary of Mary Douglas's model of religion as orientation to cosmos. The two basic variables are "grid" and "group." Grid refers to the template we use to impose order on the universe. Group refers to the relative strength of boundary maintenance and constraints upon members. The resultant four categories of "Strong Group and Grid," "Strong Group, Weak Grid," "Weak Group, Strong Grid," and "Weak Group and Grid" form radically different orientations to the universe. Ellwood hypothesizes that American culture, in its Anglo phase, began as weak group and grid, and that the alternative religions, or non-normative religions, represent those who are strong group and grid. He further argues that alternative religious movements have a continuous and coherent religious tradition. A final chapter in this section explores "Inner Worlds: The Psychology of Excursus Religion."

In the second part, Ellwood presents three case histories of "Shakers and Spiritualists," "Colonel Olcott and Madame Blavatsky Journey to the East," and "Zen Journeys to the West." In each of these excursions, one can see both the psychological dynamics and anthropological categories of grid and group at work. Whether the movement springs from conventional Christianity ("Shakers and Spiritualists"), an occult interpretation of insights of the East ("Colonel Olcott and Madame Blavatsky Journey to the East"), or direct adaptations of Oriental religions ("Zen Journeys to the West"), one can see the psycho-religious expression of that handful of strong group and grid folk in the midst of a dominant weak group and grid culture. [G.H.S.]

Elson, Ruth Miller. *Guardians of Tradition: American Schoolbooks of the Nineteenth Century*. Lincoln: University of Nebraska Press, 1964. xiii + 424 pp.

This invaluable study tackles a subject of considerable importance for teachers and scholars. It is based upon a thorough examination of more than one thousand of the most popular textbooks used during the first eight years of schooling in nineteenth-century United States. Together with a brief introduction to the history of early American elementary school textbooks, curricula, and pedagogy, this book centers its discussion and analysis on five broad themes: "God and Nature," "The Nature of Man," "Schoolbooks and 'Culture,' " and "Social Experience." These themes serve as a port of access to understand the social and cultural content of those texts and how their authors attempted to shape the average American child's world view.

At a time when Americans believed that every aspect of their culture should reflect and foster the virtue they thought absolutely essential for the maintenance of democratic government, their concern for the survival of the infant republic focused Americans' attention on schooling and the nation's children, the rising generation. It is within this social-intellectual context that Elson seeks to elucidate the national "core" values that adults in nineteenth-century United States deemed necessary for the maintenance of a virtuous republic in such diverse areas as religion, science, economics, social relations, and politics.

As her book amply documents, nineteenth-century textbook authors—most of whom hailed from New England—were more concerned with molding the character rather than the minds of children. The world contained in their pages is largely one of simplicity and brass-bolted certitude. It is a world of clearly identifiable villains and heroes, where God is just, nature is benign, racial differences are inherent and unalterable, progress is assured, virtue is rewarded, and vice is punished. And one can embrace good and shun evil by following a few simple rules. Elson's argument concerning the conservative function of schoolbooks in the creation and solidification of American traditions anticipates Frances Fitzgerald's study of twentieth-century American history texts, and it does so with a greater breadth and depth of research.

Elson offers important insights into the thinking of the nation's petit-bourgeoisie—the printers, ministers, journalists, teachers, and lawyers—who authored nineteenth-century schoolbooks. She is less successful in her attempt to prove that these texts played a decisive role in forming the world view of the nation's youth. For Elson, like the schoolbook authors she discusses, the mind of the nineteenth-century American child is a *tabula rasa* upon which adults can write anything they see fit; the notion that children might be selective about what they learn is decidedly absent in her analysis. Finally, captive to the elite bias of intellectual history, she fails to examine folktales, popular songs, and children's games of the era, which could offer valuable clues about the diffusion of the textbooks' content in American popular culture. The result is a book that tells us more about the small group of cultural arbiters who attempted to set the standards of thought and behavior in nineteenth-century American society than about the great mass of socially and economically diverse Americans who were asked to live by them.   [M.H.L.]

Erikson, Kai T. *The Wayward Puritans: A Study in the Sociology of Deviance*. New York: John Wiley and Sons, 1966. xv + 228 pp.

When Kai Erikson's *Wayward Puritans* was published in 1966, it received mixed reviews in the scholarly journals and in the popular press. Over time, however, this "Study in the Sociology of Deviance" has remained a useful example of theory and application. It exploration of the Puritan society in Massachusetts Bay provides useful insights into the social impact of religious/philosophical perspectives, and the work is still cited by scholars today.

For the student of religion, the Erikson discussion is particularly useful, because it offers an analytical approach to determining the ways in which a dominant religious group can and did shape the societal definition of deviance and, therefore, of crime.

Erikson's introductory chapter summarizes some elements of Emile Durkheim's sociological method and theory to see if the Durkheim insights "can be translated into useful research hypotheses" (p. 5). The central Durkheim idea explored by Erikson is that "Like a war, a flood, or some other emergency, deviance makes people more alert to the interest they share in common and draws attention to those values which constitute the 'collective conscience' of the community" (p. 4).

Defining "crime wave" as "a rash of publicity, a moment of excitement and alarm, a feeling that something needs to be done" (p. 69), Erikson investigates three such waves in Puritan New England: the Antinomian controversy of 1636–38; the Quaker persecutions of the late 1650s; and the witchcraft hysteria of 1692.

Using the term *boundary* in Durkheim's philosophical sense, Erikson studies Massachusetts Bay Puritanism from this perspective: "whenever a community is confronted by a significant relocation of boundaries, a shift in its territorial position, it is likely to experience a change in the kinds of behavior handled by its various agencies of control" (p. 68).

The sociological approach to Puritanism that Erikson employs in his analysis of Puritan reactions to the deviance perceived in the behavior of Antinomians, Quakers, and witches reveals much about the collective Puritan conscience. It also opens new areas for discussion on topics such as Puritan punishment techniques, harshness and severity of punishment as a potential cause of deviance, and the ultimate impact of Puritan predestination theory on the Auburn system of prison management that is dominant in twentieth-century America.

Wayward Puritans is a straightforward, clearly stated example of the way research method shapes research findings. For the student thinking about possible approaches to a field of study, it compares historiography to sociology and provides a well-defined paradigm through which to view the collective behavior of a community. [J.S.H.]

Frazier, E. Franklin. *The Negro Church in America*. New York: Schocken Books, 1964; 6th ed. New York: Schocken Books, 1971. xii + 92 pp.

Franklin Frazier was invited to give the Frazer Lecture in Social Anthropology at the University of Liverpool in 1953. At that time he was Chief of the Division of Applied Social Sciences in the Department of Social Sciences of UNESCO in Paris, France. That address was the basis for this excellent book. *The Negro Church in America* is an important document in the understanding of the religious life of the Negro in America. (This book was written before "black" became the acceptable noun.)

Frazier initiates his discussion with a description of the disruption of life caused by the slave trade. The Negro was dehumanized with nearly all vestiges of social cohesion destroyed. In that vacuum Christian religion became the new basis for structuring life.

It was not until after the Emancipation that the Negro church grew rapidly; the "invisible institution" was now becoming visible. The "free church" of the north and the "slave church" of the south merged and in their coming together each was transformed. In the pre-Emancipation church, faith orientation was primarily otherworldly. After the Emancipation, religious life took on the task of organizing the new social existence of the Negro in four specific areas: (1) sexual mores, (2) economic cooperation, (3) education, and (4) politics. In his discussion, it would have been helpful if Frazier had developed more fully his thesis that "the Negro church became the arena of their political activities" (p. 43).

This study is enhanced by Frazier's examination of certain sociological factors affecting the church. As a sociologist, the author engages in a discussion of the twin demographic shifts from rural to urban and from south to north and notes the profound effects these changes had upon the family and the church.

The reader will sense a subtle conflict within a major thesis of Frazier's book. On the one hand, he calls the Negro church the "most important cultural institution" for blacks. But he also sees his race becoming so assimilated into middle-class American culture that the uniqueness of the Negro church is disappearing.

We are saddened that Frazier did not live to continue his observations of the black church in America. He died before Dr. Martin Luther King, Jr., was assassinated. Would he still maintain that the protest movement under King was an expression of the religious heritage of the Negro more than a conscious appropriation of the Gandhi philosophy? Perhaps an even stronger case could be made today.

The footnotes provide a helpful bibliography of much of the best writing on the subject of the Negro and the church up to the time of the book's writing.

The book is brief (92 text pages). It is straightforward, direct, and almost cooly analytical. The text gives the facts without much pathos, feeling, or fervor. Perhaps it had to be written that way in order to be read by white Americans. For anyone wanting to understand the black church in America, Frazier's perspective can be tantalizing and helpful, causing the reader to want to pursue more research and study. [H.M.]

Gaustad, Edwin Scott. *Dissent in American Religion.* **Chicago History of American Religion Series. Chicago: University of Chicago Press, 1973. xii + 184 pp.**

This short, insightful work written by an eminent American religious historian was the inaugural volume in the Chicago History of American Religion Series edited by Martin E. Marty. Gaustad focuses on the broad current of dissent and conflict in American religious life. In the context of the controversy between consensus and conflict schools among American historians, Gaustad clearly comes down on the conflict side. Historically, religious dissent has been inspired by the desire to attack false, compromised, or "tame" religion for the sake of the true, absolute, "ever-discontented, ever-dissenting faith" (p. 6). Religious dissent is itself, according to Gaustad, a form of religion ("a distillation of the religious quest" [p. 5]) and a manifestation of the enduring human desire for freedom. Gaustad divides American religious dissenters into three general categories: schismatics, heretics, and misfits. Religious schism in America followed patterns long ago established in Europe. As was the case with European Christianity, schism in American religion had an inertia of its own, a kind of "chain reaction" of obstinate devisiveness. Schism invariably led to the establishment of new churches, contrary to the oft-repeated disclaimers of dissenters that they did not intend to do so. In America, pietism, the frontier, the tradition of liberal democracy, evangelicalism, ethnicity, race, and, ironically, ecumenism nurtured schismatic impulses and contributed to divisions within churches.

Heretics (Ethan Allen, Elihu Palmer, Thomas Paine) found religion repressive or irrational, insensitive or warped, obscurantist or confused, mean-spirited or simply wrong. Most devoted their time and energies to the cause of reason against the cause of religion or rejected the "nonsense" that God revealed his will in a written word that was authoritative for all humankind. Romantic heretics (the Transcendentalists) attacked the reductionism of religion. Humans have a spiritual nature; but so does the universe. Science also played a key role in the spread of heresy. The increase in scientific influence in the late nineteenth century was supposed to herald a new age that would spell the demise of religion. Intellectuals such as John William Draper (*History of the Conflict Between Science and Religion* [1874]) and the geologist John Wesley Powell saw the "spirit of the age" (science) undermining the foundations of religion. Walter Lippman and Joseph Wood Krutch trumpeted the gospel of humanism.

Misfits were religious dissenters (Roger Williams, William Miller, Dorothy Day) who were feared, destroyed, exiled, ridiculed, and patronized. Some found accommodations within establishment religions, others did not.

Although schisms, heretics, and misfits have been tough on bishops, hard on dogmatically defined creeds, and in constant tension with religiocultural currents of mainstream America, they have left an important social, cultural, and religious legacy. They raised issues of social justice, reacted against sterile reason, middle-class complacency, and bureaucratic inertia, and reinvigorated the enduring human quest for the ideal community. Gaustad paints broad outlines of both the low and the high roads of these endeavors and shows how dissenters can have a dysfunctional and destructive impact on society and work to restore or inspire new commitments and causes. This book also contains a good bibliography of American religious dissent and is valuable for use in courses on American religious history or theology. [W.D.D.]

Gaustad, Edwin Scott. *A Religious History of America*. New York: Harper and Row, 1966. xxiii + 421 pp.

The publication of this single-volume work on the role of religion in American national life is a demarcational and watershed event. With only a handful of exceptions, this work and its publication date mark the passing from the former era characterized by one-volume chronological surveys of the "rise and progress of ecclesiastical bodies" or denominations, which can be called "American *church* histories," to the new and current era when such surveys, like Gaustad's, aim at telling the far broader religious history of American life and culture. It aims at telling national history rather than institutional or denominational history. Although Gaustad knows that any history proceeds from a particular point of view, his is not a particular theological one, like most church historians; his perspective is that of a secular, empirical historian who includes a wide variety of conflicting voices, some religious and some not, some representing particular institutions and some not, but all representing differing but significant expressions of the pluralism of American national and cultural life.

Gaustad's working assumptions are affirmative of the role of religion as a formative and historical factor in culture, but not at all confessional or apologetic of a particular religious persuasion. Religion is as vital and legitimate as any other aspect of America's past and is one facet that cannot be excluded without violating the integrity of the American experience. The cacophony and variety of religious perspectives and cultural voices simply enrich rather than impoverish both the democratic and educative processes alive in national life itself.

In the body of his own historical analysis Gaustad inserts moderate-length quotes of primary source material within the context of the appropriate era or epoch being discussed. This makes the reading of Gaustad's text rather unique and a bit difficult at first; but fairly quickly the reader gets accustomed to this pattern of writing. In the long run, this material makes the text far more exciting and rewarding, because the reader is exposed not only to Gaustad's interpretive perspective but also to a host of national representatives and cultural participants speaking for themselves. It is a technique that is consistent with Gaustad's aim of producing a religious history of American culture that transcends any single religious or cultural voice. It is a technique that has the aura of honesty, openness, and integrity.

In addition to the text, its punctuating quotations of primary sources, and its generous number of interdisciplinary illustrations, there is a selective chronology of important dates in America's religious history and a carefully selected set of suggestions for further reading under particular parts and chapters of the text.

Gaustad has produced an unusually sound, balanced, multifaceted survey of American religious history, which has not been duplicated and will be difficult to supersede or displace. This plus the urbanity of his mind and evenness of his temper make this an extremely durable and companionable volume. [E.A.W.]

Gaustad, Edwin Scott, ed. *A Documentary History of Religion in America to the Civil War.* **Vol. 1. Grand Rapids: Eerdmans, 1982. v + 535 pp., and** *A Documentary History of Religion in America since 1865.* **Vol. 2. Grand Rapids: Eerdmans, 1983. xx + 610 pp.**

Compendia or documents representing American religion appeared in 1921 with a slim volume edited by Peter G. Mode and in 1931–46 with four huge denominational volumes edited by William W. Sweet. These efforts were hampered by narrow ideology and subject matter. In 1960–63 a much more inclusive set of historical records were provided by H. S. Smith, R. T. Handy, and L. A. Loetscher (see p. 122). This collection by Gaustad is their only successor worthy of the name. It improves on previous anthologies by avoiding restrictive perspectives as much as possible and by explicating the pluralistic quality of American religion that has been characteristic from the beginning. With judiciously chosen primary materials, Gaustad shows how religious viewpoints and organized structures developed exponentially throughout the American experience. His control over mushrooming growth and innovation is masterful in both its comprehensive coverage and its attention to myriad details. These documents that reflect religious life in all its vitality are accompanied by lucid introductions that place sources in their immediate context and explain their significance within the larger mosaic. Each large section also ends with suggested readings for further pursuit of particular issues.

Gaustad surpasses all others in allowing so many variegated voices to speak. He begins with native American settlements and European colonists of diverse origins. After exhibiting the complexity of early plantations he moves through awakenings, religious liberty, and more revivals to sectional strife that had ecclesiastical counterparts. In volume 2 Gaustad turns to religion among freedmen, immigrants, and women. He surveys the Social Gospel and includes resurgent interest in urban and world evangelism. A remarkably sensitive chapter probes variations on devotionalism and spiritualism, then nativist phobias, and new versions of millennialism. Final sections cover philosophy, science, and biblical criticism together with theological responses plus activities related to world churches, world wars, and the theme of national unity. All this is pertinent to his observation that "the nation's religious history is a full one: a drama with an enormous cast of characters, a story still being told" (p. xvi). [H.W.B.]

Genovese, Eugene D. *Roll, Jordan Roll: The World the Slaves Made.* New York: Pantheon Books, 1974. xxii + 823 pp.

In spite of the pioneering work of W. E. B. DuBois in *The Souls of Black Folk* and *The Negro Church*, both published in 1903, little systematic attention was given to the study of the significance of religion in the lives of African-Americans in slavery and in freedom until almost midcentury. Following the debates between Melville Herskovitz and E. Franklin Frazier in the 1940s concerning whether African-American culture was derived from African cultures or a creation of American experiences, different scholars have contributed to the whole or parts of the arguments of these two scholars. In the recent decades important works have been published that firmly establish the importance and integrity of African-American cultural traditions; Genovese's work belongs to that genre.

Genovese's work differs from his colleagues in history, folklore, and anthropology in that he attempts to analyze slavery as a system by unraveling general patterns to understand the place of slaves in the general economic and social order of the times. He further attempts to analyze the various influences on slavery and the ways in which they reinforce, contradict, and transform one another by focusing on the dynamics of the master-slave relationships and the plantation as a way of life, and by applying the notion of social class to an analysis of the dynamics of the plantation system. Genovese argues that paternalism, and its correlative of dependency, was the particular form that class relations took on the plantation.

Genovese's work shares in common with a number of scholars a plea for understanding life in slavery as producing not just silent victims or only a reaction or response to white, Euro-American culture, but a world that was shaped, bent, transformed, and sometimes transcended by African-Americans. In this world, religion was integral and complex. Not all African cultural practices and ideas were lost in the New World setting. Some were selectively mixed with certain themes from Christianity prevalent in the southern United States. These emergent new religious traditions represented an assertion of value and cultural differentiation by people whose shared African experiences and understandings of and responses to the New World helped shape daily life in circumstances of constraints and circumscribed possibilities. Services of prayers, worship, rituals, and ceremonies, individually and collectively, permitted slaves to feel themselves a *community* separate from the world of their masters. The "world the slaves made" was in part a deliberate rejection of the culture of paternalism of their masters.

Genovese's greatest strength is to argue that religion is inherently political at the same time that it is also politically ambiguous, especially in its concern with the relation of the individual to the society and the civil to the political. While his analysis of plantation agriculture as constituted by distinct and antagonistic classes in which masters and slaves shaped the lives of others is provocative, it does not account for the ways paternalism developed. Moreover, paternalism in the South is only a partial insight into the religious traditions, ideology, and racial attitudes that were integral to the antebellum life of African-Americans.   [J.K.H.]

Gill, Sam. *Native American Religions: An Introduction.* **Belmont, CA: Wadsworth Publishing, 1982. xvi + 192 pp.**

Sam Gill sets a lofty goal for himself in this book: "to introduce an academically and humanistically useful way of trying to appreciate and understand the complexity and diversity of Native American religions" (p. xiv). He attains the goal he sets.

He begins with several cautions about the sorts of preconceptions we all too frequently bring to our attempts to understand the religions of the native Americans. We carry in our minds an image of our own ideal humanity and create a view of native Americans that is in essence only a counterimage to that. "We" lump "them" together, failing at the outset to recognize their diversity. We are so conditioned by our preconceptions and limited by our tendency to look upon ourselves as the "guardians and philanthropists" of these "culturally deprived" peoples (p. 9) that we simply cannot see the richness of the religions they espouse. Gill seeks to remove these cultural blinders.

In a series of six chapters that form the core of the book, Gill develops a picture of the native American religious world view. This development has two great strengths: he both develops a humanistically satisfying overall picture and gives the reader an abundance of well-chosen specific examples. He begins with a study of creation/origin stories, those stories that set the basic categories and world view through which religion is expressed and practiced. He follows with an excellent discussion of the effect of nonliteracy on native American religions that focuses on the performative power of language, the role of face-to-face communication, and the inseparability of medium and message. The next chapter concentrates on the importance of symbols, highlighting their role in making the extraordinary world present in and through the ordinary world, transforming it, and locating individuals within a sacred cosmos. Chapter 4 discusses the life cycle and its rituals, picturing life as a "journey along a road well charted and carefully directed by the religious tradition" (p. 85). The chapter on "Ways of Life" demonstrates how physical sustenance is never isolated, but is always experienced in the context of the religious foundation of life itself. The last of these core chapters deals with the interplay of tradition and change, centering on historical development. The author examines "the processes by which tradition and cultural identity are maintained while being confronted by threatening influences" and delineates "the role religion plays in these processes as well as how religion is affected by the changes that occur" (p. 142).

The conclusion develops the theme of native American response to intercultural contact, noting that "at every level, religion plays a central role" because it is here that "the world view and broad, meaning-giving perspectives are taught, effected, and developed" (p. 172).

The usefulness of the book is greatly enhanced by its companion volume, *Native American Traditions: Sources and Interpretations*. Gill's two books are recommended without reservation to anyone who wants to learn more about the religions of native Americans. Required reading.　[J.M.C.]

Glazer, Nathan. *American Judaism*. Chicago History of American Civilization Series. Chicago: University of Chicago Press, 1957; rev. ed. Chicago: University of Chicago Press, 1972. xi + 210 pp.

Most Walgreen Lectures are delivered by professional specialists. As a professor of education and social structure in an eastern university, Glazer was an exception, but his layman's interest in Judaism made his 1955 lectures a model of sensitive interpretation. Two years later these lectures appeared as part of the Chicago History of American Civilization series, and popular response justified a revised edition in 1972. Few changes characterize the second printing beyond addition of a final chapter to cover events in the interim. Glazer has provided an accurate survey of Jewish experience in America that stands as one of the best introductions to the subject. It has stood the test of time and, amid a half-dozen rivals, still holds its own as a trustworthy approach for beginners. Glazer's treatment is not controlled by rabbinic or legalistic norms. The author is open to the many ways Jews have expressed themselves, and his open-minded approach allows the different versions to flourish without judgments about their propriety. At the same time Glazer is very concerned about survival of Jewish consciousness, so his appreciation for varying viewpoints rests on this sustaining motif.

Early Jewish experience in America was confined to Sephardic forms and the synagogues in colonial seaports where that cultural orientation flourished. By 1825 a new phase began when Germanic Jews arrived to institute their preference for Reform life and worship. Glazer shows how Reform sentiment established lasting sympathy for liberal causes in American life, a strand of Jewish identity that has lasted ever since. By 1880 new immigrants from eastern Europe constituted alternative lifestyles, and controversies arose between Reform patterns and more recently arrived Orthodoxy. Glazer shows in this context how antipathies arose between cultural and institutional definitions of Jewishness and how commitment to Israel struggled with life in America as a Jewish priority. His final chapter oriented around the Six Day War brings all these alternatives into the present and provides readers with gentle consideration of strengths found in each religious position.   [H.W.B.]

Gottschalk, Stephen. *The Emergence of Christian Science in American Religious Life.* Berkeley: University of California Press, 1973. xxix + 305 pp.

The appearance of Gottschalk's *The Emergence of Christian Science in American Religious Life* (coupled with the three-volume biography of Mary Baker Eddy by colleague Robert Peel) elevated the treatment of Christian Science to a new level. From the earliest days of the Church of Christ, Scientist, when Julius Dresser accused Eddy of stealing her ideas from her former teacher, writings about her movement have been steeped in polemics. On one side have been the exposes by ex-members, polemical broadsides by "objective" writers, and evangelical Christian attacks. Members of the church countered with defensive biographies of their founder/leader and theological apologies. The former volumes were written by individuals with little sympathy for the church and as a whole failed to understand the movement or its appeal. The latter, always having to substantiate Eddy's unique cosmic role, appeared to outsiders as little more than hagiography. Gottschalk's attempt to write a balanced assessment of Christian Science partially succeeds in moving between these two standard polemical approaches.

To arrive at his more balanced approach, while avoiding the pitfalls of sociological reductionism, Gottschalk emphasizes the religious essence of the movement, attempts to understand that essence within the context of the emergence of other religious alternatives of the time (with which it successfully competed), and traces its emergence into a position within the mainstream of American religious life. He locates its success in its pragmatic nature, by which he means its insistence upon the intimate relation of theory and practice—truth is tested by the consequences of believing it. In this respect it is somewhat analogous to the Social Gospel, which also absorbed this uniquely American approach to life.

Gottschalk presents the most detailed and thorough coverage of the first generation of Christian Science to date; it ranks far above other treatments of the subject. Yet with all its merit, it fails to escape the need to defend Christian Science and so fails to offer the balanced treatment Gottschalk sought. Its adherence to the church's traditional perspective in its first decades is clearly demonstrated in Gottschalk's lack of interest in the development of Christian Science as a movement. His work is not a study of the emergence of Christian Science so much as another biography of Eddy with emphasis upon her ideology. No interest is shown in the emergence of Christian Science outside of Boston, the activity of Eddy's capable lieutenants who actually built the movement, or the concerns of those people who left the movement and led rival organizations.

Biases aside, Gottschalk's work remains the best treatment of the subject available, and the most appropriate launching pad for future work. It is still helpful, however, to read this book in conjunction with one of the more critical works, the best of which is Charles Braden's *Christian Science Today.* [J.G.M.-n]

Greeley, Andrew W. *The Denominational Society: A Sociological Approach to Religion in America.* Glenview, IL: Scott, Foresman, 1972. 266 pp.

This work is an attempt to interpret the complexity of American religious behavior from a sociological perspective. It includes some historical background used in the interpretation of statistics leading to the creation of a morphology of American religion.

Denominationalism is viewed as a central characteristic, and the existence of a complex relationship between larger social structures and denominations is seen as uniquely American. Religion and society relate to one another through "quasi-ecclesiastical organizations" (denominations) that are a product of religious pluralism.

Religion is defined as a "set of symbols . . . that man has evolved for organizing his relationship with the sacred" (p. 28). Three theoretical positions on religion are discussed: (1) the functionalists—who argue that religion serves a need, whether explanatory or integrative; (2) Weberians—who uncover the meaning-giving role; and (3) the comfortists—who view religion as essentially providing assurance to the troubled. All three are complementary views as to both religion's existence and power in America.

Greeley moves to the practical level in an examination of the denominational form. It goes beyond the traditional sect-church dichotomy of Troeltsch and Weber, whose typology now has little value for the American experience since most Americans live out their religiousness within a denominational context.

An overview of that existence is offered, relying on statistics. Americans are shown to be basically more religious than Europeans. Education and upward mobility strengthens religious activity rather than weakens it. The denominational society is at once activist, pragmatic, optimistic, and individualistic, and also contemplative, theoretical, flexible, cooperative, and theologically innovative. This vitality is due to the pluralism engendered in part by the identification of denominations with ethnicity, and if not specifically ethnic in origin, they perform a quasi-ethnic role of group identity for their adherents.

Statistics indicate that the "secularization theory" of modern society needs reexamination; religion is not irrelevant. There may be historical cycles of religious fervor that will explain the present situation in America; there is no reason to assume previous generations were more religious.

Civil religion is noted as a phenomenon that helps explain how religion can unify a society that is religiously plural. It is perceived as a "super religion" in which all denominations participate. The growth of internal diversity within the larger denominations of Catholicism, Protestantism, and Judaism is briefly sketched as a result of interaction with the American social environment. Religious and racial prejudice are presented as regrettable effects of pluralism—but not caused by pluralism.

Greeley notes six principal areas of interreligious conflict, including church-state separation, private education, religious and public morality, and discusses the intrareligious problems of apostasy, intermarriage, and ecumenism, which touch on the religious dimensions of "meaning" and "belonging."

He concludes that, despite problems, religion will persist without radical change and denominationalism will reinforce its stability. [M.L.S.]

Gunn, Giles. *The Interpretation of Otherness: Literature, Religion, and the American Imagination.* **New York: Oxford University Press, 1979. x + 250 pp.**

Giles Gunn has become the foremost American scholar in the discipline that explores the connections between literature and religion. One evidence of that is his achievement of an integrated perspective linking those fields of study. In this book, he provides both a theoretical foundation for the interrelation of those human phenomena and a guidebook for the future of the discipline.

One way of viewing these essays is as a brush-clearing operation. Gunn aims to clean out underbrush in order to get on with more important business. From religion's side the overgrown path that requires attention is theological imperialism, the assumption of a privileged vantage point from which to judge literature. Literary criticism, on the other hand, has often run headlong into the bramble bush of studying form, methodology, and structure never to escape. Gunn recalls literary critics to their more significant work; simultaneously, he chides religionists to face the fullness of human experience without a protectionist mind set. The scythe that Gunn uses to effect this brush-clearing is cultural criticism, in which both religion and literary criticism have prominent roles. Cultural criticism also provides the foundation of his theory.

"It is now necessary," he writes in regard to the discussion between literature and religion, "to widen the terms in which it is conducted: to reconstitute the discussion on the plane of the hermeneutical rather than the apologetic, the anthropological rather than theological, the broadly humanistic rather than the narrowly doctrinal" (p. 5). Both disciplines have to do with the interpretation of experience not as though it were finally accessible to accurate description, but imaginatively, in such a way as to be productive of morally and personally enriching understandings directed toward a future.

Within that framework, a brief description of the content of each of the five chapters may be helpful. Chapter 1 reviews the history of, and criticizes the theological positions behind, the relation between literature and religion. Turning to literary criticism in the second chapter, Gunn demonstrates in what ways the task of the literary critic intersects with the subject matter, the otherness, of religion. Perhaps, the most provocative is the third chapter—in which the tasks of religion and literature are united and grounded in a theory that transcends previous formulation. This theory is bodied forth and tested in the fourth chapter, which examines nothing less than the puzzle of "the American mind." Concluding the book is an examination of the moral implications and possibilities of American literature—its ability to drive us to "felt possibility and the imagination of desire" (p. 222).

This book is irritating; in an age that seeks certainties, it advocates the value of searching for that which eludes capture. It demands that we turn to the otherness of experience in such a way as to be questioned, challenged, refined, but never complacent or certain. Thus it compliments us by calling us to be not only what we are but also what we might be. [L.S.J.]

Gunn, Giles, ed. *The Bible and American Arts and Letters*. Chico, CA: Scholars Press, 1983. x + 244 pp.

Those who have taught numerous classes on biblical literature to diverse audiences know that while the Bible might be the most frequently sold book in American culture, it is still far from being a widely read or highly understood volume! Surveys about biblical information continue to indicate an astounding level of biblical illiteracy among random American populations. Although the King James version of the Bible constituted the virtual "constitution" of the Puritan Commonwealth and was the "thumping book" of American revivalism and evangelists, its metaphors and motifs are known more by oral tradition than by intellectual investigation and literary perusal of its contents. Given the phenomenal gap between the authoritative regard for and the actual acquaintance with the Bible, it is a celebrated event to receive this insightful, enlightening volume. This work comes as part of an important series on the Bible in American culture edited by Edwin S. Gaustad and Walter Harrelson.

In his introduction, Gunn maintains that the Bible "has become America's book" in a way that has no exact parallel in any other nation. Not only have the people read and possessed it, but it has read and possessed them! Americans have cleaved to the Bible as if it were "a national cultural possession for the sake of reassuring themselves that their own history was unfolding according to biblical prescriptions" (p. 1).

In a chapter entitled "The Biblical Basis of the American Myth," Sacvan Bercovitch points out that there are not only some possibilities but problems inherent in the Puritans' and Americans' special claim on the Bible. Even a strain in the culture that would ordinarily be suspect for leading one afield from the biblical perspective ironically leads one back to "an overpowering sense of God," which is part of the tension between the Bible and American culture (Herbert Schneidau, in chapter 1).

Edwin Cady and Rowland Sherrill discuss aspects of the Bible in nineteenth- and twentieth-century American fiction, respectively. William Schurr explores a test case of the effect of the Bible on drama, Eugene O'Neill's *Lazarus Laughed.*

Edwin M. Good presents a brief but insightful overview in various eras of American music. Daniel Patterson includes music as one of a variety of folk art expressions in American subcultures that reflect the inspirational power of the Bible.

The Bible is even stimulating for the American visual arts. John W. Dixon, Jr., presents a view of "The Bible in American Painting" making clear that this is a fairly different topic than the larger one of "religion" in American painting. Clifford E. Clark, Jr., does an exemplary interpretation of the prophetic and biblical strains in American architecture.

This volume presents no final answers on the role of the Bible in the creation and re-creation of American culture. Indeed, it would be expecting too much of any single volume to do this. But any creation and re-creation of history and society involves the constant and surveillant reinterpretation of the past. This work presents some very stimulating and suggestive ways of going about this venture. [E.A.W.]

Handy, Robert T. *A Christian America: Protestant Hopes and Historical Realities.* New York: Oxford University Press, 1971; rev. ed. New York: Oxford University Press, 1984. xii + 320 pp.

A Christian America singles out a particular facet of American Protestant history—the early Protestant hope that one day America would be fully Christian. This hope provided a common orientation that transcended denominational and doctrinal differences. Beginning with the earliest colonial establishments of religion and continuing, in the 1984 revised edition, through the early 1980s, Handy documents the persistent interweaving of the evangelical commitment to Christianity and the goal of building a civilization based upon Americanized Anglo-Saxon ideals. He further documents the challenge to "Protestant hopes" continually mounted by "historical realities." Following the first, official legal disestablishment of religion, Protestant Christianity remained the norm, although based on voluntary participation. In the period from 1800 to 1860, it was thus still reasonable to speak of a "Christian America."

Five chapters treat the period between 1860 and 1940. The definitive themes for that nine-decade span, although nuanced differently, are basically two: the ongoing challenges to "Protestant hopes" and pretensions by the realities of history, and the endurance of Protestantism in the face of these challenges. The challenges themselves were varied: a nation and a church torn apart by the Civil War and the slavery issue; steadily increasing numbers of immigrants, many of whom were non-Protestant in their religious convictions; increasing industrialization, urbanization, and secularization, which challenged individualism not only in religion but in government and economics as well; a changing family structure and increasing divorce rate; and, in the 1960s and later, the struggle of blacks and women for equality and justice both within the churches and outside them.

The responses of American Protestantism were equally varied. Confidence in America's destiny as a Christian (Protestant) nation remained, for the most part, despite increasing pluralism, into the 1950s. Church people continued to view the church as God's prime agent in the Christianizing of the entire globe. Occasionally, conservatives sought, as they have in recent years, constitutional amendments to buttress their campaign for a Christian nation. Sabbath observance and temperance/prohibition remained key issues for long periods. Christianity and civilization became more and more amalgamated to one another, until the period from 1920 to 1940, which Handy aptly names the "new disestablishment." By the end of these two decades, the church had experienced a "shift in American life that was displacing evangelical Protestantism as the primary defender of cultural values and behavior patterns in the nation" (p. 169). Meanwhile, the Social Gospel movement and various approaches to interdenominational cooperation had helped to alter the face of American Protestantism. The appeal of the idea of an American civil religion indicated a felt need to replace the old Protestant hegemony with something. In the 1970s and 1980s, a resurgent conservatism again campaigned for a Christian America. This campaign was unable to reverse the tide of pluralism, however, as America had become a religiously pluralistic nation.

Extraordinarily clear organization and first-class use of primary source materials make Handy's book "must" reading.. [J.M.C.]

Handy, Robert T., ed. *The Social Gospel in America, 1870–1920: Gladden-Ely-Rauschenbusch.* New York: Oxford University Press, 1966. xii + 399 pp.

The advent of industrialization, urbanization, Darwinism, and the general nineteenth-century intellectual assault on the credibility of Scripture and traditional Christian theological claims provoked a variety of responses within the Protestant tradition. The Social Gospel movement that swept through major Protestant denominations was associated with those advocates who focused on the moral and social aspects of the economic realities of the industrial problem. These individuals, many of whom were Protestant ministers, influenced by the "new" liberal theology, challenged prevailing bourgeoisie political and economic doctrines. They worked to temper the excesses of capitalism and the struggles between capitalism and labor with a biblically inspired social ethic. Although Social Gospel leaders represented no unified point of view, they shared a common concern with the establishment of a Christocentric liberalism and the need for the churches to face economic and social "facts," especially the loss of the working class to Protestantism.

Handy's book focuses on the development and mature expression of the Social Gospel before World War I, prior to its transition, decline, and reorientation. The work includes brief biographical sketches and representative writings of three central figures in the Social Gospel movement: Washington Gladden, Richard T. Ely, and Walter Rauschenbusch. Acutely aware of the social questions of the time, these individuals took a moderately reformist position between various conservative and radical extremes in the movement. They were committed to the idea that the social principles of the historical Jesus could serve as reliable guides for both individual and social life in any age. In their writings and teachings they stressed the immanence of God, the goodness and worth of the human person, and the coming of the kingdom of God on earth. They believed wholeheartedly in "progress." They also believed that through the efforts of people of good will and through education and determined moral effort, the kingdom of God would become a reality bringing with it social harmony and elimination of social injustice.

The proponents of the movement remained a minority within mainline Protestantism. The general postwar disillusionment, especially the severe economic and social realities of the depression and the rise of totalitarianism, greatly affected the Protestant churches and evaporated much of the earlier enthusiasm for the ideas undergirding the Social Gospel movement. Nevertheless, Handy's book demonstrates how the work of individuals like Gladden, Ely, and Rauschenbusch facilitated the transition of individuals and institutions from a rural, small-town America to an industrialized, urban society.

This work is a good primary source document and is especially relevant for courses in American religious history or Protestant thought. [W.D.D.]

Hansen, Klaus J. *Mormonism and the American Experience.* **Chicago History of American Religion Series. Chicago: University of Chicago Press, 1981. xviii + 257 pp.**

Hansen interprets the Latter-day Saint experience as it relates to general American history by focusing on selected problems in the Mormon past: the origins of Mormon religion, the ways Mormonism was similar to or different from other nineteenth-century American religion, the way Mormons have coped with death, the handling of the relationship between secular and religious authority, traditions on sexuality and marriage, changing racial attitudes and practices, and the meaning of the Mormon experience.

Hansen argues that Mormonism is best understood as the attempt of a group of nineteenth-century Americans ravaged by the vicissitudes of modernization to find a religious life allowing them to cope with a world they did not like but could not change. They did this by adopting a new world view providing satisfying answers to questions uppermost in their minds not answered by contemporary evangelical Christianity. Hansen believes some elements of the Mormon tradition were found in Puritanism and some in Arminianism. Others, such as the potential godhood of humankind, were unique to Mormonism. Mormons rejected much in contemporary Christianity and provided a vision of the pre-Columbian past that placed the American continent in a primary position rather than the traditional secondary status in world history.

Although Hansen's work is at base sympathetic with the Mormons, he finds it necessary to provide a construct to try to explain the religious experiences of Joseph Smith and others in natural scientific terms. Thus part of his argument about the nature of revelation is based on an appeal to the highly speculative and extremely controversial work of Julian Jaynes and the theory of the bicameral mind. Hansen pulls away from complete acceptance of Jaynes's theory by referring to it as "metaphor." Jaynes's ideas seem to be counterproductive, since it is not clear how acceptance of the concept of the bicameral mind as metaphor helps in understanding Joseph Smith.

This book shows considerable familiarity with works ranging from William James through Freud and Jung and the various schools of psychology to more recent works on magic by Keith Thomas and Laurence Moore. The introductions to these studies seem, on occasion, to reflect Hansen's confusion about how to deal with religious experience. Perhaps he could well have benefited by using a comparative analysis based on already published work on religious experiences that accept the word of actors in times past on their own experiences as long as the experiences are consistent with their actions. The introduction of the social scientific and historical studies could then have been used for comparative purposes. This would have allowed a more straightforward interpretive narrative rather than what seem to be a number of contradictory positions in the chapter on Mormon origins.

The strongest points of the book derive from the serious attention Hansen gives to Mormon doctrine as a vehicle for understanding both the Latter-day Saints and American culture. His chapters on plural marriage and racial attitudes are insightful, in part, because Hansen recognizes that the argument that pressure from outside forced the abandonment of both fails to address the operation of the internal dynamic of Mormon doctrine and society. [T.G.A.]

Harding, Vincent. *There is a River: The Black Struggle for Freedom in America.* New York: Harcourt Brace Jovanovich, 1981; 2d ed. New York: Vintage Books. xxvi + 416 pp.

There is a River is a tale told with profound feeling. Welling up out of Vincent Harding's firm commitment to black nationalism and his years of involvement in the freedom struggles of the 1960s, it is a celebration of the undaunted spirit of black resistance in the face of insuperable odds. The passion of the true believer inhabits every page, often expressed in lyrical language. Yet this is solid history, carefully researched and documented from a vast store of largely secondary sources. It is, in short, representative of the finest Afro-American scholarship, while unflinchingly imbued with the spirit of Old Testament prophecy and judgment.

In this initial volume of a projected trilogy, Harding relates the story of "the long black movement toward justice, equity, and truth" (p. xi) from its commencement during the seventeenth century on the shores of Africa to the adoption of the Thirteenth Amendment to the Constitution in 1865. The emphasis throughout is upon the Negro's direct confrontation with slavery and active resistance to its supporting institutions.

Understandably, the primary focus is on slave rebellions and the efforts of northern blacks to undermine enforcement of the fugitive slave laws. Running throughout the narrative is a potent thematic image of black people and their struggle for freedom: like a mighty river, says Harding, the black drive toward liberty surged on, "sometimes powerful, tumultuous, and roiling with life; at other times meandering and turgid, . . . all too often streaked and running with blood" (p. xix).

In essence, this river of protest had two tributaries. One, flowing relentlessly out of the plantation and "outlyer" communities of the South, was characterized by the actions of men like Gabriel Prosser, Denmark Vesey, and Nat Turner, by hosts of runaways, and by individual acts of slave defiance. The second contributory stream emanated from the North—from its pulpits and presses, from black convocations and clandestine groups, from the forceful rhetoric of such spokesmen as Frederick Douglass, David Walker, Henry Highland Garnet, and Martin Delaney. In describing these twin streams, Harding reconsiders the impact of major slave uprisings and the work of the more prominent black abolitionists. But he also portrays such lesser-known elements of the movement as the emergence of black secret societies and the transforming effects of free black conventions.

Despite these refreshing contributions, *There is a River* does contain some questionable features. For one thing, the river metaphor itself, with its suggestion of a forward, continuous thrust of the protest tradition, implies a unity of purpose that simply did not exist in the antebellum black community. Furthermore, for students of religion, this volume has rather limited value. It does provide a rich context in which to observe both white and black religious expressions, and Harding's discussion of the messianic dimensions of black radical thought is especially insightful. Still, its relatively sparse treatment of religion's role in the struggle for freedom is disappointing. Nonetheless, Harding's book is an exciting reading experience and a welcome celebration of the black spirit in America. [L.A.H.]

Haroutunian, Joseph. *Piety vs. Moralism: The Passing of the New England Theology.* New York: H. Holt and Company, 1932; 2d ed. Hamden, CT: Shoe String Press, 1964. xxv + 329 pp.

Ostensibly a study of theology in New England in the period between the 1750s and the 1830s, the actual subject matter of Haroutunian's book is "that perennial conflict between theocentric piety and humanitarian morality which is a problem today as it was in the eighteenth century" (p. xxxii). Haroutunian has a vivid sense of Western social and intellectual history, and his particular topic is essentially treated as one important chapter in the story of the disjunction of the unstable synthesis that Max Weber described as the Protestant ethic and the spirit of capitalism. The synthesis was intensely rejoined in Puritanism, but the reunion was brief. Haroutunian takes up the story with Jonathan Edwards's heroic attempt to reclaim the piety at the center of Calvin's theology in the face of the degenerate Calvinism of early modern commercialism. The denouement is the fate of Edwards's theological brilliance in the work of followers who lacked either his piety or his intellect, or both.

Haroutunian's achievement is the recovery of Edwards's greatness—from the vapid humanism of late eighteenth- and early nineteenth-century theology and over against the sterile optimism of modern American religious thought. The goal of Edwards's theology was to glorify the God whose sovereignty was at the heart of his religious experience, and to do so without undercutting an equally strong sense of human moral responsibility. The grounds of his theology were empirical, and its methods of development were rational and philosophical. But Edwards was out of step with a vigorously independent, expanding America, and the virulent enthusiasm that subsequent Calvinism became was understandably rejected by the enlightened, successful citizens of the new republic. Civility and progressive thinking won the day. Yet the benign Christianity of the nineteenth century left Americans intellectually unprepared to cope with the horrors of the First World War and the rising specter of totalitarianism. Haroutunian clearly hopes that Edwards's more complicated thinking will offer resources for dealing straightforwardly and constructively with the massive inhumanity of the modern era.

Originally published in 1932, Haroutunian's book coincided with the efforts of Perry Miller (see pp. 92–95) and H. Richard Niebuhr (see pp. 103–6) to recover an American religious past that might be useful in the hard religious thinking their times required. As such, it contributed to the urgent revisionism that came to characterize the study of American history. Because the pendulum of piety and moralism continues to swing, Haroutunian's beautifully written, insightful work may soon fill such a role again. In any event, it stands as a substantial model for and contributes an important chapter to the history of American religious thought.   [J.G.M.-y]

Hatch, Nathan O. *The Sacred Cause of Liberty: Republican Thought and the Millennium in Revolutionary New England.* New Haven: Yale University Press, 1977. xi + 197 pp.

This is a well-written, important book for scholars of religion and politics in America. Convinced that "the convergence of millennial and republican thought forms a central theme in the complex relationship between religion and politics in Revolutionary New England" (p. 3), Hatch argues that previous interpreters of this period have failed by pursuing religious studies and political science as separate disciplines according to a conventional distinction between religious and secular spheres of life, or by investigating only the influence of religion on politics (and not vice-versa, or both together), or by dual-istically linking religious change either to intellectual or to spiritual developments.

Hatch's argument that the Old and New Light clergy were united in "a political religion of the New England clergy" (p. 8), the ante-cedents of which are found more basically in the Anglo-French wars than in vestiges of the Great Awakening, cogently revises the massive work of Alan Heimert (see p. 60). Chapters on New England clergy in revolt and on their contributions to the moral roots of Federalism square well with the pivotal works of Bernard Bailyn and Gordon S. Wood. The final chapter reinterprets the "civil religion" side of the Second Great Awakening—providing nice addenda to or critiques of the work of Sidney Mead, Perry Miller, Ralph Henry Gabriel, James F. Maclear, and Jerald C. Brauer—by showing that the "new" con-figuration of religion and politics was neither simply expedient hap-penstance nor especially novel. Once again, as during the Revolution, "the spheres of church and state became facets of a larger sacred purpose, the cause of liberty" (p. 70).

Hatch's interpretive narrative is followed by a substantive note on the printed sermons of Massachusetts and Connecticut in the years 1740–1800, in which he argues that these sermons show what laity as well as clergy believed. In addition, the author includes a selective bibliography of the sermons themselves. Because the author provides the evidence as well as the argument that religion was actually deeply involved in the period characterized by Edmund S. Morgan as "an age of politics," the book provides a sophisticated, interesting model for understanding the varied roles of religion in American his-tory. [J.G.M.-y]

Hatch, Nathan O., and Mark A. Noll, eds. *The Bible in America: Essays in Cultural History.* New York: Oxford University Press, 1982. x + 191 pp.

The purpose of this fine collection of essays is twofold: both to remind students of American history that the Bible has been central to the development of the national life and to help believers in biblical authority to recognize how the Bible's use has been influenced by American history. With the exception of a final, balancing essay from a Roman Catholic perspective, the essays treat Protestantism and pro-ceed chronologically. They are: "Word and Order in Colonial New England," by Harry S. Stout; "The Image of the United States as a Biblical Nation, 1776–1865," by Mark A. Noll; "*Sola Scriptura* and *Novus Ordo Seclorum*," by Nathan O. Hatch; "Everyone One's Own

Interpreter?: The Bible, Science, and Authority in Mid-Nineteenth-Century America," by George M. Marsden; "The Two-Edged Sword: The Fundamentalist Use of the Bible," by Timothy P. Weber; "The Demise of Biblical Civilization," by Grant Wacker; "The Bible in Twentieth-Century Civilization: A Preliminary Taxomony," by Richard J. Mouw; and "The Quest for a Catholic Vernacular Bible in America," by Gerald P. Fogarty, S. J. All of the essays are carefully researched and well written, and each thoughtfully raises the important issue its title indicates.

With neither an established church nor a normative theology, America's distinctive tradition of religious freedom and denominationalism has heightened the need and, hence, exacerbated the claims for biblical authority, while at the same time undercutting the general acceptance and intellectual cohesion of any particular version of the Bible's authority. Hence examining the role of the Bible in American culture requires all of the resources and modes of interpretation that historians can muster. The essays compiled here rise to that challenge and meet another as well, for the authors recognize that "the very survival of Scripture in America—often in the face of its defenders' best efforts to bring discredit upon it—suggests a reality about the Bible which goes beyond history to faith" (p. 12). By demonstrating that the Bible is both "in" and "more than" American history, these essays provide a model for studying other religious phenomena in American life. The distinctive, ineradicable ambiguity revealed here should be honored in all attempts to recover American religious history.   [J.G.M.-y]

Heimert, Alan. *Religion and the American Mind, from the Great Awakening to the Revolution.* Cambridge: Harvard University Press, 1966. x + 668 pp.

By comparing the rhetoric of Calvinists with that of more liberal Protestants during the middle of the eighteenth century, Heimert disputes the conventional view that the religious roots of the American Revolution lay in Enlightenment rationalism. After a searching analysis of a great many documents from the pre-Revolutionary era, Heimert concludes that religious liberalism was in fact deeply conservative, politically and socially, and that its leaders preferred the status quo to the radical changes portended by the Revolution. In political and social terms, it was instead the religiously conservative, evangelical Calvinists who were the more radical, democratic, and nationalistic. The importance of this revision of the accepted view is heightened by Heimert's debunking of another truism, for he challenges the notion that the Revolutionary era was a time when politics replaced religion as a central cultural concern. Heimert contends, rather, that "the very religious life of the colonies came to center on the crisis in public affairs, and, indeed, to be defined by it and from it to derive vitality" (p. 354). Thus the Revolution is seen to have been in some important ways a religious movement, and the Great Awakening a political one; moreover, Heimert asserts that the Awakening itself should be interpreted as a prelude to the Revolution. Hence the Calvinism of Jonathan Edwards rather than the liberalism of Charles Chauncey provided the religious ideology for political change.

Heimert's reinterpretation of these matters depends heavily upon the work of Perry Miller (see pp. 92–95), and so it is perhaps appropriate that, like Miller's masterful vision of American cultural history, Heimert's book has recently itself been challenged.

Whatever the outcome of current debates about religion and politics in Revolutionary America, however, Heimert's analysis orients the discussion, and the extent of his scholarship often supplies the evidence even his opponents use. So his book remains a landmark—the best place for students of religious and political thought to begin to examine American culture between the Great Awakening and the Revolution. [J.G.M.-y]

Herberg, Will. *Protestant, Catholic, Jew: An Essay in American Religious Sociology*. Garden City, NY: Doubleday, 1955; rev. ed. New York: Doubleday, 1960; rev. ed. Chicago: University of Chicago Press, 1983. xvi + 308 pp.

This book is one of the classic works offering a sociological interpretation of the religious aspects of the changing social structure of American society. According to Herberg, Americans have classified themselves in terms of their ethnic-immigrant origins since the mid-nineteenth century. By the post–World War II era, however, classification by ethnic nationality had been largely superseded by a "triple melting pot" (Protestant, Catholic, Jew) religious affiliation. As a result of the dynamics of assimilation, American society has been changing from a land of ethnic diversity into a culture in which religious affiliation is becoming the primary social compass and context of "belonging." This trend has had important ramifications for both religion and national identity.

After World War II, religion rode a wave of public popularity in the United States. Church attendance soared, contributions rose, ecumenical activities accelerated, and seminary and divinity school enrollment increased dramatically. The popularity of religious media figures such as Norman Vincent Peale, Oral Roberts, Bishop Sheen, and Billy Graham grew tremendously. Paradoxically, however, this era was also a period when the very same conditions that made for the postwar religious revival stimulated secularization.

Herberg argues that membership in one of the tripartite religions had more to do with a third-generation search for heritage and the necessity of maintaining social identity and group boundaries than with genuine commitment to transcendental objectives or religious absolutes. The ostensible religious revival in the early 1950s was, in fact, an expression of secularizing tendencies that were eroding doctrinal differences and reducing religion in America to the lowest common denominator. According to Herberg, religion in American had transformed into a secularized version of faith. The real religion of America is the "American way of life"—an organic structure of values, attitudes and beliefs and ideas (e.g., democracy, free enterprise, individualism, pragmatism, achievement, self-reliance, progress, idealism, an exalted perception of their own virtue, a crusading mentality, and a view of America as a new Israel) that constitute how Americans define themselves and establish national unity.

Herberg discusses the "Contemporary Upswing in Religion" and "The Religion of Americans and American Religion." This material is followed by chapters that trace the development of Protestantism, Catholicism, and Judaism in America and compare and contrast these three religious communities. This work is essential reading for courses in the sociology of religion or religion in America.   [W.D.D.]

Hill, Samuel, S., ed. *Encyclopedia of Religion in the South.* Macon: Mercer University Press, 1984. vii + 878 pp.

This reference work contains over 500 articles written by 200 contributors and edited by the leading scholar in the field of southern religious studies. It is divided into nine categories: state histories; denominations; doctrines and theological movements; biographies; sacred places; subject areas; public events and figures; offices; titles; and jurisdictions; and an eclectic miscellany of special features (including funerals and cemeteries, roadside signs, homecomings, and Bible chairs).

Hill defines the South as a sixteen state area (the Confederate secession states, the border states of Kentucky and Missouri, and Maryland, Oklahoma, and West Virginia). He suggests that this is a religious culture area, but he acknowledges subregional diversity, with articles on "Ozarks Religion," "Appalachian Religion," and the "Geography of Religion."

The *Encyclopedia* is an interdisciplinary project, drawing on the perspectives of history, sociology, anthropology, theology, and on professional scholars and lay students alike. Historians seem to predominate as contributors and the historical perspective is present in most every article. The religious developments in each southern state receive a detailed historical treatment through sixteen long articles, which have been published previously by editor Hill as *Religion in the Southern States* (1983). An appendix contains articles on the "Colonial Period" and the "Recent South," both given special attention because they have been the two least studied periods of southern religious development.

There are entries on specific denominations ranging from the powerful Southern Baptist Convention to the snake handlers of Appalachia. One of the volume's useful features is a "generic" entry on a denomination, accompanied by a separate article discussing its role in the South, that is, "Judaism" and "Jews in the South," "Roman Catholicism" and "Roman Catholic Church (in the South)." These articles are not uniform in their organization and content, with some being almost exclusively historical in focus, whereas others include longer discussions of worship, theology, polity, etc. The denominational articles include a wealth of such factual information as the founding of the group, its historical development, and its membership statistics. Entries generally contain brief bibliographies, although not in all cases.

The volume includes a generous number of biographies, although the guidelines for inclusion are not explained. There is a selective treatment of doctrines and theology: the Trinity, grace, the nature of God, and justification by faith are omitted, but sin and salvation, atonement and incarnation, holiness and millennialism, heaven and hell, revivalism and camp meetings are treated. Thematic subject articles cover church architecture, literature and religion, science and religion, music, the authority and inspiration of the Bible, and migration. Many of these represent initial, or certainly the fullest, research and writing on these subjects and thus are particularly valuable.   [C.R.W.]

Hofstadter, Richard. *The Age of Reform: From Bryan to FDR*. New York: Alfred A. Knopf, 1955; Reprint. New York: Alfred A. Knopf, 1956, 1959, 1960, 1961. xx + 328 pp.

The Age of Reform stunned the history profession in 1955 with its controversial critiques of the American Populist and Progressive movements. Since then the book has become enshrined as a classic as evidenced by its numerous reprintings. Although many of Richard Hofstadter's interpretations have been repudiated or superseded by later historians, the sterling reputation of the book rests on his sophisticated methodology. Hofstadter felt that American historiography up to and including the 1950s was too likely to resort to simplistic explanations of the sources of ideas, in general, and political behavior, in particular. He therefore drew on psychological and sociological theories to gain a more complex and nuanced perspective on human motivations.

In his interpretation of the Populists, Hofstadter looked beneath the explicit statements of these late nineteenth-century American agrarians and argued that their movement sprang from deeper and darker forces than their situation demanded. The premise of their movement was faulty, he explained, because they preferred to believe an "agrarian myth" about their individualism and self-sufficiency without recognizing the commercial realities of farm life. In this context of self-deception, Populism was an expression of deep fear of conspiracies designed by wealthy oligarchs to crush the vigor and virtue of the sturdy American farmer.

Although Hofstadter recognized that the middle-class and professional Progressives were a different constituency from the Populists, he argued that they shared a similar reform impulse, born of anti-modernist fears of large organizations and concentrations of power. Hofstadter introduced the novel concept that the impulse for Progressive reform did not stem from the need to redress actual economic grievances. According to Hofstadter, Progressives entered politics with reform ideas because of their "status anxiety." Because large business growth, immigration, and urban political machines tended to eclipse their place and prestige, this class of genteel, native-born, comfortably wealthy professionals sought to gain power in society through the alternative means of moral reform.

Even today, Hofstadter is a leading spokesman of the present generation. His interpretations have an arrestingly provocative appeal. He writes from a confidently secular and cosmopolitan perspective, and his social science methods serve his purpose of critiquing the zealous beliefs and moral stances of these prominent American reformers.   [P.J.C.]

Hutchison, William R. *The Modernist Impulse in American Protestantism.* Cambridge: Harvard University Press, 1976. x + 347 pp.

Hutchison's study is a scholarly intellectual history tracing the "modernist impulse" in American Protestantism from the 1870s to the

1930s and beyond. Although defined in different ways at various times, *modernism* has usually been associated with three core themes: (1) the adaptation and accommodation of religious ideas to modern culture; (2) the conviction that God is immanent in and revealed through human culture and development; and (3) the utopian idea that human society was moving toward the realization of the kingdom of God.

Hutchison examines the modernist impulse from its early basis in the Unitarian repudiation of Calvinism and subsequent modification of the ideas of God's sovereignty, human wickedness, and the exclusivism of Christian revelation. The evangelical emphasis on God's indwelling and humanity's direct intuitive access to the divine accelerated the emergence of modernism as did the spread of scientific epistemology and intellectual developments in German theological circles in the latter half of the nineteenth century.

The initial response to modernism in American Protestantism was favorable, especially in scholarly and journalistic circles. However, after 1890, criticism became more guided and hostile. The most consistent motif in the attack on modernism from both "fundamentalist" (and, ironically, from humanist) quarters was the allegation that modernists were claiming, in the name of Christianity, ideas that were, in fact, inherently incompatible with the historical faith.

Fundamentalists also berated liberals for the negative impact of modernist ideas on the missionary movement, for their tendency to equate the heart and essence of Christianity with social salvation (especially in the Social Gospel movement), and for diminishing the importance and primacy of doctrine. To the modernist, doctrine was the historic product of Christian experience; to a fundamentalist critic like J. Gresham Machen, there was no Christian experience without doctrine.

In the wake of the trauma of World War I, modernism began to face the decay of some of its own premises. With the rise of critical theology in the 1930s, the attack on modernism intensified. "Neo-orthodox" critics assailed modernists for harboring an unwarranted and overly optimistic view of human nature, for their tendency to minimize the depth and seriousness of sin, and for their easy acquiescence to the complacency and self-satisfaction of modern society.

Liberalism showed remarkable resilience in the face of such criticism. Liberal apologists continued to press for the reconciliation and adaptation of religion and culture and to reassert their fundamental stress upon the immanence of God. They responded to neo-orthodox criticism by complaining about the pessimism of neo-orthodoxy, about its tendency to caricature the liberal tradition, and about its alleged failure to move beyond destructive criticism to the articulate, clear lines of action.

Throughout its history, the modernist impulse has given expression to the conviction that the church and its people had to say what they really believed and then make moral action consonant with that belief. Hutchison's masterful study points out that modernism had asked Christian theology to accept realistically the entanglement of religion in culture and to make the best of that circumstance. This book is an excellent introduction to one of the constituent components of modern Protestant thought. [W.D.D.]

Hutchison, William R., ed. *American Protestant Thought: The Liberal Era*. New York: Harper and Row, 1968; 2d ed. Lanham: University Press of America, 1984. vii + 243 pp.

American liberal Protestant thought reached full flower during the six decades from the 1870s to the 1920s. Gaining a predominant position in the nation's seminaries, its characteristic ideas—confidence in human nature, the use of biblical "higher criticism," belief in the immanence of God, and the necessity of cultural accommodation in theology—molded more than a generation of students for the ministry. Consequently, the "liberal principle," as William R. Hutchison calls it, became entrenched in church and society, and even after liberal theology apparently had succumbed to the neo-orthodox attacks of the 1930s, it was still strong enough to form a base for the creedal formulations and "radical theology" of the 1960s.

The story of this tenacious movement takes on a new liveliness in this carefully compiled anthology of "manifestoes" (p. 13) from liberalism's chief theological spokesmen. As structured by editor Hutchison, the selections in this volume allow the actors in the drama of the liberal era—men like Henry Ward Beecher, Charles A. Briggs, Shailer Mathews, and Walter Rauschenbusch—to tell the tale of their own movement as it unfolded. After delineating the basic liberal ideas in a helpful introduction, Hutchison describes the stages through which liberalism passed and then organizes its representative writings in accordance with those developments.

In their early years of "initiatory explorations" (p. 9), for example, liberal theologians sought to penetrate new areas of religious inquiry. Their rejection of biblical literalism, distrust of creeds, and reliance upon the historical process brought them charges of heresy but also helped them formulate the characteristic liberal ideas. Thus in ordering this section of the anthology, Hutchison arranges his selections around those ideas.

In like manner, Hutchison organizes the writings from later stages to reflect concerns of those periods. In the 1890s liberals began to face the implications of their teachings for the church's life. Hutchison therefore includes Rauschenbusch's call for a new evangelism of public morality and George A. Gordon's reformulation of missionary goals. To demonstrate liberalism's later handling of assaults from its detractors, Hutchison chooses Harry Emerson Fosdick's classic sermon "Shall the Fundamentalists Win?" to capture the flavor of the great debate of the 1920s. He also employs the realism of Walter Marshall Horton and the wit of Halford Luccock in depicting the confrontation with neo-orthodoxy during the thirties.

This anthology is thus no mere sampler. There are genuine gems of liberal expression throughout, and Hutchison's commendable organizational pattern allows them to stand alone as well as to reflect the evolution of liberalism's history. Although the volume suffers the unevenness of most edited works, reading it in this age of growing religious intolerance is a refreshing reminder that, as Briggs wrote in 1889, "All truth should be welcomed . . . and built into the structure of Christian doctrine" (p. 36).   [L.A.H.]

Johnson, Paul E. *A Shopkeeper's Millennium.* **New York: Hill and Wang, 1978. ix + 210 pp.**

This historical monograph is a comprehensive study of the 1830 to 1831 religious revivals in Rochester, New York. These revivals played a major role in the creation of the Second Great Awakening because they sparked the religious upheaval in the entire western New York region known as the Burned-over District (see p. 32). Led by the evangelist Charles Finney, the Rochester revivals unified most Protestants around evangelical religion in this rapidly developing commercial center. The result was an army of Christian soldiers who internalized the evangelical beliefs of human perfectability and who consequently worked to restructure society around the new values of work, family, and temperance.

The volume was a pioneering effort to apply recent developments in social history to the study of religious change in American society. Paul Johnson relied heavily on sociological theory, especially the idea that religion interacts with the political, economic, and cultural fabric of the society in which it exists. He argued that the characteristics of the individual converts themselves revealed the important elements in the relationship between religion and society in western New York. By tracing the social origins of revival converts, Johnson discovered how they fit into the social structure of Rochester from 1815 to 1837.

Despite the fact that few participants left detailed biographical accounts of themselves, Johnson located information about the individual converts from quantitative sources, including church records, census reports, tax rolls, and city directories, as well as from more traditional manuscript sources.

Based on this evidence, evangelicalism was a middle-class religion, one that was most successful among the small shopkeepers of Rochester. Finney's revival converts came disproportionately from the ranks of master craftsmen, merchants, and professionals who supervised the growing manual labor force in a city dependent on commerce. Johnson speculated that economic development had broken the traditional social bonds between shopkeepers and their employees. Workers previously had lived and worked within a paternalistic family setting, but large-scale commercialization and urbanization began to separate employee residences from employer workplaces. Because entrepreneurs no longer supervised labor's every move, an evangelical theology that promoted individual responsibility and the expectation of a successful future for themselves and for their workers must have been very attractive.

Whether the revival experiences in Rochester, New York, were similar to those occurring in other locations of the Second Great Awakening is uncertain. Additional case studies of revivalism are now underway. Labor historians already have noted a strong link between Protestant evangelicalism, revivals, and the new middle-class values, but some have suggested that the workers themselves took a much more active role in promoting evangelical religion than suggested by Johnson. Whatever the overarching explanation for the Second Great Awakening turns out to be, however, *A Shopkeeper's Millennium* provides a model study of religious change within a specific social context.   [L.K.P.]

King, Martin Luther, Jr. *Stride Toward Freedom.* New York: Harper and Row, 1958. 230 pp.

Anyone who has not lived in the Deep South before 1960 will have a difficult time understanding the symbolic significance of the Montgomery bus boycott of 1955–56. Anyone who lived with the stigma of humiliating separation between the races, from "colored" drinking fountains to closetlike toilets for blacks, realizes the "small" inconveniences were symptoms of a very deep disease called racial segregation. At issue was the right to seat oneself anywhere on public transportation. At stake was the integrity of the black community against a vicious and sometimes violent system of apartheid elaborately constructed by the white power establishment over the past seventy years. It was in this context that a young, well-educated, highly articulate black minister assumed the leadership, at first hesitantly but with gathering authority, of the civil rights movement in the nation. If Montgomery became the symbol for deep-seated racial hatred by some whites and timidity by others, it also became the first focus for nonviolent resistance, born of Christian principles, as a method for achieving social and economic justice.

Eloquent and full of a sense of injustice at the very beginning of his career, King traces the development of his philosophy of nonviolence in *Stride Toward Freedom*. After the first bombing of his home, King realized both the force of hatred he was dealing with and, as he spoke to a crowd of his own people bent on retaliation, the power of nonviolence to create community and strengthen determination. Also seen here is the maturation of a man under great pressure. He was afraid in his first arrest, and often he had doubts about the strength of his support.

What emerges from these trials is first a portrait of the authority and power of the black church among black Americans. If the civil religion of white America was first hammered out in the pulpits of the American Revolution, the civil rights movement was forged from the black theology of ministers and laypersons in the black churches of the twentieth century. Second, this early book, within the movement, proves that from the start the struggle for racial equality was seen by its adherents as a contest of strategies, legal and economic, between its cause and that of its opponents.

Stride Toward Freedom cannot be read without a sense of tragedy. Its author will emerge as one of the great Christian leaders of our century, and yet, within ten years of this book's publication, King lay dying on a motel veranda in Memphis. The book itself is a qualified statement of victory for the civil rights movement. Did the boycott end the segregation on Montgomery buses or was it the Supreme Court decision that forced company compliance? One of the demands of the Montgomery Improvement Association, the hiring of black drivers, was not met until years later. And from the hindsight of thirty years of black unemployment, poor housing, and more discrete but real forms of segregation the boycott seems but as the symbol of a battle still in its infancy. [S.C.B.]

Kinzer, Donald L. *An Episode in Anti-Catholicism: The American Protective Association.* **Seattle: University of Washington Press, 1964. ix + 342 pp.**

The history of the American Protective Association (APA) is detailed in a work that is important to an understanding of religion and

American culture, especially in what may be regarded as its negative dimensions. One of the many fraternal organizations appearing in the United States in the late nineteenth century, the APA resembled the Masonic Order in that it had a women's auxiliary and a youth program, as well as a men's division that had supposedly secret signs and rituals. According to its leaders, the primary purpose of the APA was saving the nation from the "menace" of an international Catholic conspiracy.

When it appeared in the late 1880s, the APA was simply one of a variety of organizations dedicated to fighting Catholicism, opposing Irish urban political leadership, and protecting the nation's public schools. (The strategy for achieving this last aim was guarding against the hiring of Roman Catholic teachers and protesting the practice of contracting with sectarian or denominational groups for the operation of common schools.) In the 1890s, however, the APA emerged as the leading organization of its type. It reached the height of its influence in the 1893–94 elections. The APA was closely associated with the so-called patriotic press, whose goals were much the same as those of the many nativist movements that emerged in the wake of the "new" immigration of the post–Civil War years.

This monograph is a definitive study of the APA. Kinzer has followed up every clue and examined practically all the available sources. Even so, he is unable to measure the APA's political impact in national elections or to estimate the extent of the organization's influence with much precision. This well-done study nevertheless lays bare the "underside" of religion in late nineteenth-century America. Students of religion and culture will find it extremely valuable.   [J.S.]

Konvitz, Milton R. *Judaism and the American Idea.* **Ithaca: Cornell University Press, 1978. 223 pp.**

This work combines seven previously published essays by the author on various aspects of the meaning of conscience, rule of law, civil disobedience, human rights, and life, liberty, and the pursuit of happiness as these values are articulated in the Jewish tradition and reflected in American jurisprudence. Konvitz ties together biblical, Midrash, and Talmudic themes with the political writings of major English philosophers, especially Locke, and with the thought of America's founders, especially that of Thomas Jefferson. Throughout these essays Konvitz demonstrates the affinity between Jewish ideals of life, law, and civic order, and those embodied in the American Revolution and pioneering past, in Jeffersonian ideology, and in the general patterns of American cultural and institutional development.

America, from the time of its founding, has tended to see itself as a kind of new Israel, a country mandated by divine fiat. When the Declaration of Independence and the Constitution were written in the eighteenth century, the strong influence of the Enlightenment led Franklin, Washington, Jefferson, Madison, and other leaders to speak of the "laws of nature and of nature's God," and of certain "self-evident" truths and "unalienable rights." These values have acquired a quasi-religious status as American absolutes. They also have many common affinities with the religious ideals of Judaism. The belief that the national well-being of a people is dependent on the moral quality of the nation is a long-standing prophetic theme in Hebrew Scriptures. Like the intent in the Declaration of Independence, Hebrew Scriptures beckon humans to build the earthly city so that it would be hardly distinguishable from the city of God. Not escape from life but involvement in and betterment of life has been the Jewish ideal. Judaism, too, is built on the principle of law and rests on the conviction that humans are not to be used merely as a means to an end, as tools, but that each is an end in themselves, that all have an equal right to pursue life, liberty, and happiness. These pursuits are not given by government but are intrinsic to the human person as a creature of the divine.

The affinity between American ideals of liberal democracy and Jewish religious self-understanding has had an important significance for Jewish identity. These similarities have meant that American Jews have not had to suffer from problems of identity and allegiance that have haunted Jews elsewhere.

Konvitz's essays are relevant to American, religious, and Jewish studies and to political science courses. This material should also be included in any discussions of civil religion in American society. [W.D.D.]

Lasch, Christopher. *The Culture of Narcissism: American Life in an Age of Diminishing Expectations.* New York: W. W. Norton and Company, 1978. xviii + 268 pp.

Lasch's book fits easily into a niche of widely read contemporary cultural interpretations; preceding it were Alvin Toffler's *Future Shock* and Theodore Roszak's *Making of a Counter Culture*; following it are John Naisbitt's *Megatrends* and Robert Bellah, et al., *Habits of the Heart* (see p. 9). There is a significant tradition of cultural criticism in the United States, extending back to Henry James, Henry David Thoreau, Jonathan Edwards, and perhaps even John Winthrop. The question that links the luminaries and would-be luminaries in this tradition of criticism is How are we Americans to interpret the past and present so that we may be directed toward a future? Lasch's goals in this work are in continuity with that heritage: to restore a sense of the usable past and the reinstitution of a sense of the integrity of personal experience. Ultimately, he fails in realizing those goals; nevertheless, along the way his book exhibits strengths that, in concert with the reasons for the failure, make this an instructive work.

Early on Lasch states his thesis; he is *describing* "a way of life that is dying—the culture of competitive individualism, which in its decadence has carried the logic of individualism to the extreme of a war of all against all, the pursuit of happiness to be dead end of a narcissistic preoccupation with the self" (p. xv). Rather than being based on an ego strength that would enable the recognition of others and the environment, narcissism is a vortex based on inner weakness that requires constant buttressing, with a subsequent distortion of experience. Basing his cultural interpretation on this pathogenic metaphor is both a strength and a weakness. It is impressive that Lasch can illumine such a wide range of experience with this metaphor and many of his chapters—the nature of gender relations, marriage and family, and education—are quite good in terms of their diagnostic value. The weaknesses of the metaphor are that it originates from psychiatry and is applied societally, and that it is a *single* metaphor.

Lasch *has* diagnosed a central problem in America: the flight from the fullness of experience. He is sensitive to social class and alert to historical continuity. Particularly interesting are the patterns of development he traces in the history of institutions. These strengths do lead to a weakness: the obscuring of some elemental human capacities. Squeezed out of view between the vises of the human need and societal influence are conscious intentions, nuances of meaning, and the richness of human imagination.

Lasch's pessimism is consistent with the species of the work— jeremiad. A favorite of American prophets, the jeremiad both reminded the audience of its sins and pointed people back to the ideals they had violated. Lasch fails to enunciate those ideals from the past that direct us to the future. Furthermore, Lasch tells us *what* to think in diagnosing the culture but not *how* to think in ways productive of a more healthy future.   [L.S.J.]

Lewis, Richard Warrington Baldwin. *The American Adam: Innocence, Tragedy and Tradition in the 19th Century.* **Chicago: University of Chicago Press, 1955; Reprint. Chicago: University of Chicago Press, 1964, 1968. ix + 204 pp.**

The American Adam is a classic work in the interdisciplinary field of American studies, and in particular, it is a leading example of the myth-symbol approach to understanding American culture. This school of thought, which dominated American studies in the 1950s and influenced related humanities disciplines, proposed that certain symbols, such as the American image of the West or the place of technology and the machine in the American imagination, captured the central features of American culture. This methodology was a marriage of history and literature in its use of images rather than facts alone to understand the past. Lewis used a religious symbol, the biblical Adam, in his analyses of American culture. His slim but influential volume is perhaps best described as an intellectual history that uses religious ideas to examine some key figures of early nineteenth-century American literature.

Appropriately for an interdisciplinary scholar, Lewis considers the discipline of literature broadly to include philosophical and religious writings and works of history and criticism as well as poetry and fiction. His theme emerges from the familiar American discomfort with the past and the early American rejection of Europe, her habits and her history. In this pattern of rejection, Lewis sees an assertion of defiant pride in America's heroic innocence and vast potential as a nation poised at the start of a new history of great expansion and progress. In his analysis, Lewis borrows Emerson's distinction between the quintessentially American party of hope and the less distinctively indigenous party of memory, and he adds a third group, the party of irony. The "chanter of Adamic songs," Walt Whitman is for Lewis "innocence personified" and his chief example of the party of hope. The elder Henry James and Horace Bushnell offer ironic twists to Adamic innocence. To the unworldly philosopher James, the fall from grace is a fortunate one because it ironically raises the human from childlike innocence, selfishness, and naïveté. Innocence is inadequate for the full reach of human personality, according to the theologian Bushnell, who argued that conscience is higher than innocence. Lewis also offers trenchant chapters on Nathaniel Hawthorne and Herman Melville, whose dark visions might seem not to fit the Adamic model. Lewis argues that their tragic visions gain power from the prior notion of innocence against which they reacted.

Lewis's theme has enduring significance because it explains so much about the American past. Professor Lewis touches a taproot of American culture because "the myth of the American Adam was simply a formula for the way life felt to alert and sensitive Americans during the second and third quarters of the nineteenth century" (p. 154). [P.J.C.]

Lincoln, C. Eric. *The Black Muslims in America*. Boston: Beacon Press, 1961; rev. ed. Boston: Beacon Press, 1973. xxxi + 302 pp.

After a quarter century, Lincoln's *Black Muslims in America* remains an invaluable source for the study of the origins, content, personalities, and dynamics of the Nation of Islam. Written in a period when many whites and certainly some blacks saw the Black Muslims as simply a "hate" group and revised in 1973, Lincoln's work views the group as the symptom of a disease, "voiceless people" who bore witness to the unmistakable evidence that Negro-white relations were in poor repair. Although he shared a basic distaste for the Black Muslims, he understood and sympathized with the sources of their anger. Throughout, he warns the reader that the group served as a sign of worse things to come, perhaps from the "ominous" political power of the Black Muslims, perhaps from another group produced by the continuing racial conflict in America.

Lincoln's account of the inner workings of the Black Muslims provides invaluable data for historians of American religion. He describes black nationalist forerunners of the group both in the Moorish Temple of Noble Drew Ali and the United Negro Improvement Association of Marcus Garvey. He notes in detail the appearance of the mysterious prophet in Detroit during the 1930s and the passing on of esoteric-soteriological wisdom to Elijah Muhammad. Lincoln further details the mythology, moral system, and economic practices of the Black Muslims. Yet he also looks upon these developments as somehow peripheral to the "passion for group solidarity" resulting from racial tension. He believes that "Muhammad appealed to . . . newcomers not as individuals but as a crowd" (p. 107). He understood the Black Muslims as ultimately a black nationalist group, made up of lower-class blacks who rejected American culture and Negro identity and accepted "Asiatic" symbols. Their history revealed the dynamics common to all mass movements: rejection of a despised culture, avoidance of that culture, and acceptance of some of the tenets of that culture (in this case, Lincoln contends, the acceptance of inverse racial exceptionalism). Nevertheless, despite his lack of interpretive emphasis on the religious nature of the movement, Lincoln states at the end of the book that the Black Muslims were essentially "a religion of protest," powered and energized, he believed, by hate (p. 248).

Lincoln took special notice of the power of Malcolm X and correctly foresaw a power struggle within the movement after the Messenger's death. Beyond detailing the internal terms and dynamics of the Black Muslims, Lincoln locates the group in the social context of the time. He notes cranky relations with black organizations and leaders, the perverse fascination of the group for the media, and the Black Muslims' ongoing struggle to locate themselves within the broader Islamic world both in the United States and in the Middle East. The Black Muslims have divided into a group dedicated to the purity of the original message and a group transformed into the World Community of Islam in the West. Whatever further relocations follow, Lincoln's study will stand as the seminal statement on the early Black Muslims in America.   [E.T.L.]

Lincoln, C. Eric, ed. *The Black Experience in Religion*. Garden City, NY: Doubleday, 1974. xii + 369 pp.

For three decades, C. Eric Lincoln has interpreted blacks' experience in the United States. Here he focuses on the religious dimensions of that experience, bringing together essays by influential black religious thinkers of the 1970s. This important anthology provides a useful analysis of the past and offers a perspective to judge how well the United States, in the words of Martin Luther King, Jr., is living out "the true meaning of its creed."

Lincoln divides his book into five major sections: "Black Religion and the Black Church: Mode, Mood, and Music—Humanizing the Social Order"; "Black Preachers, Black Preaching, and Black Theology: The Genius of Black Spiritual Leadership"; "Black Religion and Black Protest"; "Black Cults and Sects: Alternatives to Tradition"; and "Black Religion: Africa and the Caribbean." The variety of essays by writers such as James H. Cone, Joseph R. Washington, Jr., and Lincoln himself exhibit shared convictions creating resounding unity. None is more pronounced than the belief that amid its diversity American black religion rightly possesses an identity of its own. As Lincoln says, this identity emerges from "a conscious effort on the part of black people to find spiritual and ethical value in their understanding of history" (p. 2).

Facets of that consensus appear in the volume's particular themes and essays. The black church, for example, has sustained black people and thus helped them affirm with Langston Hughes "this oath—America will be!" (p. 7). Rooting that motif in sermon and song, "black religion," contends Lincoln, "begins by affirming both the righteousness of God and the relevance of black people within the context of Divine righteousness" (p. 68). As J. Deotis Roberts, William Jones, and others understand, that affirmation makes the problem of evil fundamental for black theology. If suffering results from powerlessness, black theology must become political, and thus it must protest oppression. It also stresses God's liberating power and the responsibility of blacks to do all they can to free themselves and the United States from the shackles of racism.

Black experience in religion, Lincoln stresses, reflects "a wide spectrum of dissidence and experimentation" (p. 196). Moreover, much black religion in the United States is Christian, but that description does not fit every case. The Black Muslims and Black Jews exert an influence, as does a renewed appreciation of indigenous African religions and the black spiritual traditions of the Caribbean.

The book ends on this pluralistic note, and Lincoln lets it stand without final comment. None is needed because the book's basic message is clear: As they surveyed the varieties of black religious experience in the midseventies, black religious leaders urged that black religion in the United States was and ought to be distinctive. Utilizing its diversity to support a shared mission—the liberation of blacks from oppression—black religion would also testify its work was not for blacks only. Its efforts could redeem the nation. Were Lincoln to add a contemporary postscript, it might well read: Thanks in large measure to the efforts of black religion, that dream—still far from realized completely—has not been entirely deferred.   [J.K.R.]

Littell, Franklin H. *From State Church to Pluralism: A Protestant Interpretation of Religion in American History.* **Chicago: Aldine, 1962; 2d ed. New York: Macmillan, 1971. xxvii + 225 pp.**

At the time of this book's publication, Littell was professor of theology at Southern Methodist University, and his writing reflects his roles of American church historian and theologian. The theological dimension of Littell's work is dated; but this is not to say that it is dismissable or unusable. Rather this points out that no matter how accurate the specific historical detail collected and for this work, it is clearly selected and arranged from a perspective more directly out of the context of European "crisis theology" (more commonly called "neo-orthodoxy" in an American setting), than from the American religious-historical experience. To be sure, this theological style was very popular in major American divinity schools, mainline Protestant seminaries, and graduate schools of religion in that era. But that era has passed, and whether as theologians, social philosophers, historians, or popular culturists, American interpreters are endeavoring to explain American religious historical culture more on its own terms than on some imported precogitated point of view.

The story Littell tells is interesting and worthy, and we can profit from being reminded of it again. One historical interpretation, no matter what its other contributions may or may not be, always helps put alternative views in sharper perspective. On the surface one can justify reviewing and rereading Littell without appeal to any necessarily greater or better reason.

For him, the major problem facing American churches is a proper historical and theological "self-understanding," in particular, "the regaining of a consciousness of calling" (p. ix). One conclusion that *might* be drawn from this thesis, says Littell, is the American churches "once disciplined and faithful" have in their success and prosperity settled back into a comfortable accommodation to the secular way of the world and the once-Christian nation is having its faith eroded into "faithlessness" and a superficial, contentless Christianity (p. x).

Although there is some merit to this position, Littell contends it is more false than true because "America has never been a Christian nation except in the nominal sense" and that "true religion" has never typified American "Christian" culture (p. x). Littell's "course of American church history" then is not just an effort to "win a people back to the churches" they had abandoned when state support ceased to be compulsory (p. x).   [E.A.W.]

Luckmann, Thomas. *The Invisible Religion: The Problem of Religion in Modern Society*. New York: Macmillan, 1967. 128 pp.

According to Luckmann's influential and innovative study, the perennial question of how the individual is located in the social order has become particularly urgent in industrial society. Sociology of religion in the tradition of Weber and Durkheim avers that this question is, at its heart, "religious."

Unfortunately, in Luckmann's judgment, the "new sociology of religion" (post–World War II) avoids this question given its tendency to identify religion with the institutional church and its lack of explicit theoretical concern. It sidesteps the central question of sociology of religion: What are the conditions under which transcendent and integrating structures of meaning are socially objectivated? Thus the "new sociology of religion," while noting the marginalization of traditional religion in Europe and America, fails to pose the more significant issue: What has secularization introduced as its own socially objectivated cosmos of meaning? Is there a new religion in the making in modern society?

These questions require a theory of the place of religion in human life. From Luckmann's functionalist perspective, religion is the process by which humans move beyond a strictly biological life through the formation of a symbolic universe ("world view") that connects everyday reality with some transcendent sense ("a sacred cosmos").

In simple societies, a symbolic universe persists without explicit institutional form. But the more complex a society, the more likely it will be administered by a specialized body, especially where productive technology creates a surplus by which a group of experts can be supported. Under such conditions, socialization processes press for perfect conformity between the personal identity of individuals and the doctrines of a church-oriented religiosity.

However, the fit between personal life and official religion is never perfect. Nor is the fit between institutionalized forms of religion and the actual world view of a given society. Indeed, under conditions of rapid social change, increasing incongruence is likely. That is the circumstance in modern industrial society. But then the marginalization of traditional religion (Christianity) may be less significant than the emergence of a new social form of religion.

In exploring this new form, it should be noted that the specialization of religion was part of a more inclusive history culminating in the modern industrial system through which virtually all social institutions became specialized and governed by norms of functional rationality. Personal identity became private. Society was pervaded with a consumer orientation that shattered the unity of the traditional sacred cosmos. Variant versions of world view emerged; individuals were left to create their own; traditional religious representations were divested of public significance. In effect, the sacred cosmos of modern industrial society is a plurality of ultimate meanings available for personal selection. Such possibilities are socially expressed through secondary institutions—advice columns, magazines, popular music. Public institutions are governed by norms of functional rationality, detached from any encompassing structure of meaning.

Dominant themes in the modern sacred cosmos include: autonomy, self-realization, mobility, sexuality, familism. In sum, the modern sacred cosmos symbolizes the historical emergence of individualism. It is a new social form of religion, expressing a radical transformation of the place of the individual in the social order. [D.S.]

Maguire, Daniel C. *A New American Justice: Ending the White Male Monopolies*. Garden City, NY: Doubleday, 1980. xiii + 218 pp.

The United States of America at the present moment in its history is confronted with the need for a transformation of epochal proportions. The major moral and political problem of the coming century is, in a word, redistribution. New modes of sharing are needed if the nation is to survive. The focus of Maguire's penetrating critique is on one such mode: preferential affirmative action.

Several qualities have typified the American character over past centuries: acquisitiveness, isolationist individualism, faith in the sacramentality of wealth. But other features are also deeply etched within the American soul: racism, sexism, a zest for violence, an insistence on a minimal state. Yet at the present time, two dramatically new facts force the nation into a radical reconsideration of its fundamental structure: the end of free expansion and a passionate demand for social justice.

Preferential affirmative action—that is, any measure seeking to correct discriminatory patterns through the use of enforced numerical goals and timetables—is among the more significant means of responding to the demand for social justice. It is a means that runs directly counter to the American tradition of ideological individualism. But it is warranted by considerations of the meaning of justice.

Three forms of justice are distinguishable: (1) individual justice (right relations among individuals); (2) social justice (obligations of individuals to the common good); and (3) distributive justice (responsibilities of groups to individuals). The fundamental criterion of justice, especially social and distributive justice, is essential need, whose fulfillment may, at moments, entail sacrifice. A central deficiency of American-style individualism is its neglect of social justice, which is grounded on the principle that human life is shared life. The common good, whose exact meaning depends on historical context, is vital to a specifically humane existence even where it mandates self-sacrifice.

The realization of justice means recognizing (1) that the fulfillment of needs sometimes, as in the case of preferential treatment, requires inequality; (2) that voluntary compliance is seldom sufficient and that governmental enforcement is an indispensable means; but (3) that justice unseasoned with mercy is minimalist and ultimately imperfect.

Under contemporary conditions of American society, the obligations of social and distributive justice mandate a program of preferential treatment for certain specific disempowered groups. To qualify for enforced preferential affirmative action, groups should satisfy four criteria: (1) no alternatives to enforced preference are available; (2) prejudice against the group has reached the level of depersonalization; (3) bias against the group is systemic; and (4) members of the group must be clearly visible as such.

Given those criteria, four groups qualify for special treatment:

particularly blacks, but also women, American Indians, and among Hispanics, Chicanos and Puerto Ricans.

Preferential affirmative action, in sum, is a belated attempt to liberate groups whose lives have long been oppressed by the heavy hand of a white male aristocracy. Doing them justice may be costly, but the nation is at a point where continued injustice is no longer tolerable.   [D.S.]

Marsden, George M. *Fundamentalism and American Culture: The Shaping of Twentieth-Century Evangelicalism 1870–1925.* **New York: Oxford University Press, 1980. xvi + 306 pp.**

Fundamentalism has been approached by scholars as a social movement, a political reaction, and an economic phenomenon. This is the first book to take fundamentalism seriously as a religious movement that was shaped by and in turn shaped American culture. Older interpretations attempt to explain fundamentalism in the context of its seeming quaintness in the world of the post–World War I era. Fundamentalism, however, emerged during the late nineteenth century and took shape in the first two decades of this century. During that period, not only was fundamentalism consistent with American culture, it reflected some of the more central aspects of that culture. The culture shifted radically just as fundamentalism gained a clear and consistent voice.

Evangelicalism was the dominant religious ethos in the United States throughout the nineteenth century. Born in rural village environments, evangelicalism was able to accommodate to new social and cultural realities, exemplified by organization and the rise of a theoretical speculative science. The two major questions were, How can Christianity carry on its traditional social ministry in the changing social context? and How can the Christian message either accommodate to or establish dominance over the emerging new priestcraft, science? Dwight L. Moody paved the way for a new urban evangelicalism. The attempt by evangelicals to come to terms with the new science exposes a paradox central to fundamentalism. Postmillennialism and premillennialism, differing eschatologies within evangelicalism, highlighted the tension between those who saw religious progress and secular progress as similar, if not identical, and those who eschewed secularization and demarcated the eras of human history into periods of divine dispensation. The latter became the core of fundamentalism. Behind dispensationalism was a scientific world view based on Baconian premises, especially as expounded in Scottish Common Sense philosophy. Thus the earliest fundamentalists considered themselves hard-headed empirical scientists, just at a time when normative science was undergoing a profound shift from empirical to more phenomenological models. Intellectually, fundamentalism was in the mainstream during the time of its formation, but out of the mainstream by the time it was fully formed.

The intellectual history of fundamentalism can find parallels in other areas as well. Socially, fundamentalism was based on an assumption that the nation was dominantly evangelical, if not exclusively so. This assumption was, of course, outmoded by the 1920s. Politically, the fundamentalists were inheritors of the evangelical tradition, but that political synthesis came unravelled at least by the 1930s, and perhaps earlier. Nevertheless, fundamentalism was and continues to be an important expression of an American culture that is still active, though no longer dominant. [G.H.S.]

Marty, Martin E. *A Nation of Behavers*. Chicago: University of Chicago Press, 1976. xi + 239 pp.

Martin E. Marty's *Nation of Behavers* sets out to provide "a new map of religious America." For materials, Marty states that he will study "the visible loyalties of people as evidenced in their beliefs and social behavior and expressed in their public quests for group identity and social location" (p. 1). To a degree, Marty accomplishes this, but he does so by analyzing what scholars say about the beliefs of Americans as evidenced in their quests for identity within and through religions, not by analyzing the "behavers" themselves. In going to secondary sources, Marty actually "maps" the territories of differing approaches to the study of religious history in America.

Depending upon the purpose for which Marty's book is read, one of two "texts" can actually emerge from the study of this volume. Read as a coherent essay, the volume could well have been called *A Nation of Historians*, for Marty gives a thorough analysis of the "maps" or perspectives that have dominated the writing of America's religious history. Marty groups American religions under six headings: mainline religion, evangelicalism and fundamentalism, pentecostal-charismatic religion, the new religions, ethnic religion, and civil religion. Under each heading, he provides extensive, well-documented analysis of what religious historians have written about religious behavers. That rigorous analysis is what constitutes the second "text" which emerges, and that is, essentially, a handbook or guide for the student of American religions.

A Nation of Behavers is a useful map for the student who wants to "place" an idea, a historian, or a phenomenon in a greater context.

The volume has an excellent index—of historian's names, religious sects, topics, and trends. Each chapter provides extensive notes—indeed a rich bibliography on the subject of the chapter.

Read as an essay, then, Marty's work provides perspective for those approaching the history of religion in America. It is a beginning place in that sense. *A Nation of Behavers* is also a reference tool in its own right. It is the kind of work that should be used more than once: as one studies a denomination or as one studies a particular history, Marty's "map" can help create greater understanding of a topic by providing background and related ideas.   [J.S.H.]

Marty, Martin E. *Pilgrims in Their Own Land: 500 Years of American Religion*. Boston: Little, Brown, 1984. xii + 500 pp.

The story of religion in America is more than a mainstream. Marty honors diversity by including native Americans as well as immigrating Europeans, Spanish, and French as well as English and Dutch colonists, blacks as well as whites, rebels, and dissenters as well as establishment spokespersons, Jews and Roman Catholics as well as Protestants, women as well as men. He finds order in the distinctive ways in which all of the guiding figures saw themselves as pilgrims and pioneers.

By definition pilgrims are en route; reaching their destination calls for a new, less transitory identity. Yet Americans never fully equated geographical dominion with spiritual possession; curiously enough, when the land became their own, their sense of pilgrimage was redoubled and thus "every pioneer or shaper in American religious history promoted some commanding vision, some conquering idea" (p. 348). Marty's story is of restless people who "joined the ceaseless spiritual pilgrimage of Americans in their efforts to find more satisfying faiths and symbols—even if this meant leaving behind much of the cherished but now, they thought, shopworn church religion" (p. 319). Whether in churches, sects, or cults, Americans have characteristically sought new, or renewed, spiritual paths.

All of Marty's exemplary pilgrims began by fleeing from cultural chaos and envisioning a new community vibrantly knit together in religious truth. Yet each group came to embrace diversity and to see its vision as one of a variety of spiritual options for Americans. In the end, each helped to develop a peculiarly American "freedom *for* choice as well as freedom *of* choice in religion" (p. x). Like a master storyteller, Marty elicits the ruling design of pilgrimage by rehearsing the life stories of a broad variety of spiritual seekers and finders, from Queen Isabella to Cesar Chavez.

Given the chaos of today's spiritual marketplace and the range of ethnic heritages in American religious life, many contemporary pilgrimages are "inward journeys." Yet some visionaries still see America on the verge of gaining or reclaiming the cultural coherence of a people joined together as one spiritual body. The most truly American pilgrimage, Marty points out, charts a course "between the foreseeable chaos of total individualism and this specter of a totalist social faith" (p. 476). In showing a path between spiritual narcissism and religious fascism, Marty's delightfully readable history extends the trajectory of American religion. By leading readers to remember the many pilgrims in the American past, Marty keeps the pilgrimage alive by making it new. [J.G.M.-y]

Marty, Martin E. *Righteous Empire: The Protestant Experience in America.* **New York: Dial Press, 1970; 2d ed. New York: Harper and Row, 1977. 295 pp.**

Histories of complicated phenomena require an organizing theme or metaphor, and Marty has most appropriately selected the notion of empire as the primary symbol shaping the Protestant experience in America. The choice enables him to illumine the order and the tensions within the nation's religious life from 1776 to 1970, the time of writing. Although the notion of empire might imply treatment only of "insiders," Marty is careful to examine the mainline also by exploring its effects on such "outsiders" as Indians, blacks, immigrants, and sectarians. Thus his work is oriented but not controlled by its controlling metaphor.

In the first part of the book, covering the years from 1776 to 1877, Marty follows the formation of the Protestant empire in America, looking into its people, land, and characteristic institutions, urbanization, sectarianism, free thought, and, of course, the Civil War. Part 2 begins with the failure of Reconstruction and shows how, in response to the "perils" of an urban-immigrant environment, Protestantism became accommodated to its culture. Whereas religion became an increasingly private matter for many, others challenged the prevailing American social system, and the empire was divided into a "two-party system." The "private" party emphasized personal religious experience and took conservative stands on social and political issues. The "public" party stressed collective moral concerns and developed the Social Gospel movement. Contention between the two parties was especially bitter in the 1920s and has continued to characterize American religious life, even—and perhaps especially—when visions of empire reappear.

Extensive use of quotations gives the book the sense of being told in the participants' own words, and Marty's clear thinking and crisp writing move the story along effectively. Because of his imperial metaphor and his treatment of both its strengths and the strains within it, Marty's book is and will probably long remain the best, and certainly the most readable, single-volume examination of the mainline in American religious history. It won the National Book Award and is a fine place to begin one's study of religion in America. [J.G.M.-y]

May, Henry F. *The End of American Innocence: A Study of the First Years of Our Own Time, 1912–1917*. New York: Alfred A. Knopf, 1959. xvi + 413 pp.

Historians have usually located the great divide between nineteenth-century and modern American culture in the years immediately following the First World War. Yet to do so is to miss, May contends, the ways in which the dominant cultural tradition had begun to come apart in the years just before the war. So he terms the years from 1912 to 1917 "the first years of our own time" because they witnessed the beginning of "the end of American innocence." To make his case, May examines American literature and politics for expressions of those assumptions of value that were intact in 1912 and in disarray in 1917. He begins with President Taft's speech at William Dean Howells's seventy-fifth birthday dinner: "The dinner was really a testimonial to the unity, excellence, and continuity of American nineteenth-century civilization. Most of the speeches and press comments pledged the country's allegiance to three central doctrines of that civilization. These were first, the certainty and universality of moral values; second, the inevitability, particularly in America, of progress; and third, the importance of traditional literary culture" (p. 6). May then proceeds to analyze those who upheld these assumptions and those who rebelled against them, offering in the process insightful comments on virtually every writer, critic, thinker, and political spokesperson on the American scene.

The war precipitated a process that had been under way for a long time; when the war ended, a major cultural change had occurred. "Innocence, the absence of guilt and doubt and the complexity that goes with them, had been the common characteristic of the older culture and its custodians, of most of the progressives, most of the relativists and social scientists, and of the young leaders of the prewar Rebellion" (p. 393). Their efforts had failed because of "a permanent flaw in American nineteenth-century thought: its inveterate optimism" (p. 397). With the illusion of progress shattered, reaction set in, as seen in the racial violence, religious fundamentalism, and Prosperity First movement of the 1920s.

The conclusion is epitomized in the wartime metamorphosis of Randolph Bourne: "formally an exuberant, mystical, somewhat naive insurgent, he became in his last essays a sharp, courageous, profound inquirer, a defender of freedom in what he had learned was a hostile world" (p. 395). A corresponding lesson, May points out, is that historians should themselves get over the innocence of expecting true stories to have completely happy endings. And since then historians have generally tended to relish complicated rather than complacent cultural eras. Thus May's study, with its incredible range of examples and strengthened by an excellent bibliographic essay, both relocates an important cultural transition and helps explain the passage from continuity to conflict as the major model for the study of American history. [J.G.M.-y]

May, Henry F. *The Enlightenment in America*. New York: Oxford University Press, 1976. xix + 419 pp.

The Enlightenment in America by Henry F. May is an attempt to determine the intellectual roots of nineteenth-century American culture. One of these roots clusters about the set of ideas associated with Protestant Christianity, particularly its Calvinistic wing, which developed in sixteenth- and seventeenth-century Europe and was transplanted to America, where it expanded vigorously, especially in New England in the seventeenth and eighteenth centuries. The other root clusters about an assemblage of conceptions associated with the European Enlightenment and that also found its way to America where it again flowered vigorously.

May is not only interested in the origins, development, and demise of the American Enlightenment, but also in its effects upon various spheres of cultural experience from theology to politics and from science to social theory. He is exhaustive both in the attempt to trace how far it spread and to determine how deep it went. But the singularity of May's achievement derives in part from the way he views the American Enlightenment monolithically. Developing a clue from the European intellectual historian Crane Brinton, May argues that the American Enlightenment is best understood in religious terms and as a kind of religion. As religion, the Enlightenment centered around two propositions: that the present is more enlightened than the past, and that the best way to understand humanity and nature is through the use of our natural faculties.

Viewing the American Enlightenment monolithically, however,

does not prevent May from perceiving its diversity as well. Here is May's other distinctive achievement. Instead of one Enlightenment religion, May in effect discovers four. The Moderate or Rational Enlightenment, which developed in England around the time of Newton and Locke, remained dominant until about the middle of the eighteenth century and is associated with "balance, order, and religious compromise." The Skeptical Enlightenment, which took hold by the middle of the eighteenth century, is associated with Voltaire in France and David Hume in Scotland and made wit, invective, and intellectual suspicion its chief methodological instruments. The Revolutionary Enlightenment, which saw its beginnings in Rousseau and its culmination in Paine and one side of Jefferson, preached the need for a comparatively total renovation of institutions and values and was often associated with the possibility of constructing a new heaven and a new earth. The Didactic Enlightenment, encountered initially in Scotland, developed in response to what it viewed as the casualties of the Revolutionary and Skeptical Enlightenments. It sought to preserve the notions not only of an orderly universe but also of moral absolutes and the inevitability of progress.

May does not treat these different Enlightenment faiths as institutionally organized or systematically codified bodies of belief. He regards them instead as broad currents of thought that emigrated to America in successive waves of influence. Though his chapters include excellent treatments of standard figures such as Jefferson, Madison, Franklin, and Washington, his gaze encompasses a host of minor players and tries to take account of more general, even popular conceptions through a heavy reliance on printed pamphlets, sermons, and particularly letters.   [G.G.]

McLoughlin, William G. *Revivals, Awakenings, and Reform: An Essay on Religion and Social Change in America 1600–1977.* Chicago History of American Religion Series. Chicago: University of Chicago Press, 1978. xv + 239 pp.

William McLoughlin's *Revivals, Awakenings, and Reform* traces "core conceptions" of American culture through a series of redefinitions beginning with the Puritan experiment in the New World and continuing into our own period of social upheaval. Among these core elements are: the belief that America is a chosen nation with millennial significance; Americans are free and moral individuals, possessing inalienable political rights and rights of conscience; and that Americans are molded by the Protestant ethic, moral law, progressive laws of science, and have allegiance to a higher law engendered by the Judeo-Christian tradition.

American history, McLoughlin believes, can be understood as a history of awakenings: revitalization movements that occur during periods when these core definitions no longer fit current situations. Using the model of Anthony F. C. Wallace and the insights of Clifford Geertz, McLoughlin argues that an awakening takes place when the cultural system is in tension between "norms and experience, old beliefs and new realities, dying patterns and emerging patterns of behavior" (p. 10). Familiar religious revivals are only a part of the process of cultural transformation, as they affect individual lives, while the awakening affects the culture. McLoughlin traces the tension between ethos and world view and the changes in the core elements of American culture in the Puritan Awakening of 1610–40; the Great Awakening of 1730–60; the Second Great Awakening of 1800–1830; the Third Awakening of 1890–1920; and the Fourth Awakening that began in the 1960s and is still underway. In each period, there are times of individual stress, cultural distortion, persuasive authorities redefining the meaning of the core elements, and finally, the development of a new world view. While he charts the anatomy of the great revivals, McLoughlin's interest is in understanding the revival process within the context of basic ideological transformation.

Each of the periods has been crucial in the continuing redefinition of America and Americans. McLoughlin believes that the seeds of the culture's core elements were to be found in the "broad Calvinistic Puritan base" (p. 39) that formed the core of the colonial world view. Almost as soon as this base was established, however, it began to degenerate, and this tension was resolved in the First Great Awakening. The ferment of this Awakening restructured colonial loyalties to human and divine authority, and eventually led to the triumph of Republican ideology in the American Revolution. The Revolution, in turn, brought troubling questions about the identity and mission of the new nation, and the next awakening began to define what it meant to be an American in "Romantic Evangelical" ways, a narrowing, McLoughlin contends, of the core vision.

The next major cultural upheaval came during the conflicts at the end of the nineteenth century. Theistic evolution, progressive orthodoxy, and the different strains of the Social Gospel engendered the nativist response of fundamentalism, and set the terms of the continuing modernist/fundamentalist debate. Finally, McLoughlin contends that the loss of faith in the tenets of liberalism due to the various dislocations of contemporary times has again brought us to a period of redefinition with its attendant nativism, new spiritual options, and an as yet open-ended future.　[E.T.L.]

Mead, Sidney E. *The Lively Experiment: The Shaping of Christianity in America*. New York: Harper and Row, 1963; 2d ed. New York: Harper and Row, 1976. xiii + 220 pp.

The central thread that ties these essays together is the radically new dimension which America contributed to western Christianity through religious freedom. Mead traces this theme and its impact on the churches from the colonial era to 1930. Freedom and its corollary, persuasion, evolved from circumstances including sectarian competition, available space, and the prevalence of persuasion in the Great Awakening. By the Revolution, it was apparent that each sect, in order to survive, had to tolerate the others. But the intellectual basis for freedom was worked out by Rationalists who argued that a common core of "essentials" was implicit in all faiths and that truth would triumph in open debate. Pietists shared the Rationalists' aims but differed theologically and returned to the orthodox fold when the French Revolution inspired fears of a rationalistic subversion of the Christian faith. The intellectual premises of religious freedom were at that point obscured, and pietism typically replaced intellectual rigor in American churches. Further, religious competition in this period promoted not only revivalism and voluntaryism, but also historylessness as a cast of mind. The theology of the Republic, nonetheless, was argued by Lincoln who premised democracy on faith in God who judges all human institutions. Ironically, however, pietistic and intellectually flabby Protestants following the Civil War identified Christianity with laissez-faire economics and survival of the fittest. By century's end, the Social Gospel challenged the social system of this synthesis while evolution challenged its theology. At this point, American Protestantism split: liberals adopted social concern; fundamentalists adopted dogma. In the process, theological reflection went largely by the boards, and with it went any real awareness of "the theology of the Republic." This book is immensely helpful for anyone seeking to understand the bases for religious freedom in American life.　[R.T.H.]

Mead, Sydney E. *The Nation with the Soul of a Church*. New York: Harper and Row, 1975. x + 158 pp.

In answer to the question "what is America?" G. K. Chesterton responded, "a nation with the soul of a church." The essays in this volume represent Mead's attempt to unpack the meaning of Chesterton's apt phrase by developing an important distinction between the religious philosophy that legitimates "the religion of the Republic" and the theology professed and taught by the religious denominations of the United States.

In the title essay, Mead traces the idea of a national religion from the medieval European ideal of uniformity, through the Reformation and Puritanism, to the deism of America's Founding Fathers. They saw aspects of a universal religious truth in the variety of particular sects, believing that a synergistic cosmopolitanism should characterize religion in America—"that a definitive element of the spiritual core which identifies it as a nation is the conception of a universal principle which is thought to transcend and include all the national and religious particularities brought to it by the people who come from all the world to be 'Americanized' " (p. 63). Thus the religion of the Republic is prophetic over against the actions of the actual nation and is rooted, ultimately, in a belief in "the primacy of God over all human institutions" (p. 67). Mead concludes that "what is commonly called the relation between church and state in the United States ought to be resolved into the theological issue between the particularistic theological notions of the sects and the cosmopolitan, universal theology of the Republic" (p. 69). This, the synergistic and theonomous religion of the Republican, relativizes the absolutistic claims of all sects and also guards against national idolatry. Mead hopes, therefore, that the American religious commonwealth may provide a model for harmony among the nations in a world civilization.

The other essays collected here are "In Quest of America's Religion," "The Post-Protestant Concept and America's Two Religions," "The Fact of Pluralism and the Persistence of Sectarianism," "Neither Church nor State: Reflections on James Madison's 'Line of Separation,' " "Religion, Constitutional Federalism, Rights, and the Court," and "Religion of (or and) the Republic." In sum, Mead's reflections provide creative resources for interpreting the relations between religion and political culture in the American past, present, and future.   [J.G.M.-y]

Meyer, Donald B. *The Positive Thinkers: A Study of the American Quest for Health, Wealth and Personal Power from Mary Baker Eddy to Norman Vincent Peale.* Garden City, NY: Doubleday, 1965; 2d ed. New York: Pantheon Books, 1980. 396 pp.

One of the greatest confusions of modernity is knowing when to call a physician and when to call a priest. Beginning with Mary Baker

Eddy, one strain of American thought, neither religion nor psychology but containing elements of both, has taught that one need not make the choice. If life is fragmented for moderns, it does not have to be. Life, and indeed cosmic reality, are one if only one knows the proper formula with which to view reality. This was basic to Christian Science and has been the core of American psycho-religion to the present.

The quest for wholeness began with the discovery of cultural and personal fragmentation. The label "nervous disorders" was given to a wide variety of problems that seemed to have their origins in role fragmentation and social dislocation. Beginning with Phineas Quimby and the early "mind cure" advocates, a steady progression of suggested alleviations for these "nonphysical ailments" were produced.

Mary Baker Eddy was sensitive to the relatively high proportion of women who suffered from these maladies, and equally aware of both the male clergy and emerging, male-dominated medical establishment dealing with the problem. Her system began as theology; a radical rephrasing of Emersonian idealism. It was with her discovery of Quimby's concept of "spiritual matter" that Mary Baker Eddy became interested in "mind cure," hence psychology.

Since that discovery, psycho-religion has had a consistent, if somewhat labyrinthine, development. Both physiology and politics have been muted (in Christian Science, of course, physiology has disappeared). Individuality has been elevated, and in the 1920s a lasting identification between individualism and the business ethic was formed. This reflected the larger culture in which Henry Ford was a high priest. Through such secular evangelists as Bruce Barton and Dale Carnegie, failure to succeed was not only un-American, it was unholy. One had not only a God-given right to success, one had a divine imperative. Through the growing acceptance of the Pentecostal movement, psycho-religion gained a sacramental dimension. The source of power for success could constantly be invoked through receiving the Holy Spirit. All of these elements came to a focus in the person of Norman Vincent Peale. His enormous popularity is evidence of the pervasiveness of psycho-religion in American culture. [G.H.S.]

Middlekauff, Robert. *The Mathers: Three Generations of Puritan Intellectuals, 1596–1728.* **New York: Oxford University Press, 1971; 2d ed. New York: Oxford University Press, 1976. xii + 440 pp.**

Few families have exceeded the Mathers' contributions to the intellectual and religious heritage of the American people. Three generations of them—Richard (1596–1669), Increase (1639–1723), and Cotton (1663–1728)—distinctively marked New England Puritanism. In turn, their theological interpretations of history and politics helped build a mighty nation, although not always in ways these clergymen could have known, let alone admired.

Robert Middlekauff's study of these remarkable persons is neither biography, family history, nor a sociology of Puritan knowledge. Interests in all of those areas govern this work, but the author's seminal contribution brings them to bear on his central concern: creative elements of continuity and change, contends Middlekauff, and in that respect, they were representative of other intellectual Puritan ministers. Largely derived from his exploration of the Mathers' private as well as public writings, that outlook equips Middlekauff to tell anew the story of American Puritanism.

This revisioning of the Puritan mind that pivots on Middlekauff's finding that conventional wisdom concerning Puritanism's development has often been myopic. Specifically, numerous interpretations commonly overstress Puritan accommodation to secular pressure. That account is one of degeneration: Puritan piety deteriorated into moralism; covenant fragmented into individualism; the inroads of reason, science, and business transmuted intense religious faith into lukewarm benevolence; and in general, the church influenced society less and less. As for the Puritan clergy, Middlekauff suggests, conventional interpretation has typically portrayed them as recognizing that their continued spiritual and political leadership depended on the ability "to assimilate the new secularism to the old religion" (p. viii).

Middlekauff's alternative is not completely at odds with these ordinary views. The Puritan clergy certainly did worry about the divergence of religious and secular life. The fact that Increase and Cotton Mather were more anxious than Richard indicates that the concern grew more acute as time passed. Where the Mathers and their counterparts were involved, however, Middlekauff's point is that Puritan intellectuals did much more than respond to cultural changes in accommodating ways.

Using their formidable minds to nourish a deeply held conviction that all things should be done in a spirit of service to God, the Mathers forged in each generation a creative synthesis of piety and intellect. Their efforts did not answer every question; nor did they permanently check the erosion of Puritan ways by secular forces. Those failures helped create the impression that the Mathers and their peers were primarily leaders who would compromise to save what they could in a mission destined to fail. Middlekauff's book justly balances the scales by telling the more likely story. The Mathers were no rear guard fending off secular powers to prolong the inevitable Puritan retreat. On the contrary, although their cause did not prevail as they wished, the Mathers were an intellectual vanguard, advancing courageously a view of human existence aimed at helping people "to get the best out of themselves for the glory of God" (p. 8).   [J.K.R.]

Miller, Perry. *Errand Into the Wilderness.* Cambridge: Belknap Press of Harvard University Press, 1956; 2d ed. New York: Harper and Row, 1964. x + 244 pp.

Errand Into the Wilderness is a collection of ten essays all but one of which comprise what Miller calls a series of "spotlights on the massive narrative of the movement of European culture into the vacant wilderness of America" (p. vii). The single exception is a lengthy study of the theological mind of New England Calvinists. The remaining chapters, beginning with the frequently anthologized title essay and including "Thomas Hooker and the Democracy of Connecticut," "Religion and Society in the Early Literature of Virginia," and "The Puritan State and Puritan Society," move from the early colonial period to the era of the Enlightenment ("Jonathan Edwards and the Great Awakening" and "The Rhetoric of Sensation"), to the nineteenth century ("From Edwards to Emerson" and "Nature and the National Ego"), and on to the present ("The End of the World").

Miller's focus is ideas, particularly theological ideas that he believes provided the initial impetus for American settlement and colonization. But within this frame of reference he varies his methodological aperture considerably. Sometimes his attention is directed specifically to the ideas themselves and their own internal development and coherence, as in "The Puritan Marrow of Divinity." But more frequently he explores the continuities of experience that underlie their successive articulation and often outlasts them. Thus in "From Edwards to Emerson" Miller examines the interest that persisted from the Puritans to the Transcendentalists to cultivate in nature an unmediated relation to the divine. In "Errand Into the Wilderness" Miller isolates a pattern of reflection about the meaning of their New World mission that the Puritans inaugurated and subsequent generations of Americans have perpetuated and extended.

Miller concedes that his approach to intellectual history is somewhat unorthodox and even problematic. At the risk of personal subjectivism, it requires "not only a fluency in the concepts themselves but also an ability to get underneath them" (p. 185). It also threatens to unify, or at least to simplify, a culture that Miller is otherwise predisposed to view as a "congeries of inner tensions" (p. 1). Yet such divinatory techniques, so long as they are not willfully obscurantist, seem thoroughly consistent with a book that aims to do nothing less than explore the whole meaning of the American experience. Where the method takes its largest risks is in the imputation it encourages of an American cultural uniqueness, its susceptibility to the myth of American exceptionalism. But Miller claims in his preface to be responding to a kind of revelation that occurred to him on the banks of the Matadi in the Congo when he became convinced of the necessity to expound his own America to the generation of his peers. The title of the book thus echoes a sense of Miller's own "call" and at the same time lends it a figurative form. [G.G.]

Miller, Perry. *The New England Mind: From Colony to Province.* Cambridge: Harvard University Press, 1953; 2d–4th eds. Boston: Beacon Press, 1961, 1962, 1967. xi + 513 pp.

Perry Miller—now well known and widely quoted throughout the land as that great Harvard-based, revisionist, Puritan historian—did a fairly simple thing to understand the Puritans. He read them! So he comes with this vast reservoir of primary experiences with their writings. No matter how re-revisionized Miller's contributions might be, in this generation or the next, he will always have to be taken into account because he placed himself in such close proximity to Puritan experience due to his own saturation with their perspective on things. Miller did more than shoot down prejudiced and unfounded opinions about the Puritans; he systematically replaced unsubstantiated views with carefully researched and thoroughly reconstructed descriptions that brought his readers not only penetrating understanding but significant appreciation of the Puritan experiment on life and its unfolding for them in the American scene. Ever since Miller's scholarship, it has seemed logical, almost natural, to begin any discussion of things "American" with the Puritan as much as with the land or the aborigines ("Indians"), the continent or the Constitution!

Miller first made his name and reputation with his *Orthodoxy in Massachusetts,* published in 1933 and his *The New England Mind: The Seventeenth Century,* published in 1939 (see p. 94). However, after coming back from a stint in the armed services, Miller reflected on his earlier work and realized he needed to go back to approximately 1648—the year of formulation of the *Cambridge Platform*—to pick up on and spell out previously unannounced and unexplored themes that then would form the necessary connective tissue between *Orthodoxy in Massachusetts* and *New England Mind: The Seventeenth Cen-*

tury. Miller's scholarly instincts turned out to be correct because in true historical hindsight we can now say that while the above-mentioned 1933 and 1939 works introduced and "made" Perry Miller, its really two later works—*New England Mind: From Colony to Province* (1953) and *Errand Into the Wilderness* (1956) (see p. 92) that summarize Miller for us at his best.

Although it fits into the above writing sequence, *New England Mind: From Colony to Province* stands on its own and can be read as a self-sufficient unit. Its content is organized topically, not chronologically, because throughout this period the Puritan cosmology remains fairly standard. Difficult tests or shattering experiences could and did occur to the Puritans but without altering any major aspect of the doctrinal frame of reference on life and the universe. Consequently, the scope of this work is narrowed to the "provincial" scene and as a "case history of the accommodation to the American landscape of an imported and highly articulated system of ideas" (foreword). The system of ideas extends from the *Cambridge Platform* and Richard Mather's farewell, through the "Halfway Covenant," into the confusions about the covenant, witches and the sacraments, the fragmentation of the commonwealth, until it results in the socialization and moralization of piety/patriotism of Cotton Mather and Benjamin Wadsworth. As always, Miller tells it well.   [E.A.W.]

Miller, Perry. *The New England Mind: The Seventeenth Century.* **New York: Macmillan, 1939; 2d and 4th eds. Cambridge: Harvard University Press, 1954, 1963; 3rd ed. Boston: Beacon Press, 1961. xi + 528 pp.**

The New England Mind: The Seventeenth Century is a work conceived and composed on a grand scale. The first of a two-volume study of Puritanism in colonial New England and the most elaborate and complex of Perry Miller's numerous substantial contributions to American intellectual history, this work has grown in reputation with each of its many editions and reprintings.

The Seventeenth Century puts American Puritanism in the context of concurrent intellectual controversies in Reformation Europe and reveals it as an expression of universal human drives for religious and psychological fulfillment. Although Miller's goals are ambitious, he is strikingly successful because of his ability to enlist his broad knowledge and acute analyses in a tight focus on New England. New England Puritanism's provincial setting and peculiar intensity provide Miller with "a laboratory where the experiment can be studied under more controlled conditions" (p. ix) than would be possible in the Old World.

Contrary to the conventional stereotypes, Puritans were, according to Miller, an emotionally vibrant and spiritually vigorous group in the tradition of Platonic idealism and Augustinian piety; their zeal came from an insatiable quest for the spiritual ideal of union with God despite their human imperfections. Miller clearly admires the Puritans for the nobility of their impossible struggle. Miller's central thesis about the Puritan mind is that it was a delicately poised balance of opposites, such as the concern for this world and the next, the human and the divine, reason and faith. The resultant Puritan synthesis affected the "plain style" of their preaching; it was the mainstay of Puritan politics, society, and economics that operated by the dictum to live fully in the world and reap the fruits of its God-created riches, but to enjoy them with "weaned affections" (p. 42); the Puritan synthesis also shaped the narrow path Puritans trod between reasonable, ethical religious thought and uncontrolled zealous piety. According to Miller, Puritanism's difficult synthesis lent the movement an urgency that quickened the life of every Puritan.

Miller's large yet intricate volume is too sophisticated for casual browsing, and it "treats the whole literature as though it were the product of a single intelligence" (p. vii) to a greater extent than is acceptable by current historiographical trends, but after four decades, it still serves as a starting point for the study of American intellectual and religious history. His is a special form of history that is grounded in a profound religious sensitivity. In the late professor's own words, "students of the soul and students of the past" (p. 490) may both be richly rewarded for the rigorous exercise of reading this difficult but profoundly important classic.   [P.J.C.]

Morgan, Edmund Sears. *The Puritan Dilemma: The Story of John Winthrop.* **Boston: Little, Brown, 1958. x + 224 pp.**

John Winthrop was the principal founder and first governor of the Massachusetts Bay Colony. As later Americans from Cotton Mather to Sacvan Bercovitch discovered, the course of Winthrop's life reveals something crucial about the meaning of America.

Morgan's masterly biography begins by noting how thoroughly modern Americans have misunderstood the Puritans—"We have to caricature the Puritans in order to feel comfortable in their presence. They found answers to some human problems that we would rather forget" (p. xi)—and quickly points out how important a correct view of them may be: "Actually the central problem of Puritanism as it affected John Winthrop and New England has concerned men of principle in every age, not least of all our own. It was the question of what responsibility a righteous man owes to society" (p. 8). Given what Winthrop saw as the perversions of his native land's government and church, the only way to keep the problem alive, and thereby to keep his covenant with God, was to move to New England—for the sake of reforming Old England. In Massachusetts he met the problem head on in the persons of "well-meaning zealots" who "failed to recognize God's kingdom on earth must still be a kingdom of flesh and blood, and their misdirected zeal soon indicated to Winthrop that he faced a far more difficult problem to control the good than to punish the wicked" (p. 73). As Winthrop soon learned, "the people of Massachusetts had in fact undertaken an almost impossible task: they had accepted a commission which required them to follow a specific body of religious principles; but among these principles was one which encouraged the development of schism and another which denied them the means of preventing it" (p. 80). As governor, Winthrop confronted this classic Puritan dilemma in dealing with the separatism of Roger Williams, the antinominianism of Anne Hutchinson, the uneasy coordination of church and state, and the religious, economic, and political consequences of deciding to remain in America after the Puritans came to power in England. Winthrop's achievement was to keep the dilemma alive until death brought "what in life he had never sought, a separation from his sinful fellow men" (p. 205).

Morgan's achievement is to bring Winthrop back to life and thus to lead contemporary American readers to appreciate a dilemma that cannot ultimately be avoided. His lucid, moving book shows how biography can contribute to the study of American religious history and, indeed, to a fresh understanding of one central issue of American life. [J.G.M.-y]

Morgan, Edmund Sears. *The Puritan Family: Religion and Domestic Relations in Seventeenth-Century New England.* **Boston: The Trustees of the Public Library, 1944; 2d ed. Boston: The Trustees of the Public Library, 1956; rev. ed. New York: Harper and Row, 1966. x + 196 pp.**

In what has become a classic in the literature on American Puritanism, Edmund Morgan suggests that we look at Puritan domestic relations in the context of their theological and philosophical perspective. Morgan begins with a brief review of Puritan doctrine, reminding readers of the tension between the belief that sanctification follows justification and the belief that there is some connection between faith and works. Those without any evidence of good deeds were presumed to be far from the mercy of God. Morgan outlines the Puritan belief that covenantal relations structured all areas of life, from the grandest cosmic agreements at the time of creation to the humblest accords between masters and servants. Even though the Covenant of Grace was first of all individual, the promise of grace was commonly extended to Christian households. Other covenants, such as the various domestic agreements and the state or national covenant, required obedience in return for temporal blessing; thus while outward morality was not efficacious for salvation, it was necessary for the prosperity of the community.

Philosophically, says Morgan (following the lead of his mentor Perry Miller), the New England Puritans, like most other westerners at the time, saw creation in terms of superior and inferior relations. The logic that articulated this sense that all life is relationship they borrowed from Petrus Ramus. The social order that follows from such a theological and philosophical matrix supposed that one's place in society was that of relationship. Clergy, for example, could only exercise their vocation when they had specific calling from and connection with a congregation. In terms of the domestic scene, Morgan devotes chapters to the "relative" relations of husbands and wives, parents and children, and masters and servants. In each case he demonstrates that mutuality rather than authoritarianism marked domestic life.

Other large-scale institutions, notably church and civil government, undergirded the family in its various roles and checked behavior that seemed to threaten the family's centrality. Civil government required that single people live in family settings and chastised family leaders who neglected their duties. Indeed, argues Morgan, the entire Puritan experiment begins to resemble an extended family. Puritan preference for their families began to contradict the theological emphasis on the saving grace of God to save whom God wills. Morgan points out that seventeenth-century Puritans assumed that "God casts the line of election in the loins of godly parents" and that those outside the Puritan tribe found it nearly impossible to be included in the "circle of grace" (p. 182).

The Puritan Family, first published as a book in 1944, was Morgan's doctoral dissertation and stands at the beginning of his influential career as a scholar and teacher of American colonial history. Morgan relied on "literary" sources rather than the quantified sources of more recent social historians, but his insights are largely borne out by the work of later scholars. As a teaching tool and basic text in Puritan studies, *The Puritan Family* has indeed become a classic in the literature. [B.A.R.]

Morgan, Edmund Sears. *Roger Williams: The Church and the State.*
New York: Harcourt, Brace and World, 1967. 170 pp.

This intellectual portrait of a prickly Puritan is a classic in its genre.
Edmund Morgan's discernment of a powerful, intellectually fearless
mind at work creates a landmark study that redefines the place of
Williams in American intellectual history.

Morgan begins with a sketch of currents in England that shaped
Williams between his birth in 1603 and his arrival in New England in
1631. In Elizabeth's England, apocalyptic schemes to uncover deep
meaning in current great events and in expected greater ones were
the order of the day. "Englishmen persuaded themselves they were
a favored people, a people whom God had cast in a role paralleled
only by that of the Jews before the coming of Christ" (p. 7).

Williams pursued these accepted ideas to their outer limits. He
concluded that neither the facts of English history nor scriptural evidence supported them, and so placed himself in opposition to the
millennial fervor of his countrymen.

In similar fashion, Williams the Puritan accepted the premises of
Puritan theology and, thinking them through to the end, became a
Separatist. Finally he arrived at "the awful conclusion to which his
ideas had led him and from which there was no escape: Christians
had lost their church, and there was no present way to recover it" (p.
53). For Williams, self-constituted, covenanted Puritan congregations
could not undo the vast chasm of apostasy that stood between the
Emperor Constantine and the seventeenth century. Only a direct,
divine intervention (which Williams did not expect soon) could rein-
stitute a legitimate church with a legitimate ministry.

Similarly, the conflicts between Williams and the Massachusetts
authorities who banished him to Rhode Island were rooted in a view
of the state that Williams developed by pursuing Puritan principles
to their logical ends. If God no longer was in covenant with the church,
then any state's claim of a covenant-imposed divine responsibility for
the church and public morality was a delusion. "Williams demanded
the separation of the state not merely from the church but from God"
(p. 85). Among other unpopular consequences of his view was a denial
that the English king, because he was a Christian, had more right to
give away land in Massachusetts than the heathen native Americans.

Morgan pictures Roger Williams as a man possessed of rare intellectual courage and capacity. Morgan locates the importance of his
subject not merely in defense of religious liberty and separation of
church and state. "His greatness was simpler. He dared to think" (p.
142).   [L.W.]

Mulder, John M., and John F. Wilson, eds. *Religion in American History: Interpretative Essays.* **Englewood Cliffs, NJ: Prentice Hall, 1978. xi + 459 pp.**

This helpful book includes essays that analyze "the United States as a new nation which, although derived from European sources, was from the outset stubbornly independent in self-understanding and patterns of behavior" (p. x), in order to "supplement to existing narrative studies" and "collections of primary materials" (p. xi). The essays range historically and perspectivally and are consistently erudite, interesting, and well written. The book will broaden the views of scholars working on particular periods and give students a sense of the variety of methods employed in the study of religious history. Brief headings serve as transitions between the essays, and there is a convenient bibliography of primary and other secondary sources.

The essays are sound and distinguished; the authors are often eminent and established. The contents include: "Understanding the Puritans," by David D. Hall; "The Covenanted Community," by Alan Simpson; "The Halfway Covenant," by Edmund S. Morgan; "The Myth of Declension," by Robert G. Pope; "The Election Sermons," by A. W. Plumstead; "Piety and Intellect in Puritanism," by Robert Middlekauff; "Underlying Themes in the Witchcraft of Seventeenth-Century New England," by John Demos; "Jonathan Edwards as Great Man," by Richard L. Bushman; "The Great Awakening as Watershed," by Alan Heimert; "From the Covenant to the Revival," by Perry Miller; "American Protestantism during the Revolutionary Epoch," by Sidney E. Mead; "The Republic and the Millennium," by James Maclear; "The Second Great Awakening as an Organizing Process, 1780–1830," by Donald G. Matthews; "Religious Benevolence as Social Control: A Critique of an Interpretation," by Lois W. Banner; "The Emergence of Immediatism in British and American Anti-Slavery Thought," by David Brion Davis; "The Formation of the Catholic Minority in the United States, 1820–1860," by Thomas T. McAvoy, C. S. C.; "Religion and Resistance Among Antebellum Negroes, 1800–1860," by Vincent Harding; "The Negro Church: A Nation Without a Nation," by E. Franklin Frazier; "A Critical Period in American Religion, 1875–1900," by Arthur Schlesinger, Sr.; "Protestantism and the American Labor Movement: The Christian Spirit in the Gilded Age," by Herbert G. Gutman; "Immigration and Puritanism," by Marcus L. Hansen; "Lay Initiative in the Religious Life of American Immigrants, 1880–1950," by Timothy L. Smith; "Judaism in America," by Will Herberg; "American Catholicism and American Religion," by David O'Brien; "The Origins of Fundamentalism," by Ernest R. Sandeen; "The

American Religious Depression, 1925–1935," by Robert T. Handy; and "The Radical Turn in Theology and Ethics: Why It Occurred in the 1960s," by Sydney E. Ahlstrom. Thus the volume's chief virtue lies in its accurate sounding of important channels in the main stream of religion in American history. [J.G.M.-y]

Murray, John Courtney. *We Hold These Truths: Catholic Reflections on the American Proposition.* New York: Sheed and Ward, 1960. 336 pp.

This is a collection of occasional papers delivered over a ten-year period. Topics covered include: the American consensus, the Constitution, religion, morality, war, and foreign policy. Also, the private school question, censorship, and the relevance of traditional Catholic natural law theory and philosophy to the problems of today's world are discussed. The first example of Catholic natural law theory applied to the American experience, and from an American Catholic perspective, these reflections, particularly as they relate to religious liberty and pluralism, were foundational for the Vatican II *Declaration on Religious Liberty.*

Murray examines the founding, forming, and validity of the consensual "public philosophy of America" (p. viii). The American consensus accepts God's sovereignty over nations and government by consent. The Bill of Rights can be traced to medieval natural law and is not simply Enlightenment rationalism. What is operative, however, socially, is not the tenets of our founding documents but an ethic of success-seeking, positivism, and pragmatism at all levels. Protestantism has largely abandoned American roots and Catholicism has preserved them in its Thomistic natural law. All citizens need to look into the moral and political philosophy on which the nation is founded and engage in a continual dialogue regarding the common good and a workable world view from which consensus on fundamental issues can be gleaned. Diversity can remain but only as long as there also exists reasonable assent and loyalty to a set of constitutional principles or propositions.

The First Amendment ought to be understood as an "article of peace" (p. 56) in regard to church-state separation and the realities of religious pluralism. It is not a negative comment on religion or the avoidance of state support for religion. The amendment should not be turned into a "doctrine" of separation.

This is particularly true when reviewing the problem of the private school in American society. Murray argues that the "canons of distributive justice" (p. 146) demonstrate the rightness of aid for private schools. The Catholic population is large and supports a viable alternative to public education and nothing in the First Amendment permits "non-preferential aid to all religions" (p. 150).

A discussion of censorship distinguishes between private and public morality in positing that the state is concerned with crimes, and the private religious arena deals with sin. The two should not be mixed by an imposition of specific denominational beliefs about moral behavior. A public consensus on values is better; censorship by the state is just only when "possible"—when minimally acceptable by the general populace.

The last four essays apply natural law theory to the debates and problems of national security and the risk of war. Natural law can serve as an ideological counterpoint to Communist rhetoric and dogma and will serve as the American perspective on the nature of the social order, injustice, and human rights. Murray sees limited nuclear war as a possible necessity; but in any event, Americans should not view their national purpose as simply "survival." That would indicate a political bankruptcy. An effective national policy on the use of force is needed, preferably one based on a return to natural law. [M.L.S.]

Needleman, Jacob. *The New Religions.* **Garden City, NY: Doubleday, 1970. xii + 245 pp.**

Jacob Needleman's first major work on nonconventional religions in America became a launching pad for many scholars to examine (in a much more positive vein) what had for a generation popularly been termed *cults*. Looking at the flowering of different "new" spiritual alternatives that seemed to suddenly appear in the San Francisco Bay area in the late 1960s, Needleman became convinced that he was witnessing a great spiritual movement that would transform everything the modern West had thought about God and religion, the most significant change since the dawn of the scientific revolution. He was impressed by the "inward turn" and the search for transformation that he saw as a basic similarity shared by the new groups. Selecting five of the more prominent and promising ones, he devoted a chapter to more in-depth descriptions of Zen Buddhism, Meher Baba, TM (Transcendental Meditation), Sabud, Tibetan Buddhism, and Krishnamurti. In addition, the author highlighted some of the new ideas growing in popularity, such as astrology, reincarnation, and esotericism.

Standing at the beginning of the most productive decade of research on new religions as his volume did, it was inevitable that Needleman's work would be superseded. From the perspective of that body of research, his vision of a new religious consciousness remaking Western religion has faded. The burst of new alternative religions that he saw in the late 1960s was merely the first phase of the large-scale movement of Asian religion into America initiated by the removal in 1965 of the restriction imposed by the Oriental Exclusion Act of 1917. A new religious consciousness did not arise to replace Western religion (which as a whole continued to grow and thrive); rather, Asian religions grew to the point that they had to be recognized as additional protuberances, however small, on the American spiritual landscape. The more lengthy descriptions of the selected groups to which he devoted a chapter became outdated due to the rapid change in the groups during the decade and years since.

As important as any factor, Needleman (like all of his colleagues) failed to see the rise of the intensely hostile anticult movement or the tragedy of Jonestown, which would so distort the public's image of nonconventional religion and alter the development of even those not directly attacked by deprogrammers and accused of brainwashing their followers.   [J.G.M.-n]

Neuhaus, Richard John. *The Naked Public Square: Religion and Democracy in America.* **Grand Rapids: Eerdmans, 1984. xii + 280 pp.**

During the civil rights struggle, Richard John Neuhaus marched with Dr. Martin Luther King, Jr. During the Vietnam War, he protested United States policy long before it was popular to do so. Now Neuhaus is identified as a spokesperson for conservative issues.

Neuhaus is a Lutheran pastor, theologian, and critic of the political environment. His purpose in writing this book is "to address some of the major questions raised by (the religious new right) and by the reaction to it" (p. 5). The author believes that the mainline churches have sold out to sectarianism and acquiesced when transcendence was eliminated as legitimate in the public square. The Moral Majority has sensed a vacuum in the public square and has rushed in with sectarian solutions to every problem.

Heavily reliant upon Jesuit John Courtney Murray, Neuhaus reviews the American experiment. Acknowledging that many of the early leaders of this fledgling nation were not orthodox Christians, he maintains that a sense of the transcendent was at the very center of this unique attempt at a new form of government. Neuhaus fears that the experiment may go down the drain if the church capitulates in a process of redefining our culture without any reference to religiously grounded values.

The transcendent values needed to both move the American experiment forward and keep it loyal to the past heritage sound very similar to orthodox Lutheran theology.

While Neuhaus has done a splendid job of raising important issues, some of his interpretations of history and projections are dubious at best. For instance, he says freedom can be found through obedience to the normative. The blacks of 1850 (or 1920) would hardly believe that the normative expression of American culture gave them great freedom.

He asserts that Methodist Social Principles follow the left wing of the Democratic party. It could equally be claimed that the left wing of the Democratic party chose to follow the Methodist church and tried to co-opt its positions. The author seems to say that the only alternative to a Christianized transcendence for America is privatized religion. Even if persons do stake their lives on a Christian's understanding of transcendence, it does seem presumptuous to narrow the alternatives to those two.

Neuhaus claims that "on balance and considering the alternatives, the influence of the United States is a force for good in the world" (p. 72). No real basis is given for that moral judgment. Neuhaus focuses on the church and state as primary forces shaping America. Advertising gets a brief passing comment. Economic forces are not directly mentioned.

In spite of gaps and weaknesses in the book, Neuhaus has done a great service to raise important issues for a vision of the future of America. He recognizes that compromise is essential, that persuasion is better than coercion, that theological roots and sociological observations must interact. In his call for a critical patriotism, Neuhaus has dared to struggle with an issue others ignore. Perhaps other writers will continue the dialogue.   [H.M.]

Niebuhr, H. Richard. *The Kingdom of God in America.* New York: Harper and Row, 1937; 2d ed. Hamden, CT: Shoe String Press, 1956; 3d ed. New York: Harper and Row, 1959. xvii + 215 pp.

Niebuhr's interpretation of American Christianity as a movement centered in faith in the kingdom of God is guided by three basic convictions. First, Christianity, "particularly in Protestantism and in America, must be understood as a movement rather than as an institution or series of institutions" (p. xiii-xiv). Second, this movement is not a matter simply of progress or of a static dualism, but "requires of those who seek to be obedient to the divine imperative a dialectical movement" that is expressed both in the direction of worship toward

God and in the direction of work in the world (p. xiv). And third, "apart from God the whole thing is meaningless and might as well not have been," for "apart from God and his forgiveness nationality and even Christianity particularized in a nation become destructive rather than creative" (p. xvi).

Although Niebuhr recognizes that religion is nothing if not a matter of economic and social institutional realities, he avoids a sociological interpretation because "the instrumental value of faith for society is dependent upon faith's conviction that it has more than instrumental value" (p. 12). He adopts an interpretive perspective from within the movement, therefore, and attempts to view the meaning of American Christianity through its own central images and symbols. This internal point of view reveals that Protestantism's stress upon the sovereignty of God provides excellent principles for criticizing all human institutions—including a standing religious order—but provides little guidance for and in fact undercuts the construction of lasting Protestant institutions. Hence, although people will always try to secure their faith within social and intellectual structures, the life of faith transgresses such boundaries and the enduring elements of a vital tradition express different meanings at different times.

Thus Niebuhr discovers that in the foundational period of American life, "kingdom of God" meant "sovereignty of God"; in the era of awakenings and revivals, it meant "reign of Christ"; and in the modern period, it has come to mean "kingdom on earth." These different meanings of the same central symbol are the heuristic devices with which Niebuhr organizes his study, though he is aware that the idea of the kingdom of God requires all three emphases for adequate expression. As he concludes, "there was no way toward the coming kingdom save the way taken by a sovereign God through the reign of Jesus Christ" (p. 198). So he shows the thematic continuity within the various periods of the history of American Christianity.

Written between Niebuhr's study of *The Social Sources of Denominationalism* (see below) and his treatise on *The Meaning of Revelation,* this book is valuable theologically as well as historiographically, for it shows that an understanding of history is one of the resources for the task of theology and that through the study of religious history one may come to see the present and future America, as well as its past, in a new way.   [J.G.M.-y]

Niebuhr, H. Richard. *The Social Sources of Denominationalism.* **New York: H. Holt and Company, 1929; 2d ed. Hamden, CT: Shoe String Press, 1954; 3d ed. New York: H. Holt and Com-**

pany, 1957; 4th ed. Cleveland: World Publishing, 1962. viii + 304 pp.

This extended essay, originally published in 1929, remains one of the most influential and controversial analyses of the denominational divisions within Christianity. Niebuhr felt that theological distinctions alone did not adequately explain these partitions within the Christian church. Historically, denominations have reflected the same social segmentation as the secular society, including differences based on class, nation, region, ethnicity, and race. In this volume, he suggested why Christianity has been unable to transcend these social sources of Christian denominationalism, and he traced their evolution from their beginnings among the followers of Jesus, through the Roman Catholic and Protestant Reformation centuries, into the colonial New World, and finally into his own early twentieth-century United States.

This volume has important theoretical implications for two uncomfortable allies in the study of American religion, Christian ethics and the sociology of religion. Niebuhr believed that Christian differences based on social cleavages were morally wrong and he drew on the secular science of sociology to explain the failure of the Christian religion to overcome this "denominationalism." Although Niebuhr borrowed his initial constructs from Max Weber and Ernst Troeltsch, he developed a distinctive interpretation of the interaction between religion and society in this book.

Niebuhr argued that the Christian ideal of human oneness has failed because of the ethical compromises that religious organizations make with the society in which they exist. He based his analysis on two analytical categories, the "sect" and the "church." The church is an inclusive religious group into which a person is born, whereas a sect is an exclusive voluntary association which people choose. Niebuhr believed that sects are created by the "disinherited," especially those who suffer extreme economic deprivation, because their special needs are overlooked by churches trying to accommodate the larger society. He additionally suggested that a sect-church dynamic creates a perpetual religious reorganization based on the divisions within society. Sects originally are hostile to the secular society and its churchly agents, but the sect increasingly conforms to social norms in order to maintain itself and grow. As the sect becomes more like a church, the needs of the poor and other social outcasts once again will be ignored, thus recreating the preconditions for the rise of new sects.

Subsequent controversy over this book has been intense. In a later work, *The Kingdom of God in America* (see p. 103), Niebuhr himself argued against this attempt to locate the origins of religious change in a secular society. Others have refined or modified the sect-church typology. The most disputed issues include whether the poor provide the most vital impulse within the Christian churches; whether the sect-to-church-to-sect process is sequential and inevitable; whether sects lose their distinctive organization after the first generation; and whether sect-church categories are useful for non-Christian religion. Nonetheless, *The Social Sources of Denominationalism* remains the foundation for any conceptual exploration of religious institutions in relationship to American society.   [L.K.P.]

Niebuhr, Reinhold. *The Irony of American History*. New York: Charles Scribner's Sons, 1952. 174 pp.

Reinhold Niebuhr (1892–1971), one of the most perceptive social analysts the United States has produced, believed that "the powers of human self-deception are seemingly endless." He expressed that opinion in one of his best books, *The Irony of American History*. It focused on the Soviet-American cold war that loomed so large at midcentury; but his insight gives the book lasting relevance.

Niebuhr's vision of American history contained two premises that are especially important for grasping his philosophy of irony. First, human beings are infected by *original sin*. Niebuhr's understanding of that concept was down-to-earth, for he located its significance in the fact that all human beings "are persistently inclined to regard themselves more highly and are more assiduously concerned with their own interests than any 'objective' view of their importance would warrant" (p. 17). Second, Niebuhr located the American version of original sin in the nation's unwarranted assumption that its ways not only represent a clean break from a corrupted past but also remain so innocent and virtuous that they can rightly be identified with God's will for the world. Niebuhr saw the situation differently: "The irony of our situation," he argued, "lies in the fact that we could not be virtuous (in the sense of practicing the virtues which are implicit in meeting our vast world responsibilities) if we were really as innocent as we pretend to be" (p. 23).

Power, affirmed Niebuhr, is neither won, used, nor even lost innocently. But American experience is riddled with irony when people persuade themselves differently. To make his case, Niebuhr distinguished irony from pathos and tragedy. Pathos resides in unmerited suffering resulting from events in which none of the agents can rightly be held responsible or guilty. Tragedy arises from conflict of another kind as life's many claims are not always harmonious. One good must sometimes be sacrificed for another; life often involves what Niebuhr called "conscious choices of evil for the sake of good." Such choices define tragedy. Contrasted with pathos and tragedy, irony dwells in the gaps between intention and consequence that yawn neither by accident nor by conscious design alone.

The point was not that American life lacks pathos, tragedy, or even an abundance of blatant wrongdoing. But neither did Niebuhr think the United States was the most corrupt nation. Just the opposite struck him as closer to the truth; and, therefore, he anguished about the Americans' propensity to wreak havoc because they know themselves insufficiently. In *The Irony of American History,* Niebuhr showed Americans that their virtues contain hidden defects, that the nation's strength is weakened whenever it becomes vain, that its yearnings for security breed insecurity if they go too far, that America's considerable wisdom may be reduced to folly unless limits are better understood. Grandiose pretention, excessive pride, and unwarranted self-righteousness—these perennial idols were Niebuhr's targets. Wanting Americans to do their best, he urged them to learn, before it became too late, that the United States cannot save the world or even itself singlehandedly. [J.K.R.]

Oates, Stephen B. *Let the Trumpet Sound: The Life of Martin Luther King, Jr.* **New York: Harper and Row, 1982. xiii + 560 pp.**

Unlike other biographical accounts by journalists, academics, and long-time personal associates, Stephen Oates's book is the first effort by a professional biographer at recounting the life and times of one of the stellar figures in modern American history—Martin Luther King, Jr. This work is the fourth in a quartet of biographies by Oates about Americans who played key roles in the national saga of slavery and race-class oppression (others are Nat Turner, John Brown, and Abraham Lincoln). Materials used in this biography have been drawn from the Martin Luther King Collection at the Martin Luther King Center for Non-Violent Social Change in Atlanta, the John F. Kennedy and Lyndon B. Johnson libraries, and the Ralph J. Bunche Oral History Collection at Howard University. Oates skillfully weaves together the parental, cultural, spiritual, intellectual, and social forces that shaped the drama of Martin Luther King and the civil rights movement with which his name is inseparable.

As a child, Martin Luther King was deeply influenced by his dominating minister father. As a gifted and sensitive college student, he came under the influence of intellectual mentors at Morehouse College (Gladstone Lewis Chandler, George D. Kelsey, and Benjamin

May, president of Morehouse). Following graduation from Morehouse, King entered Crozer Theological Seminary. At Crozer and then at Boston University where he completed his Ph.D., Dr. King synthesized his own Baptist background in the black church with the teachings of Henry David Thoreau and Gandhi, the Protestant liberalism of the Social Gospel movement, Hegelianism, and the philosophy of personalism. The struggles and social upheaval of the civil rights movement, which catapulted the young minister into a messianic role, are all well narrated in Oates's biography.

Even though few new revelations are added to standard accounts of these events, Oates's work does capture personal and private aspects of Dr. King's inner struggles (especially with depression), insecurities, and doubts about his ability to bear the burden of leadership and to act as the instrument of God's will (as he clearly believed he had been called). The resistance Dr. King faced in struggling to emancipate both black and white Americans from the yoke of race-class oppression was formidable: intransigence in society at large, conflict, jealousies, and rivalry within the organizational structures of the civil rights movement, opposition from conservative elements within the black church, militancy and impatience on the part of an increasingly hostile, urban, black underclass, and duplicity and harassment on the part of the federal government.

Oates sheds new light on Dr. King's increasingly troubled relationship with the Johnson administration following his early, outspoken condemnation of the war in Vietnam. He also provides new insights into the vendetta by J. Edgar Hoover and the FBI in their attempt to discredit Dr. King and sabotage his political and moral effectiveness as a national leader. Oates's biography will be the standard reference work on Martin Luther King, Jr., for the forseeable future. [W.D.D.]

Pfeffer, Leo. *Church, State, and Freedom*. Boston: Beacon Press, 1953; rev. ed. Boston: Beacon Press, 1967. xiii + 832 pp.

"Congress shall make no law respecting an establishment of religion or prohibiting the free exercise thereof." According to Pfeffer, these words epitomized a "radical experiment" unique to human history. The object of those who framed the political institutions of this "experiment" was to create a sociopolitical environment in which neither church nor state could ever be used as an engine for the objectives of the other. The purpose of Pfeffer's book is to examine how this experiment evolved, to explore its implications and consequences for democratic living in America, and to identify the forces seeking to "frustrate and defeat" that experiment.

The first part of this study covers the historical events leading to that "radical experiment." The entire history of church relations in Europe up to the time of the Constitution sharply demonstrated two salient facts: (1) with minor exception, the history of church-state relationships was a history of persecution, oppression, bloodshed, and war, all in the name of the God of love; and (2) with equally minor exceptions, that history was the history of the unscrupulous use of religion by secular powers to promote their purposes and polities, and the acceptance of that role by "guardians" of religion in exchange for benefits. During temporary periods and in scattered areas, the church has dominated the state; but overwhelmingly the state has dominated the church and used it for its own purposes. Those who wrote the Constitution were fully aware of the religious wars, the persecutions, and all other evils that inevitably accompanied the union of church and state. They "sought forever" to keep these evils from the American experience.

The second part of Pfeffer's study treats that aspect of the "radical experiment" relating to the legal separation of church and state: state aid to religion, church use of state property, tax exemption, prayer in school, and a variety of other establishment clause issues. Pfeffer argues that the separation aspect of the First Amendment was intended to be as absolute as could be achieved within the limitations of human communal society.

The third part of the book is concerned with issues related to the exercise of religious freedom: public morals, conscientious objection, blasphemy and sacrilege, and religious liberty in reference to marriage, family, and the welfare of children.

Pfeffer's study was one of the first full-length treatments of the church-state issue by a specialist in law. Although somewhat dated (revised in 1967), it is a carefully documented work that contains a wealth of pertinent information on church-state law up to that time.

The conclusions of *Church, State, and Freedom* are clear: in the modern world, religious liberty is generally secure where church and state are most completely separated. If the "radical experiment" in America has demonstrated anything, it is that under the system of separation of church and state and religious freedom, religion has achieved a high estate unequaled anywhere else in the world. History has justified the experiment and proved the proposition on which it is based—that complete separation of church and state is best for both the church and the state, and secures freedom for both. This book is an excellent reference/resource work on the church and state question. [W.D.D.]

Pope, Liston. *Millhands and Preachers: A Study of Gastonia.* **New Haven: Yale University Press, and London: H. Milford, Oxford University Press, 1942; 2d ed. New Haven: Yale University Press, 1967. xvi + 369 pp.**

This work is one of the classic community case studies of the relationship between religion, social structure, social change, and social conflict. Pope examined the historical background and events surrounding a bitter strike that occurred in a textile mill in Gastonia, North Carolina, in 1929. The protagonists in the conflict were working-class poor whites and small farmers who had lost land and taken work in the mills, and the textile entrepreneurs whose basic motives revolved around the desire to maximize profits and maintain the status quo.

The textile operators were accepted as benevolent altruists. They exercised paternalistic control over the mainline churches (especially Baptist and Methodist). They built and maintained the churches and parsonages, subsidized the salaries of the ministers, and arbitrated church issues. Ministers, in return, rarely attacked any of the labor abuses in the mills (e.g., they remained silent on the child labor issue), refused to criticize the textile industry, adamantly opposed unionization, screened workers applying for jobs in the mills, repeatedly denounced "communist influences" trying to organize the workers during the 1929 strike, strove to divert the workers' attention from the strike to "religion," and refused to condemn the mob and police violence directed against the workers.

The only religious groups that tended to support the strikers' cause were the newer "sects" (Holiness, Pentecostal). These groups—regarded with great disdain by the establishment church ministers—drew their membership from the lower-class constituency.

Pope's study clearly shows the failure of the religious institutions of Gastonia to act as a source of transformation and to disturb the cultural and economic life of Gastonia. The ministerial leadership refused to act in any way that would jeopardize or challenge the economic system from which they benefited. They contributed unqualified and effective sanction to the system of paternalistic social control and cultural conditioning that characterized class relations in Gaston County.

Aside from insights into the relationship between religion and economic structures, *Millhands and Preachers* also provides an expansion and critique of Troeltsch's classic church-sect typology. Pope criticizes Troeltsch for too static a definition of "sect." Based on his observations of the religious organizations in Gastonia, Pope argues that sects are dynamic; they always move in the direction of becoming a church. They do so because their members inevitably seek social respectability and attempt to control their social environment. Pope rejects the view that sects are the product of ignorance, transiency, or culture shock associated with urbanization and industrialization. Instead he views them as a product of religious dissent and dissatisfaction with a parent body and as socially and psychologically compensatory mechanisms. The sects provided the disinherited underclass with opportunities for excitement, escape, and status reversal.

Millhands and Preachers touches a multitude of research interests. The work contributes insights into the relation between social class and religion, the distinction between church and sect, the impact of economic development on rural community, tension between management and labor, the struggle for industrial unionization, race relations in the South, and the causes and dynamics of mob behavior. [W.D.D.]

Porterfield, Amanda. *Feminine Spirituality in America: From Sarah Edwards to Martha Graham.* Philadelphia: Temple University Press, 1980. 238 pp.

In this carefully researched and extraordinarily incisive study, Porterfield traces the development of a distinctive form of spirituality in America. Alongside the religious imagination exhibited by theologians and churches, Porterfield contends, some remarkable American women have shaped a specifically feminine spiritual tradition, one that derives from their "domestic consciousness," their ability to sacralize their living space and thus be "at home in the universe" (pp. 4–5). This intriguing phenomenon, unlike churchly spirituality, centers upon beauty rather than truth and thus enables its adherents to express their spirituality through aesthetics and human services.

Porterfield joins William James in defining spirituality as one's "total reaction upon life" (p. 6) and, like him, she chooses to examine it through the study of exemplary lives. Along the way she also exposes her indebtedness to her mentor, William A. Clebsch, and to such pioneering students of femininity as Ann Douglas and Kathryn Kish Sklar. But it is to the Puritans that she owes her greatest debt, for it is with them that she begins her "inner history of femininity" (p. 11) and from them that she derives the basic patterns for her portrayal of female religious consciousness.

The Puritans, according to Porterfield, held a bride-conscious view of the religious experience. They drew an analogy between a woman's surrender to her husband and a saint's submission to God— a dual relationship best typified by Sarah Edwards, the wife of the renowned Northampton theologian. Edwards, who is a normative figure for Porterfield, saw her dependence on her husband, Jonathan, as a subordinate reflection of her higher surrender to her divine Lover. These twin submissions enabled her to yoke Christian virtue with feminine beauty.

The late eighteenth and early nineteenth centuries witnessed an unfortunate softening of theology that transformed the Puritan vision into a sentimental "pietism of domesticity" (p. 70) in which God became feminized, women deified, and sexuality was associated with evil. In this milieu, significant American women took feminine spirituality in new and often diverse directions. Frances Wright, for example, dissented from conventional orthodoxy and found in free love a liberation of religious consciousness, while Mother Seton and Catharine Beecher institutionalized female spirituality through sacrificial service. Likewise, Emily Dickinson, a pivotal character in the path from Sarah Edwards to her modern daughters, found "religious virtue in life at home" (p. 144), but women like Mary Baker Eddy, Jane Adams, and Charlotte Perkins Gilman located it in more public spaces. Lastly, Martha Graham, through her modern dance forms, gave a new meaning to grace as beauty and a new vitality to the feminine religious quest.

Amanda Porterfield's examination of these women should have a significant effect on a number of fields. Her astute use of source material and sensitive interpretation of biographical and literary information will be invaluable to scholars in American Studies, and her cogent case for using literature in "doing theology" should appeal to theologians. The author's own mysticism, for those not attuned to it, does create a sense of vagueness at points. But this weakness, if it be that, is more than offset by an abundance of strengths.   [L.A.H.]

Raboteau, Albert J. *Slave Religion: The "Invisible Institution" in the Antebellum South.* New York: Oxford University Press, 1978. xi +382 pp.

Albert J. Raboteau's *Slave Religion* is a testament to the human ability to invest life with dignity in destructive social situations. Through his use of slave narratives Raboteau has detailed the creative interchange between a people living in extreme situations and the European Christian traditions that became available to them.

Raboteau believes that slave religion, in its institutional and folk forms, was not merely the continuation of African religion in any pure form, or simply slaves' appropriation of the Catholic or Evangelical Protestant traditions. In North America, "the gods of Africa died" (p. 86). The survival of a "continuity of perspective" engendered instinctive familiarity with certain elements of Evangelical Protestantism, particularly the interracial responses to the awakenings of the late eighteenth and early nineteenth centuries. The ecstatic experience of conversion introduced slaves to Protestantism through familiar categories of experience. In addition, Raboteau depicts the persistence of Africanisms (such as systems of conjure) in folk beliefs, which merged easily with European folk beliefs.

The curious interchange between a people and a tradition was, in this case, ambivalently mediated by the slave masters, for the dangers of the gospel were evident to the owners. Raboteau believes that it was not until the awakenings that slaves were introduced to Evangelical Protestantism in great numbers and began to make the tradition something other than what it had been. It was also at this time that the egalitarian spirit of the awakenings revealed itself in interesting ways, particularly in the growth of independent black churches. The fruits of the awakenings had to be taken to the plantations, however, to reach the majority of slaves who had not yet been exposed to the Christian message. The role of the plantation missions raised further problems for the slave owners: it called into question their treatment of slaves, the status of slave marriages, and the appropriateness of slaves as religious leaders for blacks and whites.

The process of making a tradition one's own also took place in the rich folk traditions of slave communities: the secret prayer meetings, revivals, the importance of life-cycle rituals (baptisms, weddings, funerals), the centrality of slave preachers and conjurers, and, looming over all this, the centrality of the Bible. Scripture clarified the difference between the religion of the slavemaster and the religion slaves experienced in their conversions. The symbol of the Exodus came to life in the performance of spirituals. Slave religion, Raboteau argues, was not only otherworldly and compensatory, but as the slaves modified Christianity to fit their particular situation, it became something new, something with "this-worldly impact." It spoke to slaves about the ultimate meaning of their situation and how they could act as full human beings in the face of that situation.

Slave Religion treats the religion of the slaves as autonomous religious expression, connected to West African roots, nourished by evangelical piety, but always translated through the continuing reality of life in slavery.　[E.T.L.]

Reynolds, David S. *Faith in Fiction: The Emergence of Religious Literature in America*. Cambridge: Harvard University Press, 1981. 269 pp.

Tracing the rise of religious fiction in America between 1785 and 1850, Reynolds shows how authors of Oriental and visionary tales undermined orthodox Calvinism without engaging in directly theological polemics, how subgenres developed to illustrate Calvinist, Liberal, and Roman Catholic doctrines and to embellish biblical texts, and how these led into both combative, satirical fictions and affirmative novels of mainstream religion. Many books and writers are surveyed, and major figures in each category are studied in more depth. In each of the subgenres, as in the careers of individual writers, Reynolds finds a "movement away from static otherworldly contemplation and polemical precision toward an experiential faith involving sentiment, secular conflict, and objectification" (p. 195). Moving away from determinism and sin, the secularizing process was optimistic in its emphasis on divine fairness and human perfectibility. On the popular level, which is his main subject, Reynolds demonstrates how "religious fiction provided elixirs and cordials in a time of widespread spiritual uprooting" (p. 215).

Well written and exhaustively researched, Reynold's book will enrich our understanding of the role of religion in American culture between the Revolution and the Civil War and will, by providing a context for contrast, help us better appreciate major artists like Hawthorne and Melville. Popular religious fiction, Reynolds concludes, was "an exercise in wish fulfillment, in compensatory affirmation, and especially in the evasion of the kind of shattering self-scrutiny and intellectual inquiry that, if carried too far, threatens to bring one up on the side of doubt" (p. 215). Thus Reynold's analysis is interesting even when some of the fiction he interprets no longer is. His achievement is to demonstrate how the analysis of works of popular literature can complicate and enrich the study of American religious history.　[J.G.M.-y]

Richey, Russell E., and Donald E. Jones, eds. *American Civil Religion*. New York: Harper and Row, 1974. viii + 278 pp.

This volume is a compilation of articles addressing Robert Bellah's structural-functional concept of civil religion. An introduction expands the definitions of the phenomenon to a fivefold typology: civil religion as folk religion; as Protestant civic piety; as faith in democracy, or the democratic faith; as a zealous religious nationalism and finally, as the transcendent universal religion of the nation (Bellah's normative concept).

Bellah's seminal 1967 *Daedalus* essay, "Civil Religion in America" (see p. 145), serves as prologue to the discussion and the lead essay under the category of "theme." Sidney Mead's "Nation With the Soul of a Church" (see p. 88) argues that the universalism of a neutral "religion of the republic" or political religion helps preserve denominational pluralism by preventing the heteronomous imposition of a particular tradition over other belief systems. W. Lloyd Warner surveys the implicit and explicit religious nationalism found in Memorial Day observances, and Will Herberg defines the topic as a folk religion with its sociological sources in the American way of life more than in any national self-transcendent ideology.

A section discussing "method" contains John F. Wilson's thesis that, from an historian's perspective, little exists to substantiate the discrete existence of a civil religion over and above instances of rhetoric and political activities from which extrapolations are taken. Martin Marty finds two kinds of civil religion—priestly and prophetic—and argues that each mode can be found in both the nonidolatrous "one nation under God" national image and in the more suspect "nation as self-transcendent" understanding that can border on self-deification.

Four disparate essays appear under the "criticism" section. Herbert Richardson posits civil religion as inherently idolatrous because a nation as such has no ultimate value, and pretensions to ultimacy by civil powers is a corruption of the New Testament concept of the state. David Little examines the religion of Thomas Jefferson, finding it simplistic. He concludes that one cannot, as civil religionists do, extract a nascent civil religion from Jefferson's writings.

Charles Long develops the disparaging thesis that the American version of civil religion creates a hermeneutical mask of concealment. He asserts that there is a bias within the recounting of the normative, white, male, European deeds in the New World preventing a truthful look at American history and concealing minority contributions, rendering them non-normative. All this calls for a radical revisioning, a new *episteme* in the American psyche.

Leo Marx examines the use of obscenity by writers such as Norman Mailer as a vehicle for deflating the egotistical American self-consciousness (see p. 189). Various writers have challenged, through their use of obscenity and crude language, any claims to ultimacy by nation or government. The language often found among rural or working classes is both an expression of a democratic egalitarianism and a desacralizing of Bellah's type of civil religion rhetoric.

Bellah's final article insists that civil religion exists, whether or not another term eventually replaces the word, and that the reality is subject to change from other religious influences.   [M.L.S.]

Scott, Nathan A., Jr. *Three American Moralists: Mailer, Bellow, Trilling.* **Notre Dame: University of Notre Dame Press, 1973. 230 pp.**

Over against the apocalypticism of contemporary American culture stands the courage for going onward through the concrete materiality of historical existence that Scott finds disclosed in the literary works of Mailer, Bellow, and Trilling—these "public moralists" who offer "not only a mirror of the age but also, from quite various perspectives, a releasing view of the stoutness of the human spirit" (p. 11).

With his staunch commitment to selfhood and to a politics of salvation for the reconstruction of America, Norman Mailer is read as "our Whitman," revealed by his many works to be "one whose vocation it is to supervise language in ways that will invigorate the imagination of the people of his age" (p. 82). In a similar vein, the phenomenology of selfhood developed in Saul Bellow's novels progresses through the despondence of existentialism toward a radically religious vision of the "axial lines" that, while offering no short cuts to ecstasy nevertheless ultimately support the human bond that justifies life. And Lionel Trilling's tendency "to see literary situations as cultural situations, and cultural situations as great elaborate fights about moral issues" (p. 155) leads to a view of "the 'modulated' reality of man in his full human autonomy, at once responsible and conditioned, neither beast nor angel" (p. 170) and thus to a vision described by Scott as an "anxious humanism"—an affirmation of both the authenticity and the fallibility of selfhood.

His insightful review of the works of these three modern American writers leads Scott to conclude that "in a time of the eclipse of God, the most characteristic form of the religious question becomes the question of authenticity, of how we are to keep faith with and safeguard the 'single one' or the 'true self'—in a bullying world" (p. 221). Hence Scott lauds their protests against "the terrible potency of the ideas and attitudes and systems of life that constitute the otherness represented by the vast collectives in which modern men dwell" (pp.

222–23). He confirms not simply their inculpation of these forces but, more fundamentally, their knowledge that "the world supports and confirms the sacrament of selfhood only in the degree to which it is organized along the lines of some viable form of coexistence" (p. 224). This conviction is shared by and affirmed in the works of these "men whose testimony can have the effect of recommitting us to the common tasks of the human city, in (to use Buber's phrase) this 'radically demanding historical hour' " (p. 224). Thus Scott demonstrates brilliantly how literary interpretation can discover religious insights and thereby renew and strengthen the moral courage required for revisioning America. [J.G.M.-y]

Shipps, Jan. *Mormonism: The Story of a New Religious Tradition.* Urbana: University of Illinois Press, 1985. xviii + 211 pp.

In her study, Jan Shipps argues that the Latter-day Saints have a "peculiar understanding . . . of themselves and their Hebraic-Christianness, which grew out of their past as peculiar people" and which makes "Mormonism . . . a new religious tradition" (p. 149).

To make the case, this book compares the history of Mormonism between 1830 and the present to the first 150 years of Christianity's emergence as a tradition that, at first, believed itself to be the only true Judaism, and then came to be an altogether different religious tradition distinct from Judaism.

Mormonism was born in and shaped by the same millennarian social and religious ferments that produced other, mostly sectarian Christian movements in the early decades of nineteenth-century America. Although its language of doctrine, ritual, and mythic history is heavily influenced by Jewish and Christian Scriptures, it developed, very quickly, its own canon of sacred texts and its own understandings of election and the kingdom of God that set it apart from, and at odds with, both Jewish and Christian communities.

In *Mormonism,* Shipps creates an interpretive framework to assess the question of "whether Mormonism has become just another religion of the American mainstream, an idiosyncratic subdivision of Christianity, or whether it is a separate and distinct religious tradition in its own right" (p. xi). A close reading of the Mormon texts (both texts written on paper and texts written on the hearts and in the behavior of Saints) buttresses a convincing argument for the third option.

The book's clarity is achieved by keeping a sharp focus on the stream of tradition embodied in Utah Mormonism that chose a literal interpretation of the revelations experienced by Joseph Smith. The

Missouri "Reorganization" Mormons, who early on understood the revelations in a more metaphorical way, do not come so clearly into focus.

This study is important in several connections. As a reliable interpretive introduction to Mormonism, it has won praise from both Mormon and non-Mormon (Gentile) readers. Its careful analysis of how Mormonism has managed continuity and change in its historical development is a case study that suggests a way of looking at other religious communities in struggle over the same issues. In her willingness to allow the history to say that Mormon religious symbols meant very different things to different people—and to the same people at different times—Shipps creates a hermeneutical method that is applicable to the study of other religious traditions in processes of formation and re-formation.   [L.W.]

Simpson, Alan. *Puritanism in Old and New England.* Chicago: University of Chicago Press, 1955; 2d ed. Chicago: University of Chicago Press, 1961. vii + 125 pp.

This felicitous book is a splendid introduction to Puritanism as an historical movement. It sketches the impact of Puritanism on English and American institutions in the seventeenth century and briefly appraises the Puritan tradition. Perry Miller's weighty studies of Puritanism (see pp. 92–95) preceded this slender volume, but Simpson, believing that those works stressed the Puritan mind at the expense of the Puritan's feelings, emphasizes Puritanism as a species of enthusiasm. "It is the stretched passion which makes [the Puritan] what he is" (p. 21).

Simpson defines Puritanism broadly, as embracing a Right, Center, and Left, not excluding Quakers, all of which shared a distrust of the established churches. The essence of Puritanism was an experience of conversion, which led to insistence that the natural man must be reborn. Genuine Puritans, a small minority, wanted to gain control of England and carry the Reformation to completion. When they met resistance, their ranks fragmented into Presbyterians, Nonseparating Congregationists, and Separatists.

The Puritans' first opportunity to realize their goals came in New England, and Massachusetts led the effort to translate the ideal of a covenanted community into practice. The new Israel was a tribal community in which orthodoxy permitted no division of opinion. The state was to be a "nursing father" to the church, the author notes, but he overstates the case in viewing the state as "simply the police department of the church" (p. 40). The original spiritual intensity soon declined, and obedience to external order became the criterion.

Some saints refused to be confined within orthodoxy. Their rebellion led some to repudiate society, others to accept freedom of worship in principle, and still others to become militant millennarians. The author discusses the problems created by Puritans who sought salvation through separation and examines Rhode Island as an effort to fulfill the Puritan mission within the forms of religious freedom.

According to Simpson, the Puritan crusade to establish Zion in England was shattered by its own contradictions. The search for a constitutional and religious compromise broke down, England drifted into civil war, and after the war, Presbyterians, Independents, Levellers, and Millennarians each offered their own programs of reconstruction. A negotiated settlement was impossible, and Cromwell imposed unity on the nation at great cost. Puritans had aimed at producing a holy commonwealth, but "the rule of the saints was a prodigy of stultification" (p. 88).

As for its enduring influence on English and American make-up, "the continuing history of Puritanism," Simpson writes, "must be the continuing history of attempts to solve problems in a Puritan spirit" (p. 100). This point is valid though imprecise. The author adds that the Puritan had a moral sense, stimulated the tradition of religious revivalism, and fostered the heroic virtues. Yet the Puritan had a limited sense of humor, contributed little to literature outside of didactic literature, and regarded the fine arts as trimmings. The Puritan left a legacy of limited government and self-government and of commitment to education and morality. Not least, the Puritan insisted that righteousness ought to prevail.   [W.U.S.]

Singleton, Gregory H. *Religion in the City of Angels: American Protestant Culture and Urbanization, Los Angeles 1850–1930.* **Ann Arbor: UMI Research Press, 1979. xxxi + 262 pp.**

Drawing on the fields of religious history and urban history, Gregory Singleton studies the connections between Protestant "culture" and the process of urbanization in Los Angeles between 1850 and 1930. Singleton argues that Los Angeles was a city dominated by Protestant churchgoers who hoped to combine civic growth and prosperity with Christian influence and thus forestall the secularism and pluralism evident in eastern U.S. cities at the turn of the century. Rather than seeing the story of Los Angeles as a steady movement from localism to nationalism, from familiar and small-scale to impersonal and immense, Singleton sees the city as persisting in its local allegiance long after other cities had succumbed to corporate and national influence.

Until the late 1860s, Los Angeles was a largely Hispanic and Catholic pueblo with a few wealthy gringos in evidence. Protestant clergy recoiled from Los Angeles, seeing it as an uncivilized and un-Christian place. But by the 1870s, with increased migration from the eastern U. S., Protestant churches gained a foothold. By the 1880s, the economic life of Los Angeles was in the hands of gringos, and the old Catholic-Hispanic culture was clearly on the wane. City government, police protection, banking, and commerce were all in the control of American migrants. Equally, in the 1880s, Los Angeles experienced residential segregation that reflected the growing dominance of "whites."

Singleton is interested in showing that the Protestant control of Los Angeles comes not from all non-Catholic Christians in the area, but from a particular kind of Protestant whom he calls the "voluntarist." Voluntarism, says Singleton, emerged in the early nineteenth century as a result of the disestablishment of religion following the Revolution. By the mid-1880s, voluntarist Protestant churches were losing their influence in an increasingly incorporated and interconnected America. Los Angeles Protestants, however, were determined that their influence would not wane, and indeed, as Singleton shows, their influence was crucial until the 1920s.

Like voluntarist Protestants elsewhere, Los Angeles' Protestants sought to extend their influence in their community by establishing schools (the University of Southern California by the Methodists, Occidental College by the Presbyterians), by organizing cultural groups (choral societies, the historical association), and by dominating government. Between 1899 and 1920, ninety-one percent of all Los Angeles city officials were members of voluntaristic Protestant churches. Although voluntaristic Protestants never made up more than seventeen percent of the total city population, they clearly ruled the city's cultural and political life before 1920.

Los Angeles' leadership encouraged industrial growth in the early twentieth century, but were less enthusiastic about corporate relocation to their city, since corporate control and loyalty were exercised elsewhere. By the mid-1920s, however, such voices of resistance were silenced. Throughout the decade, Los Angeles became increasingly tied into corporate, state, and national structures, and the local Protestant hegemony was shattered.

Religion in the City of Angels is clearly a book for urban historians and historians of religious institutions. It is marred by too many typographical errors and much awkward phrasing, and the author is self-consciously proud of his use of quantitative methods and sources rather than "impressionistic" evidence. [B.A.R.]

Sklare, Marshall. *Conservative Judaism: An American Religious Movement.* Glencoe, IL: Free Press, 1955; rev. ed. New York: Schocken Books, 1972; rev. ed. Lanham, MD: University Press of America, 1985. 330 pp.

"[T]he present study may be considered as a case history of the development of a particular American religious group," Marshall Sklare writes in his introduction to this volume (p. 16). But *Conservative Judaism,* first published in 1955, is actually much more, for it pioneered the sociological study of American Judaism and introduced both methodologies and theoretical paradigms that continue to influence students of the subject to this day. When Sklare began his work, Conservative Judaism was the newest and fastest growing movement in American Judaism; some (wrongly) believed that it would soon become predominant. Sklare endeavors to explain this popularity in sociological terms, describing the rise and development of Conservative Judaism, the nature of Conservative Jewish worship and education, the new style Conservative rabbi, and the problem of Conservative ideology in terms of the "changing needs and values" (p. 19) of the American Jewish community. As he puts it, "the signal contribution of Conservatism would seem to be that of offering an acceptable pattern of adjustment to the American environment for many East European-derived Jews" (p. 249). Conservative Judaism thus fits somewhere between Orthodox Judaism, the religion of the immigrants, and the more liberal Reform Judaism, originating in Germany.

Sklare's analysis is particularly notable for its honest portrayal of the Conservative movement's ongoing tensions between rabbis, the laity, and the faculty of the Jewish Theological Seminary, where Conservative rabbis are trained. Whereas the laity, according to Sklare, views Conservative Judaism as a "halfway house between Reform and Orthodoxy" (p. 207) and is untroubled by the movement's lack of ideology, rabbis seek ideological clarification and agonize over the day-to-day tensions between Jewish tradition and the demands of American life. Meanwhile, Seminary faculty members, remote from these practical concerns, continually berate their movement's rabbis for capitulating to lay demands and for neglecting their traditional scholarly roles. Looking at the problem afresh in 1972, for a new edition of his book, Sklare finds the malaise deepening, "morale . . . on the decline"

(p. 261). Notwithstanding enviable success in terms of numbers and institutional growth, he describes a pervasive crisis of confidence in the Conservative movement, a sense of anomie, a loss of direction, and as a result, growing fears for the future.

Sklare's analysis has never been without its critics. He receives and analyzes some of the early criticisms he received in a new preface to the third edition of his book. More recently, stinging criticisms have come from those who charge him with having underestimated the strength of Orthodox Judaism. The December 1984 issue of *American Jewish History*, entirely devoted to a reexamination of *Conservative Judaism*, offers four new perspectives on its analysis by young scholars, as well as a brief history of the volume by Sklare himself. All of this interest testifies to the enduring value of *Conservative Judaism*—a classic of American Jewish religious sociology. [J.D.S.]

Smith, H. Shelton, Robert T. Handy, and Lefferts A. Loetscher, eds. *American Christianity: An Historical Interpretation with Representative Documents*. 2 vols. New York: Charles Scribner's Sons, 1960–63. xv + 615 pp.; xv + 634 pp.

The strength of these two volumes is that they interpret and document an impressive amount of American religious and "church" history from 1607 through 1960. Each volume has its contents organized under major chronological periods, with about one-third of the space of each being given to historical commentary and the remaining two-thirds being devoted to primary sources. Volume 1 covers the eras and documents from 1607 to 1820, and volume 2 includes epochs and texts from 1820 to 1960. Topical chapters are necessarily and understandably grouped flexibly rather than rigidly under given historical periods, as is the case with most edited anthologies. The only major question that might be raised is why the authors/editors chose to break the two volumes right in the middle of the National period, approximately 1790 to 1860. The historical break should have been made earlier in volume 1, and the last two chapters in that volume should have more appropriately begun volume 2—but that is easily accomplished in the critical reader's own mind and judgment.

The historical interpretations in these volumes are sound and carefully rendered, but fairly predictable and standard; the reader ought not to expect any radically new, ground-breaking theses to come out of this sort of publication. Such novelty, however exciting to the imagination, is probably out of character for this type of enterprise.

The documents included as primary texts are of a consistently high quality, having passed the principles of selectivity of not just one historical mind but the even higher standards of three such discriminating minds in dialogue with each other.

The value of this collection resides more in what it excludes than in what it includes. The focus is on American "Christianity"—that is, Roman Catholicism and "mainline" Protestantism. It was assembled in the late 1950s and early 1960s by American "church historians"— a decade or so before it became popular to pursue the more secular and more encompassing history of religion in American culture. Consequently, these two volumes do not really endeavor to embrace the scope of topics and documents that are of necessary interest for the whole of American religious history. One will not find in them adequate material on such common current topics as the religious cultures of American aborigines (so-called Indians), black religion(s), Judaism, Black Islam, right-wing or conservative Protestantism, indigenous American denominations (Mormons, Jehovah's Witnesses, etc.), political religion, nonchurchly moral reform groups, religious ethnicity, religion in "pop culture," and religion in the media. For these and other relevant topics one will have to range well beyond the scope of the Smith, Handy, and Loetscher volumes, no matter how well they document the more traditional churchly history of America.   [E.A.W.]

Smith, Timothy L. *Revivalism and Social Reform: American Protestantism on the Eve of the Civil War.* **Nashville: Abingdon Press, 1957; 2d ed. New York: Harper and Row, 1966; rev. ed. Baltimore: Johns Hopkins University Press, 1980. 269 pp.**

Since the original publication (Abingdon Press, 1957), Smith's book has proved a signally important study of American evangelicalism from the National period through midcentury because it then drew forward, and has continued over the decades to provide, special nuances on that emergent pattern of Protestant experience and commitment—from denominationalism to sectarianism, to revivalism, to evangelicalism—which has been a controlling interpretation for scholarship in the field. Smith's fundamental purpose, as suggested by his title, is to correct the notion that revivalist and evangelical Christianity, by dint of its soteriology, eschewed any efforts of broad social reformation: far from simply cleaving to an otherworldly doctrinal orientation, Smith contends, these Protestants, especially the postmillennialists, frequently engaged the secular realm in their own particular terms for activism in American culture and did so in ways cutting quite across sectarian and denominational lines. Indeed, at an odd moment or two, various stripes of premillennialists found themselves animated, perhaps more in effect than with full intention, by social and cultural questions that seemed to require their particular kinds of Christian answers.

These objectives in tow, Smith plots a course across the currents of vast evangelical tides of the day—the revival waves of the 1840s and 1850s, the oceanic year of 1858, the depths of a revival ecumenism, the swells of scattered holiness and perfectionist groups, some Methodist islands of "entire sanctification," the evangelical wash on social Christianity, the gales of the major issues of poverty and slavery—and charts throughout the social and political concerns and actions that belonged to these channels of American Christendom. Along the way, Smith's huge range enables him to gather in a veritable treasury of sources and resources in American religious history, and the story that emerges is therefore all the more valuable and convincing for not being made simply a matter of the Wesleys, the Beechers, the Finneys, and the Whitefields; also sailing these seas are the Pecks, the Ladds, the Earles, the Colwells, the Huntingtons, as the William Millers and Phoebe Palmers beat across the wake. The hold is filled to brimming, the style is streamlined, and the cargo even after three decades is generally, impressively, timely.

If Smith's narrative ship sometimes wallows with the sheer weight of its documentation and if the upshot remains by and large a portrait of a revivalistic disposition to convert sinners one-by-one as the means of social reform, Smith's study nonetheless delivers indispensable freight. Especially valuable and significant are the bibliographical leads into journals and tracts, the interpretations of the "westering" movement of evangelicalism, the pointed inquiries into the antinomous relationships between evangelical reform efforts and liberal, "secular" ones, and the insights into distinctively American facets of evangelical Christianity. [R.A.S.]

Solberg, Winton U. *Redeem the Time: The Puritan Sabbath in Early America.* Cambridge: Harvard University Press, 1977. xii + 406 pp.

Why has Sunday observance been so important in American culture? Solberg traces Sabbatarianism from its scriptural origins, through the Continental and English Reformations, to its modern roots in the Puritan-Anglican controversies in England, showing how it flourished in the spiritual atmosphere of Reformed, covenant theology and grew in the soil of early modern political, economic, and social developments. The full flowering was, of course, in the "fluid and plastic environment" (p. 299) of the New World. Fascinating examples show how the Puritan Sabbath spread throughout—and was enforced—in nearly all of the American colonies. The importance of the Sabbath influenced national life well into the twentieth century because "at stake was not simply the religious observance of a stated day of the week, but a whole way of life involving man's relations with God and the entire realm of work and play." Moreover, Solberg points out, "since the American colonies used the power of the state to foster religion and morality, Sabbatarianism brought theology and religion into contact with politics and law, with lasting consequences for American culture" (p. 3). Thus Solberg demonstrates how the ritual organization of time endures beyond the period of its most central importance and continues to shape the national life.

While recognizing that "Puritanism was indeed varied and complex," Solberg contends that "the Sabbath was a common denominator and a unifying element in Anglo-American Puritanism, perhaps the leading one" (p. 300). In the massive, entertaining evidence he provides for this claim, Solberg broadens our understanding of the nature of Puritanism beyond the more usual focus of attention upon theology and politics. Indeed, the institution of the Sabbath becomes a mirror of the way spiritual and social life were united in early New England. This enables Solberg to reveal the distinctive character of Puritan experience and also to suggest how, when times changed, Puritanism lived on in America.

A sixteen-page bibliographical essay and rich notes augment Solberg's interpretive argument, making his book at once a model for exploring "the social and political ramifications of a religious idea" (p. 67) as well as for studying the history of a living, changing religious tradition. [J.G.M.-y]

Sontag, Frederick, with John K. Roth. *The American Religious Experience: The Roots, Trends and the Future of American Theology.* **New York: Harper and Row, 1972. xiii + 401 pp.**

Theology has been vitally important in American history and, Sontag and Roth argue, will likewise be crucial for an American future. In the past American theology and religion have been constantly concerned with the source and nature of evil in the world, the character and significance of freedom, and the possibility of fulfillment and meaning in both individual and communal life. Above all, the American tradition has been one of diversity and pluralism. In addition a missionary spirit, an ongoing revivalism, and the separation of church and state have characterized American religious life.

In surveying the past, the authors highlight resources and requirements for the future. Thus they foresee no single normative

American theology but "several 'free theologies'—ones which never seek justification by their institutional or historical connections alone," and these new religious reflections "will need to be built around a theme of the need for national—and thus individual—rebirth" (p. 20). Furthermore, "all religion in the future of America must at the same time fill a spiritual need and serve a social purpose, or its theology will not be found compelling" (p. 21). Accentuating freedom, future American theologies "will have to remain politically independent but morally oriented" (p. 27).

With these prescriptions in mind, an extensive, interesting review of American religious thought is undertaken, moving all the way from Cotton Mather through the middle-class materialism of the 1960s and concluding that "it would be a neat twist of fate befitting the action of a free God if the saving note in American religious life came back to us from the men we brought here in bondage" (p. 349). Whatever its ultimate theological formulation, Sontag and Roth stress that a contemporary American spiritual pilgrimage must recover vital resources from the past, confront the hard problems of the present, and accept the high adventure of helping to make a new future.

The main strength of this clearly written book springs from the authors' conviction that history is an essential ingredient in the construction of a new American theology. They recognize that religion in America has involved yet included more than the history of the churches. By acquainting readers with the intellectual resources of America's diverse cultural traditions, they demonstrate the importance of religious history for the revision of American life and thought. [J.G.M.-y]

Strout, Cushing. *The New Heavens and New Earth: Political Religion in America.* New York: Harper and Row, 1974. xv + 400 pp.

Here is a highly qualified and reasonable statement suggesting that the relationship between religion and democracy in the United States has been more symbiotic than accommodating. Through careful research the author trims the fat from claims, on the one side, that the denominations have been purified of their parochial flavor by the political process and, on the other side, that the history of American Protestantism has been a history of continual concessions to the demands of secular crisis.

Tocqueville is both Strout's guide and his foil in this analysis. Strout believes that the historical facts have borne out Tocqueville's contention that American religion would help shape the character of democracy. Tocqueville saw in the respect for religion a moral check on the prospect of unbridled "mobocracy" and a positive influence in the development of a philosophy of individualism. Strout, however, maintains that denominationalism helped to create a politics of majoritarianism only at the expense of a developing notion of individual expression. Consequently, while religion is not the handmaiden of American politics, it is a conditional factor in the types of rationale deemed publicly acceptable in political theory.

For example, blacks in American history have been viewed with an irony borne of Christian vision. Their suffering in slavery has earned them a superiority in terms of the messianic "suffering servant" concept. But this same concept, as religious romanticism, has undercut a realistic appraisal of the economic and social needs of the race. Hence a recurring religious motif plays an unintentional, but unsavory part in the indifference many Caucasians exhibit toward minority group political goals. Strout's interpretation of the historical significance of *Uncle Tom's Cabin* is typical of his skillful treatment of how the interests of politics and religion are interwoven.

There are some puzzling inclusions and omissions in this book. The author goes on at great length about the legal implications of disestablishment and the separation of church and state. Yet this section adds little to his contention that it is in the larger social context that religious influence has counted. The courts have still offered no conclusive authority in this matter and from a historical vantage point there is good evidence that the founding fathers—Jefferson in particular—did not think that specific religious doctrines were ultimately important or threatening in matters of political polity. Finally, Strout neglects any full treatment of Roman Catholicism—the one faith that felt the barbs of accommodation in its approach to democratic institutions. Yet it was Tocqueville himself, in anticipation of Americanists Isaac Hecker and John Ireland, who insisted that Catholicism, with its universal laity, offered the best model for republican religion. [S.C.B.]

Tocqueville, Alexis de. *Democracy in America*. Translated by Henry Reeve. Vols. 1 and 2. London: Saunders and Otley, 1835–40. Subsequent editions including New York: Washington Square Press, 1964. xv + 333 pp.; viii + 365 pp.

Widely regarded as the most important study of American culture in the nineteenth century, Tocqueville's work, based on his travels in the United States from May 1831 to February 1832, has retained its singular interpretive relevance since its publication in 1835 (vol. 1) and 1840 (vol. 2). Tocqueville caught the broad cultural power of religion and its imagination in shaping American behavior. He saw that imagination as a major channel through which religion influenced the moral life of Americans and thus often indirectly, but nonetheless powerfully, its political life. "The religious aspect of the country was the first thing that struck [his] attention" (1:365), and he came to see religion as a major bulwark of the democratic republic. "Religion in America," he noted, "takes no direct part in the government of society, but it must be regarded as the first of their political institutions" (1:362). The most important discussions of religion are in two long chapters of volume 1 (chaps. 2 and 17) and several short chapters of volume 2 (Bk. 1, chaps. 5–8, and Bk. 2, chaps. 9, 11–12, 15, 17).

The reasons Tocqueville offers in explanation of this distinctive situation are complex—primarily the "customs, manners, and opinions," that is, the "habits of the heart" of the people, for religion is most powerful "when it reigns in the hearts of men unsupported by aught beside its native strength" (1:34). More particularly, he found the religion of the culturally dominant Anglo-Americans to be "democratic and republican" (1:355), such that "politics and religion contracted an alliance which has never been dissolved" (1:355). Tocqueville says that one manifestation of this alliance is that even most of the people's religion was republican because it submitted otherworldly truths to private judgment and free election. For Tocqueville it was especially important that Puritanism "was almost as much a political theory as a religious doctrine" (2:22). He saw America's destiny embodied in the first Puritans for they set in motion something really new in the world that led in time to the admirable combination of two distinct elements generally at odds elsewhere— "the *spirit of religion* and the *spirit of liberty*" (1:32).

Never hostile to religion, even when puzzled by "religious madness" or the "striking American regard for the Sabbath," Tocqueville was more interested in the usefulness than in the truth of religion. Concerned about the American love of material gratification, he saw "the greatest advantage of religion" to be its tendency "to purify . . . and to restrain" a passion he knew Americans would not try to eradicate—"the excessive and exclusive taste for well-being that men feel in periods of equality" (2:30). He wrote perceptively about the problematic as well as promising features of religion in America, the complex relation it bore to the dynamics of individualism. Further, he discussed what he thought about the ingredients he found in religion of both self-interest and high idealism, and about the delicate (even precarious) balance among religious, political, social, commercial, and moral factors in American society.   [R.A.D.]

Tuveson, Ernest Lee. *Redeemer Nation: The Idea of America's Millennial Role.* Chicago: University of Chicago Press, 1968. xi + 238 pp.

Redeemer Nation shows how early to middle nineteenth-century American millennialist thought was an unusual merging of the religious and the secular. Tuveson traces its origins to early Christians who expected the imminent return of their Messiah. In secular terms, this expectant hopefulness was extremely pessimistic. But eighteen centuries later, in the American context, some of these same Christian impulses created secular optimism because of the widespread belief that the American nation could prepare the world for an earthly millennium.

According to popular American millennialism, which was especially strong in the decades before the Civil War, the United States was God's chosen nation, destined for progress and perfection. Nineteenth-century American millennialism provided a persuasive organizing principle because it revealed all seemingly random events to have an orderly place in the world. It was also a great boost to optimism because it assured success in the great cosmic battle of good and evil. In that battle, millennialism made pain and suffering bearable or even welcome, provided they served the force of good.

The millennialism that Tuveson describes had a host of ennobling and sordid influences on American history. It helped to quicken the social conscience of many who sought to participate in the improvement of God's chosen nation through moral reform. Others saw in millennialism a rationale for territorial expansion of the United States even at the expense of native American Indians who would be either Christianized or displaced by the juggernaut of America's manifest destiny for progress and greatness. By the middle of the nineteenth century, millennialism provided a psychological preparation for the Civil War, especially among citizens of the northern states. This ideology was premised on a vision of good and evil in locked combat and of terror and desolation as a necessary first step to the hoped-for victory. Julia Ward Howe gave popular expression to this militant millennialism in "The Battle Hymn of the Republic."

Tuveson's theme provides a profoundly important insight about American culture and helps to explain a host of disparate trends. The millennialism he describes has recurred in various forms countless times in United States history. His work is especially valuable because he describes millennialism as the ironic flip side of secularism. As traditional religious expressions have declined in the modern world, religious ideas have often spilled into worldly arenas to give them a zealous, ideological edge.   [P.J.C.]

Tyler, Alice Felt. *Freedom's Ferment: Phases of American Social History from the Colonial Period to the Outbreak of the Civil War.* **Minneapolis: University of Minnesota Press, 1944; 2d and 3d eds. New York: Harper and Row, 1962, 1965; 4th ed. Freeport, NY: Books for Libraries Press, 1970. x + 608 pp.**

The numerous reprintings this volume has received speak to the value of this pioneering study in American social history. Professor Tyler presents succinct pictures of the fundamentals of the faith of the republic and that faith's manifestations in various crusades, reforms, and reformers that developed during the period between the end of the colonial period and the beginning of the Civil War. The author wrote this book on the basis of the belief that "religious movements and the adventures in reform of the early years of the republic were the truly significant activities of the men and women of the age, and they contributed much to the way of life of twentieth-century America" (p. v).

The first section of this three-part work deals with the background upon which the reform tradition was built. This section examines the faith of the young republic with particular emphasis on the notion of dynamic democracy during the early 1800s when people were asserting their choices in faith and theory and an examination of the evangelical religious movement of the time. That portion of the discussion dealing with the dynamic democracy presents a sweeping overview of the underpinnings of American democracy from its European roots with special emphasis on the frontier aspect of the American experience. The ideas of progress and the importance of each individual citizen were complemented by the renewed religious fervor as evidenced by the formation of various sects, cults, and reform movements.

Part 2 presents a look at numerous cults and utopian communities that bloomed during this period. Each movement is explained with a brief overview of its belief system and with sketches of key figures leading the movement. Groups ranging from the Transcendentalists to the Mormons to the Shakers to the utopian socialists receive attention.

Part 3 deals specifically with various humanitarian crusades that flowered during the period covered in this book. The author says that the reformers felt a burden to educate the younger people, saw society's responsibility to those less fortunate, and viewed all of their activities as being designed to perfect the institutions of contemporary society. The book's final section covers numerous reform activities including the education of younger Americans in things related to the American faith, criminal reform, temperance, denials of democratic principles (and the threats these denials presented), the crusade for peace, women's rights, and slavery.

Even though the Civil War changed the American "scene," Tyler feels that the "fundamentals of the American faith and the American way of life had been set by the pioneers and the crusaders of the early years" (p. 549). With the underlying theme of dynamic democracy and evangelical religion as the foundation, Tyler succeeds in tracing these fundamentals of American life as its citizens sought to fulfill "the destiny decreed by their inheritance from the past, by the circumstances of space and resources, and by the spirit of the century in which they lived" (p. 548). Of course, much more has been learned about this country's social history since the first printing of this book; but because of its pioneering nature, Tyler's work remains a classic in the field.   [A.T.F.]

Warner, W. Lloyd. *The Family of God: A Symbolic Study of Christian Life in America.* New Haven: Yale University Press, 1961; 2d ed. Westport, CT: Greenwood Press, 1975. x + 451 pp.

In this dauntless book, Warner presents a compendium of his previous work in the "Yankee City Series," published by the Yale University Press in the 1940s and 1950s as a venture in what is now called symbolic anthropology. Here, with a new theoretical introduction, the major chapters treat the broad themes of "God's New Kingdom" (in Protestant symbolism), "The Living and the Dead" (in the allusive evidence of cemeteries, funerals, war memorials, and the like), "The Family of God" (in the familial symbolism of Christianity), and "Transition and Eternity" (in implications of clock, calendar, and communal rite). These queries explore the nonrational life of Americans as Christianity, in its family-symbolism, consecrates the biological and psychological structures of family life and is in turn reinforced in collective subjectivity by those elementary structures.

At a time when vast social changes would seem to stymie the American family as a bearer of religious and other cultural values, Warner seeks to discover the means by which a unifying core inheritance, preserved nonrationally in the nation, can sustain itself and, more specifically, to discern how the "sacred symbols . . . of the human family can help re-order the meanings and values of science . . . and, in so doing, . . . can strengthen and give energy to religious symbols and the collective unity" (p. 6). His working contention is that Christianity, suffused with the symbolism of family life, answers to a primal psychic need for a "reality" that science and rational culture cannot supply, inscribes the sacred primacy of family and kinship structures, and affords rational culture with fundaments of meaning and order for its own maintenance.

Although disjointed, the book provides fine insights into the ways that elements of Christian imagination have been absorbed tacitly, but ineluctably and forcefully, into important nonrational forms of American existence. Warner's argument concerning these less "visible" entanglements of Christianity and American culture precedes Robert Bellah's "civil religion thesis," and it possesses a surer account of the dynamics—in family structures—for the persistence of such faith, even if the conclusions perhaps square more fully with John Wilson's conception of "public Protestantism" (see p. 134).

If Warner's approaches disclose some signal possibilities of inquiry into symbolic forms of American faith, wariness is warranted at several crucial points. Marching under the banner of a neutral social anthropology, the interpretations nevertheless occasionally betray the long, purposeful strides of normative theological rectitude stepping in beat with religious conviction. For Warner, America is monolithically Christian—the nation's Judeo-Christian heritage bereft of Judaism—and his Christianity permits few distinctions between Protestants and Catholics, much less among "kinds" of Protestants. Finally, captive to social science, he surrenders so much to gross determinisms that prophetic figures and movements can only be regarded as aberrations, arriving in those who have suffered lesions in psychic life. Indeed, Warner's drive for "unity" disdains virtually all elements of cultural heterogeneity and social pluralism in favor of a permanent containing pattern. What is gained in this strategy might be a provoking sense of the *possibilities* of the whole; what are lost could well be major rudiments of *actuality*—diversity and change—in the conditions of contemporary American existence. [R.A.S.]

Wilmore, Gayraud S. *Black Religion and Black Radicalism.* **New York: Doubleday, 1972; rev. ed. Maryknoll: Orbis Books, 1983. xiii + 344 pp.**

Wilmore argues that black religion has had a "vacillating and paradoxical relationship" (p. xii) with radicalism for at least 300 years.

Radicalism, according to Wilmore, is a point of view that regards white society as having a sickness of soul, an illness that is deeper than racism. There are three characteristics of the radical tradition in black religion: (1) the quest for independence from white control; (2) the revalorization of the image of Africa; and (3) the acceptance of protest and agitation as theological prerequisites for black liberation.

Wilmore develops these themes by reflecting upon selected aspects of the black religious experience in America from its beginnings in slave religion to its contemporary expression in black theology. He argues that the Christianity provided to the slaves was enriched by the volatile ingredients of the African past, and thus strengthened was able to serve as a vehicle of resistance. Likewise, the religious vision of the major black revolutionaries such as Walker, Prosser, Vesey, and Nat Turner represent a significant stream in the undercurrent of black church life. However, Wilmore interprets the rise of the independent church movement among blacks, during and following the Revolutionary War, as the prime expression of resistance to slavery—the first black freedom movement. The development of black nationalism is seen to be rooted in the black theology of missionary emigrationism and racial destiny that evolved from the aggressive thrust of black folk religion toward liberation and the African homeland.

The author reviews the deradicalization of the black church in the twentieth century and traces the dechristianization of black radicalism through Garvey and Malcolm X. Wilmore argues that the career of Martin Luther King, Jr., reversed the deradicalization of the black church and that his assassination heightened and consolidated the Black Power movement, which he, ironically, had opposed. An examination of the themes of black theological renewal and survival and liberation in black faith close the study. Wilmore's work is an outstanding contribution and is required reading for anyone interested in American religion, black radicalism, or black history. [R.G.B.]

Wilson, Charles Reagan. *Baptized in Blood.* Athens: The University of Georgia Press, 1980. 256 pp.

"The South's kingdom was to be of culture, not of politics" (p. 1), writes Wilson, who then traces the "religion of the Lost Cause" that dominated the South from 1865 to the twentieth century. The core of this faith was its theology; in spite of defeat, a divinely chosen South was chosen still, but for a greater work in purifying and evangelizing both the nation and the world. Slavery, proponents urged, was divinely ordained. Confederate leaders like Lee, Davis, and Jackson were Christ-like in their virtue, and the South was at once the most Christian of regions, a new Israel, and a continuation of the basic ideals of the American Revolution.

A virtual evangelical consensus formed around these perspectives, which were celebrated especially by preachers and by former Confederate chaplains. An elaborate ritual evolved around these themes including fast days, memorial glass windows, monuments, hymns, poems, and patriotic oratory at public gatherings. Through education, proponents sought to keep the Lost Cause alive for later generations, with two schools in particular serving as centers for Lost Cause ritual and celebration: Sewanee (University of the South) and Washington and Lee.

By 1880 Lost Cause proponents criticized the New South, claiming that northern materialism and industrialization were eroding old southern values. But by 1900, and especially after World War I, southerners were reentering and reaffirming American civic piety, though claiming that the South could make an important contribution to the nation since the South's values were, after all, only the original American values revived. This book enhances our understanding of the civic religion phenomenon of the American South and of the larger American culture to the extent that the South embodied larger American themes. [R.T.H.]

Wilson, John F. *Public Religion in American Culture.* Philadelphia: Temple University Press, 1979. ix + 198 pp.

This inquiry into the utility of public religion as a working concept uses this term rather than "civil religion." Wilson attempts to clarify and delineate the latter by analyzing the concept itself. Bellah's structural-functional definition, which posits a discrete civil religion (see pp. 8, 145–47), is questioned as being an academic construct that takes on a life of its own. As an historian, Wilson sees the examination of public aspects of denominational religion and instances of civic piety as more productive.

The empirical evidence offered in support of a civil religion is found to be episodic and changeable—ranging from once-normative evangelical Protestant republicanism to the tripartite society of Herberg (see p. 61), to the cultural transformation of the 1960s.

Yet Americans have always understood that within their culture some form of public religion has been present as a basic and significant religious medium. This does not mean that one can extrapolate a single, perennial civil religion per se. Study should focus on the cultural assumptions about the nature of religion in American society, for example, the religious materials in the public realm that serve as a given *mythos*.

These materials include: (1) the civic piety exemplified in presidential rhetoric; (2) the ritual behavior expressing a common sense of "America"; (3) the normative self-understanding betrayed in the "array of meanings" usually attributed to the nation; and (4) institutions that support a civic cult.

Study of these materials leads to a tentative conclusion that there is much evidence for a diffuse civic piety, but it cannot be identified as a differentiated civil religion. Clusters of meanings and images of American self-identity are always present, but are subject to change and reflect a changing social order rather than a closed set of beliefs associated with a distinct religion, whether civil or denominational. There may be a public religion, but the data do not support the claims to an *institutionalized* civic religion. This underscores the ambiguity in Bellah's work and that of other civil religionists. Is there a separate and differentiated religion apart from denominations, or are Bellah and others elaborating a dimension or aspect of American society present within the *whole* of society, including specific religious traditions? Wilson gravitates toward the latter interpretation.

Theoretical arguments for a civil religion have been constructed on systematic ambiguities produced by using mixed modes of analysis and confusing various models of civil religion. Wilson describes four constructions stemming from differing premises.

Yet whether or not a civil religion does exist now, or will in the future, does its emergence as a concept and its proposed existence have implications for our contemporary national experience? Wilson suggests this may point to a political-religious revitalization movement taking place. As we move to new global arrangements based on economic factors and toward increasing secularization, the civil religion proposal may be an attempt to distill and conserve an American political culture now threatened by social change. The question is not *whether* civil religion exists, but why it has been proposed at this time. In answering these and other questions, denominational leaders need to become involved along with the sociopolitical discussants.   [M.L.S.]

Zaretsky, Irving I., and Mark P. Leone, eds. *Religious Movements in Contemporary America*. Princeton: Princeton University Press, 1974. xxxvi + 837 pp.

This work is a collection of interdisciplinary articles presenting historical, empirical, and theoretical research on marginal religious movements, their ideologies and goals, and their impact on contemporary American culture. Although slightly dated (no articles on tel-evangelism or the conservative evangelical right), Zaretsky and Leone's anthology contains a wealth of information on "sects" and "cults" that are now well established on the American religious landscape.

The papers collected for this book were the result of two research meetings organized by the editors in November 1970 and April 1971. Three types of religious movements are examined: marginal nineteenth-century American Protestant churches that maintain active membership today (Christian Science, Spiritualism, Mormonism, Pentecostalism); recently founded religious groups (Scientology, Jesus Movement); and syncretistic groups of Eastern derivation (Meher Baba, Hare Krishna). Issues discussed in the articles include: church-state relations raised by new religious movements; ritual studies (particularly linguistic and communication forms that transmit information about a group); the nature of religious experience, the psychological aspects of participation in religious movements; the dynamics by which religious movements resocialize disaffected individuals and help them overcome personal problems; and the problematic issue of classifying the wide range of extant religious movements.

These essays demonstrate the need (now generally accepted) to rethink classification systems such as the church/sect typology, the social pathology model, and the defective individual model that have been employed in the past to explain sects and cults. The editors of this collection worked from the assumption that there is a dialectical relationship between the rise of new religious movements and social, cultural, and historical factors. New religious movements are a response to societal change and a type of religiocultural innovation and adaptation that impacts society.

While *Religious Movements in Contemporary America* does not focus directly on the merits of the theological or belief aspects of new religious movements, its essays do not espouse a negative or exclusively secular treatment of religion. The focus, instead, is on the relationship of religious movements to the larger society.

The quality of articles in this as in other anthologies varies. Noteworthy pieces include John Richard Burkholder on "Marginal Religious Movements and the Courts," Raymond Price on "Cocoon Work: An Interpretation of the Concern of Contemporary Youth with the Mystical," Dick Anthony and Thomas Robbins on "The Meher Baba Movement: Its Effect on Post-Adolescence Social Alientation," John

F. Wilson on "The Historical Study of Marginal American Religious Movements," and Virginia H. Hine on "The Deprivation and Disorganization Theories of Social Movements." Collectively, the essays in this work reinforce the validity of a number of presuppositions associated with the literature of new religious movements: (1) religious revivalism follows cyclical patterns; (2) groups are most successful that synthesize cultural elements shared by the general society; (3) groups evolve to meet the shifting needs of their members and ongoing societal pressures; (4) religious renascence generates its own impact on social change; and (5) new religious movements tend to emphasize individual perfection. [W.D.D.]

ARTICLES

Ahlstrom, Sydney E. "National Trauma and Changing Religious Values." *Daedalus* **107, no. 1 (Winter 1978): 13–29.**

Sydney Ahlstrom both roots the impulses of the 1950s (the placid decade) and the 1960s (the traumatic decade) in the restless energy of American religious history and suggests that this time the criticisms may have had more fundamental impact.

The growth of the institutional church, the popularity of "peace of mind" thinking, the infatuation with believing in belief, and the celebration of a kind of civil religion in the postwar period belie the "creeping malaise of latter-day capitalist civilization" that underlies it all (p. 19). The sixties are the pivotal period in American history. He compares the great changes of those times to the Great Awakening of the mideighteenth century. Racism, war, the role of the sexes and sexism, environmentalism, the new morality, and the "utlimate trauma," the misuse of government power, altered the nation's conception of itself. In place of a complacent civil religion there was only "ideological confusion and disbelief" (p. 22).

Trauma extended into religious traditions. Roman Catholicism, Protestantism, and Judaism were shaken by internal disorders, controversial relations with society at large, and in the confusion, new religious alternatives that promised a "meaningful structure of moral and religious values" competed for allegiance in the religious marketplace (p. 28). The future, Ahlstrom believes, is uncertain. He expects the "new comprehensive agenda of expectations and reforms" to endure (p. 28).   [E.T.L.]

Ahlstrom, Sydney E. "Problem of the History of Religion in America." *Church History* **39, no. 2 (June 1970): 224–35.**

Noting that comprehensive American religious histories followed a Protestant orientation for over a century, Ahlstrom declared that the sixties inaugurated an "earthquake of revisionism" (p. 224). Less moral conformity aided by Supreme Court decisions, an electorate no longer stridently anti-Catholic, and the black revolution forced historians to recognize that the country had entered a post-Puritan, post-Protestant, post-Christian, post-WASP era. Ahlstrom argues that historians must face the fact that old landmarks are gone, and long accepted views of the religious past must give place to new ones. He calls for a new set of priorities sensitive to the ferment of contemporary life. He looks for new angles of vision shaped by current pluralisms that will shed light on how modern circumstances occurred. In this search for a new plot or rationale, Ahlstrom expands the concept of religion beyond that expressed in institutional churches in order to look comprehensively at the full moral and spiritual history of all the American people. [H.W.B.]

Ahlstrom, Sydney E. "Religion, Revolution and the Rise of Modern Nationalism: Reflections on the American Experience." *Church History* **44, no. 4 (December 1975): 492–504.**

The first great European democratic revolution coincided with the high tide of European Romanticism, Sydney Ahlstrom points out in this essay, first delivered as an address in 1973. The French Revolution had a direct bearing on the great outpouring of creative energy in the work of Goethe, Schiller, Beethoven, Chateaubriand, Madame de Stael, and many others. The birth of the American nation, also at the end of the eighteenth century, had no such literary, artistic, or philosophical parallel. How do we account for this difference?

In this essay, the late professor of religious studies and American church history at Yale argues that Europeans saw the American Revolution and nation-building as demonstrative of that "spirit of revolt" that was sweeping their continent at the end of the eighteenth century. Yet the birth of the American Republic had virtually nothing to do with European-style nationalism and Romanticism, except indirectly as that birth nurtured European revolutionary movements that in turn stimulated American Romantics. American nationalism is instead indebted primarily to Puritanism. English and American Puritanism adopted the Hebrew notions of a chosen people and a sacred history. Long after the specific theological tenets had been modified, the Puritan ethic continued to fit American circumstances, particularly the emerging democratic capitalism.

However, argues Ahlstrom, the combination of Puritanism and Enlightenment that marked the nation's birth seems ever more strained. Perhaps the genuinely innovative thinking that marked the Romantic revolution needs to be as much a part of the American character as Protestant ethics and Enlightenment rationalism. [B.A.R.]

Ahlstrom, Sydney E. "The Religious Dimension of American Aspirations." *Review of Politics* **38, no. 3 (July 1976): 332–42.**

Ahlstrom discusses the religious dimension of national aspiration as it has to do with those mysterious bonds of affection and loyalty that provide whatever degree of psychic unity and collective aspirations a country may possess.

With regard to self-conscious nations, he argues, some form of civil religion becomes an almost inevitable presence unless that nation has become so filled with injustice and resentment that its very existence is threatened. National or political identity becomes associated with a specific doctrinal position; providing its citizens with a sense of personal identity. They become aware of the state as a transcendent reality that exists above and beyond one's finite personhood, a source of moral norms, summoning them to the ultimate sacrifice—often in an unjust cause. Each person in each nation is for all practical purposes incapable of changing the course of human events and is committed to a given place, a given government, and a given social order.

Ahlstrom argues that in the conflict of the 1960s in the United States, patriotism of the old sort became an abomination to many and a credibility problem for many others, making it appear that these 30 million Americans were living outside the social covenant. Writing during the American bicentennial, the author notes that traditional civil religion no longer sounded in the public consciousness.   [V.T.A.]

Albanese, Catherine. "Requiem for Memorial Day: Dissent in the Redeemer Nation." *American Quarterly* **26, no. 4 (October 1974): 386–98.**

This article traces the gradual decline of an American cult of the dead, which once was celebrated in the ritual of Memorial Day. The author discusses its Civil War-era origins and shows that later generations of Americans have been unable to sustain the initial sacrificial fervor, especially during the wars in Korea and Vietnam. During the 1960s, in fact, Memorial Day became too closely identified with right-wing ideology to be a national communal event.

Albanese posits four possible meanings for the decline of Memorial Day: (1) the American symbol system may be in a deep crisis; (2) Americans may have turned away from the earlier Enlightenment concept of the Divine Absolute, which has been identified with the national civil religion; (3) contemporary social and cultural conditions may have brought a decline in the communal bonds within American society; and (4) all mythic structures have solemn and secular aspects and the changes in Memorial Day may be a natural, perhaps only temporary, movement toward the secular.

Albanese concludes that the nation is in a symbolic crisis, but the decline of Memorial Day may simply be an inevitable cultural event, reflecting changing American life.   [C.R.W.]

Anthony, Dick, and Thomas Robbins. "Spiritual Innovation and the Crisis of American Civil Religion." *Daedalus* **11, no. 1 (Winter 1982): 215–34.**

Dick Anthony and Thomas Robbins have sought to analyze the contemporary American spiritual ferment in terms of American civil religion, largely described by Robert Bellah (see p. 8, 145–47) but with some nuances of their own. They summarize three approaches that try to account for the "surprising upsurge of cults and new religions" in the 1970s and subsequent to the counterculture turbulence of the 1960s: (1) the simplest theory blames secularization; (2) another approach cites a "crisis of community" caused by traditional mediating and stabilizing structures being undermined by an impersonalized mass society and bureaucratized world; and (3) another points to increased societal complexity, "cultural confusion," and a subsequent loss of value consensus—leading to a spiritual void (p. 215).

Anthony and Robbins suggest that there has been an "erosion of a dominant politico-moral ideology, or civil religion" (p. 230), which has given legitimation to a common core meaning system in the past. This overall system of moral and spiritual legitimation has been eroding over a lengthy period due to several contemporary, societal phenomena such as conspicuous consumption and the lost sense of personal autonomy, which the authors discuss in some depth.

A civil religion is inherently pluralistic, as America's is, but its center will only hold if there is a reasonable cluster of shared values that legitimate common American identities and moral affirmations. America's moral attitudes and religious commitments are now too polarized and mutually exclusive leading the authors to conclude its civil religious center may not hold.　[E.A.W.]

Baltzell, E. Digby. "The Protestant Establishment Revisited." *American Scholar* **45, no. 4 (Autumn 1976): 499–518.**

In this article Baltzell reviews developments since the publication of his book *The Protestant Establishment: Aristocracy and Caste in America* in 1963 (see p. 7). And indeed, a great deal has occurred! The erosion of the influence and power of the WASP establishment has continued at a greater pace, and dramatic developments on college campuses and in the political arena have been symbolic of that erosion. One needs only think of the assassinations of the Kennedys and Dr. King, Watergate, Vietnam, and student uprisings in Berkeley, Columbia, and Kent State and the point is made.

Baltzell describes the erosion of this power and influence in terms of changing lifestyles and values of the children and grandchildren of the landed aristocracy. He sees a moral vacuum being created due to this decline in authority. Baltzell goes on to cite trends in political and religious life, changes in college enrollments, increases in inter-marriages, and access to mass media information sources as specific causes for waning influence.

Baltzell defines *establishment* as that "means by which a society is led by a class of men who act according to an agreed-upon code of manners" (p. 502). So long as it is in power, it is fairly clear what is to be done and what is not to be done. However, based on the changes that have transpired, Baltzell sees no way that America will ever return to the dominance of the WASP establishment. Instead, he says, we should cultivate a hierarchical society where all aspire to be like Washington or Jefferson. [W.C.O.]

Beam, Christopher M. "Millennialism and American Nationalism, 1740–1800." *Journal of Presbyterian History* 54, no. 1 (Spring 1976): 182–99.

Christopher Beam details the anticipation of an earthly millennium that so entranced Americans of the colonial and early national period by focusing on optimistic interpretations by Presbyterian clergy. He argues that they perceived in historical events clues to the fundamental transformations that were soon to come about. Historical events became part of the great tradition of salvation history, soon to be brought to its fulfillment, either in or because of America.

For example, during the French and Indian War, the Antichrist was clearly identified with the state of France and the Catholic church. After 1765 the British wore the mantle of the Antichrist and the Revolution became the opening chapter of the millennial saga, a saga to be played out by those American Protestants who brought about the possibility of an American millennium born out of political and military action.

Beam argues that the optimistic sense of expectation at work at least since Jonathan Edwards's time was upset initially by the excesses and then the substance of the French Revolution. But, Beam asserts, the Second Great Awakening laid to rest many fears about the diminution of religion's influence on public life and inspired voluntary reform movements many thought necessary before the final chapter of human history could be written. [E.T.L.]

Bellah, Robert N. "Civil Religion in America." *Daedalus* 96, no. 1 (Winter 1967): 1–21.

One of the reasons this classic article on American civil religion has proved to be such a powerful stimulus to the study of the subject lies in the author's ability to encapsulate within twenty-one pages practically every subtopic and criticism of the topic.

Bellah is capable both of making the case for the importance of civil religion as a statement about providential charge to the nation in presidential speeches and founding documents and of specifying the key symbols of public piety in our national holidays. The rhetorical power of such parallelisms as "just as Thanksgiving Day . . . serves to integrate the family into the civil religion, so Memorial Day has acted to integrate the local community into the national cult" (p. 11) should not be slighted for what they are—masterful constructions in the English language. Second, Bellah outlines the work that occupied him for the next fifteen years.

The three times of trial in American history and the evocation and evolution of civil religion in each of them first receive full treatment in *The Broken Covenant* (see p. 8). The loss and possible recovery of personal commitment to a national covenant in our time has received Bellah's attention in the more recent *Habits of the Heart: Individualism and Commitment in American Life* (see p. 9).

This article, then, serves as a model for what Bellah proposes to do on a full scale in later extrapolations. It is his equivalent of the theological prolegomenon.   [S.C.B.]

Bellah, Robert N. "Religion and Legitimation in the American Republic." *Society* **15, no. 4 (May/June 1978): 16–23.**

The United States has no state religion and no official civil religion. Yet religion has played a significant role in American history. According to Robert Bellah, this role has been blurred by lack of clarity arising from two fundamentally antithetical ideas about the nature of the American regime. Is America a republic and therefore dependent on the ethical commitments of its citizens, or is it a liberal constitutional regime "governed through artificial contrivance and the balancing of conflicting interests" (p. 18)? The answer, Bellah suggests, is both.

In Bellah's view, religion has been a means by which America has balanced the liberal elements of the Declaration of Independence with the republican elements of the Constitution. Early American rhetoric established a place of permanence for a suprapolitical sovereignty who judges the nation and justifies its existence. The persistence of this symbolism supports Bellah's assertion that there is a civil religion in America. By itself, however, the American civil religion could not support the ethical needs of the republic, because, as Bellah suggests, its formality and its marginality prevent it from becoming an encompassing world view. The "national community," which exists outside of formal political structures, takes up the slack by producing what Martin Marty has called a "public theology," a theology that is rich in biblical symbolism and capable of influencing national purpose. The future of America, Bellah argues, will depend on continued reflection and discussion of religion's role in balancing the nation's twin identities. [C.J.]

Bercovitch, Sacvan. "The Typology of America's Mission." *American Quarterly* 30, no. 2 (Summer 1978): 135–55.

Focusing on millennialism, Bercovitch reveals a persistent typology of America's mission within Puritan, Yankee, and Revolutionary rhetoric. Jonathan Edwards crucially adapted the Puritan design into an authentically American millennialism by enlarging the theocratic errand beyond the bounds of New England to embrace the whole (white male) American New World. Edwards and his followers unified sacred history, local progress, and spiritual self-fulfillment, thereby enabling Yankee Americans to usurp the types of Scripture for national ends, imaging "one grand spiral of fulfillment from theocracy to democracy" (p. 152). But in the hermeneutical process, Bercovitch observes, Puritan figuralism was turned inside-out. Whereas the Puritans saw their efforts in terms of the biblical Exodus, Edwards saw the Great Awakening as fulfilling the Puritan errand, and eighteenth-century Whigs viewed the Revolution as the antitype confirming the meaning of American experience as such. Instead of assessing their trials in terms of biblical events, these later Americans employed biblical imagery to express the promise of America itself. Men of the Revolutionary era read their own times as completing a process begun by the Puritans and expanded by the revival, adapting the original biblical frame of reference to sanction symbolically a new order of the ages that the Puritans themselves would hardly have recognized.

By outlining the complex process of inverse hermeneutics that Bercovitch examines in *The American Jeremiad* (see p. 10), this article introduces the ongoing revisioning that contemporary scholars have discovered at the center of early American history. [J.G.M.-y]

Berens, John F. "Religion and Revolution Reconsidered: Recent Literature on Religion and Nationalism in Eighteenth-Century America." *Canadian Review of Studies in Nationalism* 6, no. 2 (Autumn 1979): 233–45.

Since the 1970s, the relationship linking religion, nationalism, and the American Revolution has received extensive scholarly attention. Berens discusses six major monographs published between 1975 and

1977 that address this issue and present scholars with a sophisticated portrait of the nuances of religion in America in the eighteenth century.

Berens cites three works that address nationalism and revolution: Carl Bridenbaugh's *The Spirit of '76: The Growth of American Patriotism Before Independence* (1975), Catherine L. Albanese's *Sons of the Fathers: The Civil Religion in the American Revolution* (see p. 5), and Henry F. May's *Enlightenment in America* (see p. 85). These works argue that religion was important in pre-1776 nationalism, that perceptions of God's will changed during Revolutionary times, and that the true liberals of the period were the Calvinists. Two more recent monographs, James West Davidson's *Logic of Millennial Thought: 18th Century New England* (1977) and Nathan O. Hatch's *Sacred Cause of Liberty: Republican Thought and the Millennium in Revolutionary New England* (see p. 58) focus their attention on the millennial aspects of American Protestantism.

A summary of the themes of the previous volumes is found in Mark A. Noll's *Christians in the American Revolution* (1977), a starting point for reflection and research. Berens says that these writings offer students of American religion a reconsideration of the American Enlightenment illustrating that rationalism and secularism were conquering the providential interpretations of nature and that for Americans during the eighteenth century, religion and politics were central elements of the American mind.   [V.T.A.]

Berens, John F. "The Sanctification of American Nationalism, 1789–1812: Prelude to Civil Religion in America." *Canadian Review of Studies in Nationalism* **3, no. 2 (Spring 1976): 172–91.**

Judged by research methodology currently in vogue among many practitioners of the social and behavioral sciences, this essay by Berens doubtless would receive a poor grade. That it warrants the appellation "essay" is itself something of a damning judgment. Berens draws selectively upon early American source material to buttress his thesis. The sources themselves constitute subjective assumptions about the characteristics of American nationalism.

Nonetheless, Berens makes an important case: many spokespersons for America, including preachers and politicians, took for granted the fundamentally religious nature of American national character and the nature of its political institutions. He finds this thinking imbedded in ideas about the Revolutionary War itself as foreshadowing our "civil religion," as, for example, in the future importance of the Fourth of July "as an occasion for remembering God's intervention during the Revolution" (p. 176).

Americans found in references to religious roots a basis for reassurance in an era when the infant country's material future in a hostile world was far from secure. "Most of the psychological needs of the American people were also met by the popular conviction that America was God's New Israel" (p. 177).

In our present age of uncertainty, it is helpful to reflect on a conclusion of Berens: "The sanctification of American nationalism after 1789 is evidence, not that the patriots of Early National America were supremely confident of their national future, but rather that they were deeply disturbed" (p. 186).   [R.W.H.]

Bowden, Henry Warner. "A Historian's Response to the Concept of American Civil Religion." *Journal of Church and State* **17, no. 3 (Autumn 1975): 495–505.**

The sociologist Robert N. Bellah gave wide currency to the notion that an elaborate civil religion has existed in America alongside of and rather clearly differentiated from the churches (see pp. 8, 145–147), but Henry W. Bowden contends that this concept creates more problems for the historian than it solves.

Bowden argues against uncritical acceptance of civil religion as if it were a positive entity. Adherents of the concept usually refer to certain ideological themes (e.g., America as a redeemer nation), certain national leaders who embody this ideology, and the symbolism of national holidays to make their case, but Bowden finds the evidence insufficient to demonstrate the existence of a common civil religion. Moreover, the criteria essential to verify the presence of such an entity in America are lacking.

Writers may have given the concept more positive status than it warrants. One possible reason is faulty logic—ascribing to civil religion the type of influences that the major religious traditions have exerted in American life. Another possible reason is viewing civil religion as a rival faith responsible for decline of the older orthodoxies.

The concept of civil religion may nevertheless have limited value. One way to enlist it positively is to emphasize the religious dimension as a functioning social reality, which Bellah has always done, rather than to define religion ontologically. Historians should avoid using "civil religion" to refer to a socially differentiated entity, but they might constructively employ the concept as a category or linguistic symbol to illuminate historical reality.   [W.U.S.]

Bowden, Henry Warner. "Landmarks in American Religious Historiography: A Review Essay." *Journal of the American Academy of Religion* **42, no. 1 (March 1974): 128–36.**

Bowden's review essay of Sidney E. Ahlstrom's *A Religious History of the American People* (see p. 3) shows how American religious history has been and might be studied. Placed in the context of other major works, Ahlstrom's book is analyzed as synthesizing three related interpretations of religion in American life: first, religion as the thoughts and behavior of people working in organized churches; second, religion as various spiritual impulses that flourish alongside of traditionally organized channels; and third, religion as reciprocally connected with social and political life.

Reviewing Ahlstrom's historiographical commitments (having no special privileges, religious historians must cast a wide net, recognize diversity, and be aware of social context), Bowden finds much to praise but concludes that although Ahlstrom's rather standard history is rich with new materials, it is disappointing as an answer to Ahlstrom's own call for a new way of doing religious history that is commensurate with distinctive ways of life and thought in "post-Puritan" America. Thus Ahlstrom's book is usefully seen as the most definitive work to date, a book that will serve both as a reference source book and as a landmark summarizing recent work and clearing the way for further research into the history of religion in America.   [J.G.M.-y]

Bucher, Glenn R. "Options for American Religious History." *Theology Today* **33, no. 2 (July 1976): 178–88.**

According to Bucher, the question of American identity is closely related to the issue of how America's religious past is conceived. His article constitutes an illuminating interpretation of trends in American religious history and a proposal for a new historiography in the discipline.

Sidney Ahlstrom, in a typically synoptic and encompassing overview (*A Religious History of the American People*, see p. 3) claims that, until the 1960s, Puritanism dominated the American ethos. Countering that thesis, Sidney Mead argues that the Enlightenment instead provided the religious legitimation for American pluralism. However, both assume an identifiable center in American religious history. That assumption is now under serious question. Thus Martin E. Marty (*Righteous Empire,* see p. 83) brings a critical perspective to bear on mainline Protestantism by drawing attention to its neglect of and contribution to the plight of blacks and native Americans. Similarly, Robert T. Handy (*A Christian America,* see p. 52), while concentrating on evangelical denominations, is critical of the compromises and destructive effects of Protestantism throughout American history. Moreover, Edwin S. Gaustad (*Dissent in American Religion,* see p. 40) asserts that dissent, not consensus, may constitute the most vital characteristic of American religion. These works of Marty, Handy, and Gaustad suggest a transition is underway, directed toward the need for a new methodology in American religious history.

Bucher suggests that, in perspective, the new historiography would require histories written from locations outside of mainstream Protestantism. In focus, the new historiography would concentrate on multiple and diverse centers of faith and, as such, would more adequately disclose the actual patterns and shape of American identity, what it has been and what it ought to become in an increasingly revolutionary world.   [D.S.]

Bushman, Richard L. "The Book of Mormon and the American Revolution." *Brigham Young University Studies* 17, no. 1 (Autumn 1976): 3–20.

Bushman tests the claims to Thomas O'Dea that American political sentiments common in antebellum New York permeate the *Book of Mormon.* He examines these claims by comparing the political perspectives of the *Book of Mormon* with political views common in the *Wayne Sentinel,* in upstate New York oratory, and in the school books sold in Palmyra's bookstore. Three areas for comparison emerge: (1) whereas American rhetoric praised the Revolutionary heroes for their resistance against tyrants, the *Book of Mormon* extols divine deliverance, not resistance; (2) whereas Americans were antimonarchical, persons in the *Book of Mormon* demanded monarchy and delighted in subjection to kings; and (3) most of the principles central to the American constitutional government are slighted or missing in the *Book of Mormon.* Bushman concludes that the *Book of Mormon* does not owe its genius to the American milieu, but rather to biblical paradigms.   [R.T.H.]

Butler, Jon. "Enthusiasm Described and Decried: The Great Awakening as Interpretive Fiction." *Journal of American History* 69, no. 2 (September 1982): 305–25.

Historians invented the "Great Awakening," Butler argues, and because the term "distorts the character of eighteenth century American religious life and misrepresents its relationship to prerevolutionary American society and politics" (p. 322), it should be abandoned. In its place, Butler offers a four-part model of the colonial revivals. First, they were—with the exception of Whitefield's itinerancy—

primarily regional events that occurred in only half the colonies. Second, their theological origins were international and diverse rather than narrowly Calvinist and uniquely American. Third, the revivals affected colonial religion only moderately—reinforcing ministerial rather than law authority and stimulating demand for organization, order, and authority in the evangelical denominations. Fourth, with the ambiguous exception of Virginia, the link between the revivals and the American Revolution is virtually nonexistent. Thus after critically reviewing conventional interpretations, Butler asserts that the revivals actually emerge as nearly perfect mirrors of the regionalized, provincial society of eighteenth-century America.

Since an article-length essay almost necessarily caricatures some of the alternative views it analyzes, one might take issue with some of Butler's critiques. Nevertheless, in the main he demonstrates well the revisionism that makes the contemporary study of American religious history such a lively enterprise.   [J.G.M.-y]

Butler, Jon. "Magic, Astrology and the Early American Religious Heritage: 1600–1760." *American Historical Review* **84, no. 2 (April 1979): 317–46.**

During the 1960s, scholars began an important new look at the traditions of the less-conventional and less-formal religious life of America. In this essay, Butler adds to that ongoing search by surveying the occult religion that was brought by European colonists to the United States along with Christianity. Quite apart from the Salem incident, colonial records indicate widespread attention to the ideas and practices of witchcraft, astrology, alchemy, and magic. As was previously noted in relation to Europe, Butler discovered a marked decline of occultism after 1720 and began tentatively to explore the difficult problem of explaining that decline (not to mention the sudden reappearance of occultism in the nineteenth century and its astounding revival in the twentieth). Placed together with the other exploratory studies that have come from scholars in religion, folklore, and the natural sciences (alchemy), a picture of the occult tradition is emerging and some understanding of its hidden century (1720–1820) is beginning to be reconstructed.   [J.G.M.-n]

Cherry, Conrad. "Two American Sacred Ceremonies: Their Implications for the Study of Religion in America." *American Quarterly* **21, no. 4 (Winter 1969): 739–54.**

Robert Bellah's celebrated article on civil religion (see p. 145) in America concentrated on the religious language of the American presidents to make the argument for the existence of this independent national religion. Conrad Cherry looks to national rituals as evidence of this civil faith.

Cherry details the preparations for and activities of Memorial Day in a small American community. For Cherry, Memorial Day is part of a larger American sacred calendar, a "modern cult of the dead" (p. 741), a day when Americans transcend their sectarian persuasions to witness to the power of patriotic ideals that both inspired warriors to make the ultimate sacrifice for the nation and must now inspire the living to ensure that the sacrifice was not in vain.

Funerals for national leaders such as Robert Kennedy also witness to the power of patriotism and the deep faith in the nation's destiny under God. Simultaneously a Catholic and national funeral, citizens were urged to respond to the dilemma of death by rededicating themselves to Kennedy's dream of reconstructing the nation's task in the world.

Like Bellah, Cherry notes the dangers inherent in a religious nationalism that uncritically sanctifies the national purposes. He favors a national religion that communicates a Lincolnesque humility in the face of a transcendent power. [E.T.L.]

Cole, William A., and Philip E. Hammond. "Religious Pluralism, Legal Development, and Societal Complexity: Rudimentary Forms of Civil Religion." *Journal for the Scientific Study of Religion* 13, no. 2 (June 1974): 177–89.

Cole and Hammond, sociologists and colleagues in the Department of Sociology of the University of Arizona, address the question why civil religion arises or exists in the first place. Their central line of argument is that: (1) "the condition of religious pluralism creates special problems for social interaction"; (2) in such a condition social interchange is undergirded and facilitated by "a universalistic legal system"; and (3) such a universalistic legal system may, out of social necessity and possibility, be "elevated to the sacred realm" (p. 177). Cole and Hammond include a reasonable amount of abstract and theoretical considerations, but what distinguishes their study from a traditional social, intellectual, or religious historian's approach is their reference to quantitative sociological data and their global interests. The latter gives these sociologists perspectives that contribute to provocative ideas on religious pluralism and its relation to notions about pluralistic nations.

Their conclusions are rather straightforward, presenting food for thought for Americans in the 1980s and beyond. They say if people experience conflict, they seek to resolve it. In a pluralistic society, part of the conflict includes the clash of "meaning systems"; if two or more persons or groups cannot accept each other's bases of value, a different, overriding, and "higher" plane of resolution must be found. This higher level or plane, if it is found and if it is effective, becomes respected, obeyed, and sanctioned—it becomes a "civil religion." [E.A.W.]

Davis, David Brion. "Some Themes of Counter-Subversion: An Analysis of anti-Masonic, anti-Catholic and anti-Mormon Literature." *Mississippi Valley Historical Review* **47, no. 2 (September 1960): 205–24.**

David Brion Davis first published this influential article in 1960 when Richard Hofstadter's themes of "the paranoid style" and "status anxiety" dominated historical understanding of the American past. Davis analyzes how mainstream Americans reacted to three minority groups: the secret society of Freemasons and the Mormon and Roman Catholic churches. His interpretation, which has been frequently referred to and anthologized, is still a major starting point for our understanding of antebellum culture. Davis's subject is the paranoid reaction of many native-born Americans to the imaginary conspiracies of Masons, Mormons, and Catholics, who they thought were attempting insidiously and ruthlessly to seize political power. These minority groups supposedly planned the subversion that the nativists worked to counter.

Although Davis admits that the distinct opposition movements that arose in response to the Masons, Mormons, and Catholics were not unified or identical, he discovers common traits that display broad characteristics of American culture in the four decades before the Civil War. Masons, Mormons, and Catholics generated similar fears and produced a common, evil stereotype in the minds of the opponents because each allegedly subversive group was "an inverted image of Jacksonian Democracy and the cult of the common man" (p. 208). The Freemasons were a secret society; the Mormons were supposedly despotic and lustful; and the Catholics brought forth the traditional Protestant fear of the tyrannical pope ruling over unthinking minions. The lack of outward distinguishing traits among these groups fanned the fears of conspiracy.

Davis discovers broad significances among the American "themes of counter-subversion" (p. 205). In a new nation still searching for a cultural identity, these enemies provided, at least by contrast, a sense of American selfhood. The noble cause of counter-subversion unified many Americans at the cost of publicly sanctioned discrimination that established American traditions of both identity and prejudice. [P.J.C.]

Dean, William. "An American Theology." *Process Studies* 12, no. 2 (Summer 1982): 111–28.

Empirical process theology is a quintessentially American theology, drawn from the single philosophical movement truly indigenous to American history. Though neglected of late, its perspective is corroborated by recent intellectual movements: phenomenology (Merleau-Ponty), deconstructionism (Derrida), and theoretical physics (Bohr and Wheeler).

Empirical process theology is derived from American radical empiricism, which from its beginning rejected German idealism, Cartesianism, and British empiricism. Radical empiricism is represented in the thought of Jonathan Edwards (the "sense of the heart"), William James (the "wider self"), Alfred North Whitehead ("causal efficacy"), and John Dewey (the sense of "quality").

Out of this background, empirical process theology is developed in the work of Henry Nelson Weiman ("mystic consciousness"), Bernard Meland ("structure of experience"), and Bernard Loomer (the priority of "physical feelings"). A rationalistic form of process theology (Charles Hartshorne, Schubert Ogden, and the early John Cobb) has partially eclipsed empirical process theology, which alone is heir to American radical empiricism.

Empirical process theology, Dean asserts, however, is lacking in a disciplined method of investigating the events of history and, thus, for interpreting the concrete activity of God. In constructing such a method, he suggests empirical process theology might develop an idea of a history of nature; it might counterbalance its preoccupation with science with a more predominant focus on the arts; or it might conceive reality as itself composed of chains of historical interpretations (á la Richard Rorty, Jacques Derrida, and Hillis Miller). [D.S.]

Deloria, Vine, Jr. "Completing the Theological Circle: Civil Religion in America." *Religious Education* 71, no. 3 (May-June 1976): 278–87.

Beginning with Bellah's thesis that the American civil religion has emerged "out of the American historical experience interpreted in the dimension of transcendence" (p. 279), Deloria asks whether or not that has ever been examined from the perspective of the metaphysical context from which it arises—the a priori view of reality that becomes the vehicle for interpreting the white Christian American experience. This experience is, in turn, transformed as it encounters the exigencies of the historical situation.

This metaphysics provided an internal integrity and foundation for self-interpretation for all experience—war with England, persecution of Indians and their denial of political status. Deloria states that these metaphysical assumptions, unexamined beliefs, make it *impossible* to view the experiences and world view of the Indian as a distinct metaphysics not to be simply interpreted from the white religiously undergirded world view.

For good or evil, the metaphysics of American civil religion function as the "latest denominational expression of Christianity" (p. 279), for it possesses "the spontaneous reversion to doctrines for justification for actions that characterizes the status of an institution" (p. 285), that is, a particular world view from which critical judgments, laws, and political activity arise. It is a false distinction to posit a civil religion that appears to exist simply parallel with, but not identical to, denominational religion. Deloria asserts that study of the relationship and interaction between the white Christian government and that of the Indian who has never shared the operative metaphysics reveals the fallacy of viewing American civil religion as anything but a denominational expression of white Christianity. [M.L.S.]

Diggins, John P. "Slavery, Race and Equality: Jefferson and the Pathos of the Enlightenment." *American Quarterly* **28, no. 2 (Summer 1976): 206–28.**

Diggins argues with major studies of Thomas Jefferson, since 1943, that deal with the problems of slavery, racism, and equality in the American Enlightenment, and introduces "a crucial theoretical problem which Jefferson failed to perceive and [Winthrop D.] Jordan failed to resolve—the incompatibility of the doctrine of equality and the doctrine of natural rights" (p. 207).

Jordan's *White Over Black: American Attitudes Toward the Negro, 1550–1812* (1969) saw that Linnean classification and the Great Chain of Being concept—Enlightenment pillars in Jefferson's thought— "spelled death to the idea of equality" (p. 212) and bound the Negro to an inferior status in the presumed order of nature. Puritans, knowledgeable about sin, challenged slavery, not Enlightenment rationalists.

The Enlightenment's belief "that the human mind can draw its principles from the 'nature of things' " was in conflict with "the conviction that the mind can impose its rational will and moral imagination on the environment" (p. 228). Jefferson stood on the side of naturalism and "science" and was unable to include black people in the self-evident circle of "all" who are "created equal." Jefferson's pathos was not just personal, it is an enduring perplexity of social thought in the Enlightenment tradition. [L.W.]

Eisenach, Eldon J. "Cultural Politics and Political Thought: The American Revolution Made and Remembered." *American Studies* **20, no. 1 (Spring 1979): 71–97.**

This article examines three areas of conflict in America from 1763 to 1787 with a view to showing two different modes of political and historical understanding at work. One was an institutional perspective that emphasized ideas; the other an anti-institutional perspective that emphasized events. These perspectives have continued to characterize the historiography of the American Revolution.

In religion the Great Awakening led to division into two camps. Rationalist liberals opposed revivalism, retreated from Puritan millennial thought, and became more attuned to a politics shaped in England. Evangelicals, insisting that the converted could make an authentic community, reasserted the Puritan vision that America had a prophetic place in Christian history.

In law, conflict arose over the authority of English legal precedent and over the relation between common law rights and natural rights. Some wanted closer adherence to English models, institutionalization of the law, and emphasis on the common law. Others opposed legal technicalities, condemned the common law, and favored return to the purer colonial past in law as in religion. The conflict was also evident in thought on constitutionalism during the revolutionary era, and this issue was transformed into one of contending theories of politics.

These conflicting ways of understanding have persisted in American historiography. Progressive historiography is anti-institutionalist and defends American uniqueness. It bypasses the history of ideas. Whig historiography stresses the importance of institutions and ideas. History remains an important source of political understanding in America; but, the author asserts, we lack a Progressive historiography of ideas which is tied to major political events. [W.U.S.]

Endy, Melvin B. "Abraham Lincoln and American Religion: A Reinterpretation." *Church History* **44, no. 2 (June 1975): 229–41.**

Whereas most interpreters have argued that Lincoln was a prophetic figure who sensed a radical distance between the ways of an infinite God and the judgments of himself and the nation, Endy argues that Lincoln's understanding of revelation and providence and his attitude toward the Negro and slavery rendered him less prophetic than most have thought. Convinced that God controlled the events of the nation in an often deterministic way, Lincoln often expressed his belief that he perceived the ways of God through direct intuition, thus circumventing his own notion of history as suspenseful drama. Further, Lincoln was never greatly concerned for justice for the Negro, but rather for preservation of the nation, convinced as he was that America was the "last best hope" of humankind. For this reason, he favored gradualism and due process of the law at the expense of black liberation. [R.T.H.]

Engel, J. Ronald. "Sidney E. Mead's Tragic Theology of the Republic." *Journal of the American Academy of Religion* **44, no. 1 (March 1976): 155–65.**

Sidney Mead's constructive *theological* role as an apologist for the Republic of America is both described and criticized in this article. Beyond his historiography, Mead provides a systematic perspective on the American democratic faith that can best be comprehended as tragic. The "religion of the Republic," understood through the dialectic of finite-infinite, sought an ever-widening theonomous community of the whole. Through actual inclusive communities and universal ideals of community, knowledge of the infinite One could be mediated to individuals as a source of stable and saving identity. However, the hope of this republican religion has gone unfulfilled; American churches fell prey to the *hybris* of sectarianism, refused to accept their finitude, and absolutized the relative. Fragmentation, rather than ever-expanding unity, inhibited the realization of the ideals of New World religion.

Mead later began to look beyond the human species to "Nature and Nature's God" for the transcendent community of identity. Only the natural universe appeared to have enough immensity, universality, and permanence in time to manifest the infinite. There Mead sought the emergence of a universal and inclusive religious outlook.

Engel's analysis is instructive in that it reveals how distant the ideas of the American experiment have become and how little loyalty particular communities exhibit toward the ideal of the public good. He is exactly right, in criticizing Mead, when he points to the religious importance of concrete, practical human interaction in space, the need for an ecological perspective on the "Republic of the World." [L.S.J.]

Fichter, Joseph H. "Religion and American Values: An Update." *Thought: A Review of Culture and Idea* **58, no. 229 (June 1983): 224–33.**

Contemporary social scientists work from the premise that religion has become highly privatized and compartmentalized. In short, religion is largely irrelevant to the major concerns of the social order. New religious movements challenge this assumption. They give expression to the deprivatization and reinstitutionalization of religion.

Fichter argues that highly valued behavior is likely to be institutionalized. Freedom of choice is highest where values are lowest. In American society, the highest agreement on values is found in the major institutions of business, government, and education. These bureaucracies pattern thought and social relationships and constrict freedom of choice. Lifestyle practiced in the family, leisure activity, and religious spheres are devoid of many of the rigid controls operative in the institutionalized public sphere. Values in these "private" realms do not carry the weight of authority and social pressure.

In American culture the traditional value loci have been reversed: public instrumental institutions are sacralized while the expressive institutions of the private sphere are secularized. However, norms of the institutionalized public sphere do not promote satisfactory values of ultimate significance. The values of these institutions are differentiated and sometimes conflicting. Their traditions resist differentiation and manifest a "de-modernizing impulse" among those whose lives are characterized by sterility and an absence of meaningfulness. Religions currently growing the fastest are the ones that make the most demands in merging the quest for community with the quest for certitude. [W.D.D.]

Forrer, Richard. "The Puritan Religious Dilemma: The Ethical Dimensions of God's Sovereignty." *Journal of the American Academy of Religion* **44, no. 4 (December 1976): 613–28.**

Forrer shows how several American thinkers—from Puritan theologians to Transcendentalist writers—wrestled with tensions between ethical and religious values. Like the Puritans, later Americans faced the dilemma of proving the necessity for commitment to ethical values in a world that often contradicts them. After noting its interesting resemblance to Søren Kierkegaard's formulation of "the teleological suspension of the ethical," Forrer investigates how Urian Oakes, Jonathan Edwards, J. Hector St. John de Crevecoeur, Nathaniel William Taylor, and Ralph Waldo Emerson tried to answer this Puritan dilemma, or at least to render it comprehensible for their contemporaries.

While observing that other religious traditions, as well as political writers, have also contributed to the ways Americans have defined the relationship between ethical and religious values, Forrer's main achievement is to demonstrate that American literature could insightfully be studied in terms of the extent to which writers variously reformulate and explore the Puritan dilemma in terms commensurate with our changing experience. By illuminating the important role that religious symbols have played and continue to play in the development of the American imagination, Fòrrer provides a promising interdisciplinary model for the study of American religious history. [J.G.M.-y]

Gaustad, Edwin S. "Restitution, Revolution and the American Dream." *Journal of the American Academy of Religion* **44, no. 1 (March 1976): 77–86.**

In 1717 John Wise (a Congregational pastor in Ipswich, Massachusetts) charged that a set of proposals put forward in 1705 (under the leadership of Increase and Cotton Mather) were threatening to the all-important "congregational way." In broad terms, these proposals threatened "individualism and liberty" and invited "priestly pomp and arbitrary exercise of power" (p. 77). On the occasion of the American bicentennial, Gaustad chose to reflect on the American dream using material from a Wise text as the basis for his discussion. From Wise's text, Gaustad derives three themes (antiquity, nature, Scripture) that, to him, point out that the Revolutionary era looked backward as well as forward, that the sentiments of restoration and restitution were very strong in the eighteenth-century American climate, and that the American dream included some intense nostalgia side by side with its millennial hope.

For Gaustad, the American dream is a deliberate remembrance and recollection of some things past—to antiquity for its opposition to tyranny and its love of liberty, to nature for virtual perfection, lawful order, and artistic simplicity, and to Scripture for its pure morals, clear truth, and available authority. These three constituted major authorities for Americans to chart their progress into the future as a restitution of an ancient order of things, combining time past and time future. His perceptive article is a reminder of the depth and persistence of the themes of antiquity, nature, and Scripture in the history of American religion; and they are not likely to lose relevance in the near future. [E.A.W.]

Gilkey, Langdon. "Social and Intellectual Sources of Contemporary Protestant Theology in America." *Daedalus* **96, no. 1 (Winter 1967): 69–98.**

The main sources of contemporary Protestant theology in America are those characterizing all modern Western thought: first, the broad influence of science; second, the general acceptance of the historical nature of all human experience and thought; third, the pervasive, this-worldly emphasis of modern culture; and, fourth, a shift in ethics from personal holiness to love of neighbor as the central obligation of Christianity. Yet the special style of American theology springs from its peculiar cultural environment and reflects a distinctively American relationship between religion and culture. Here secular and religious elements of society are understood as harmoniously interactive. Religion is known primarily as personal and inward rather than as social and institutional, and the "world" of culture and society is thought of as benignly "unfallen." Thus American religion has been inherently secular in orientation.

Given these general and particular characteristics, Gilkey reviews the history of American theology, compares European and American religious thought, and analyzes Reinhold Niebuhr as a typically American thinker whose main intellectual categories stemmed from European sources—to which he was driven by social concerns—and whose ideas had explicit secular relevance. Gilkey foresees the future philosophical influences on American theology as process thought, linguistic philosophy, phenomenology, and pragmatism. He forecasts continuing theological commitment to national and international social justice and hopes that America's familiar, dangerous pattern of national messianism will be checked by a renewed message of transcendent judgment, mercy, and hope. Thus Gilkey insightfully surveys the resources and challenges, both intellectual and social, of current American theology. [J.G.M.-y]

Gleason, Philip. "Blurring the Line of Separation: Education, Civil Religion, and Teaching About Religion." *Journal of Church and State* **19, no. 3 (Autumn 1977): 517–38.**

Philip Gleason demonstrates that the U.S. Supreme Court, during the period from 1947 to 1977, applied an "increasingly stringent interpretation" (p. 524) of the separation of church and state in cases involving devotional practices in public schools and public assistance to parochial schools. At the same time, he argues, attempts were made to use the public schools as an arena to merge religious and political interests. This was fostered by those who discovered American "civil religion" and believed that it should claim the loyalty of citizens and those who called for the academic study of religion in public schools.

Both are "quasi-religious goals" that ignore the First Amendment's prohibition against the establishment of religion. This is the case because "civil religion" is presented as a "national religion"—something "precisely . . . Americans are not supposed to have" (p. 538), and because the academic study of religion as encouraged by Supreme Court justices and academicians tends to be "naturalistic" (a quasi-religious position) and is used to sanction and inculcate American civil religion. [N.P.]

Gleason, Philip. "Identifying Identity: A Semantic History." *The Journal of American History* **69, no. 4 (March 1983): 910–31.**

This semantic history of *identity* does not deal directly with religion in American life. Nevertheless, it reveals so much about the way in which scholars since the midtwentieth century have understood this concept that its inclusion here is appropriate.

Part of ordinary discourse since the 1500s, identity has long had technical algebraic and philosophical meanings. Around 1950 scholars started using the concept to explore (1) how individuals come to understand who they are and (2) the relationship of individual personalities to "the ensemble of social and cultural features that [give] groups their distinctive character" (p. 926). Following Erik Erikson, who coined the phrase "identity crisis," many psychologists believe that, although shaped and modified by interaction between individual and surrounding social milieu, identity is imbedded in a person's deep psychic structure. Sociologists tend not to understand identity as fixed, but as a product of interaction between individuals and society.

Erikson's theoretical work and biographical studies brought his position to the fore in the 1960s. But the first major work using identity as a significant explanatory factor, *Protestant, Catholic, Jew* (see p. 61), was written from a sociological perspective. In this book, Will Herberg argued that Americans use religion, not ethnicity, as their primary indicator of identity. Events soon demonstrated that ethnicity was more important than Herberg thought.

Despite its imprecise meaning, scholars since have pictured identity as the key to national character and crucial to the relationship between individuals and mass society. As useful as this concept is, scholars employing it should exercise care. [J.S.]

Goen, Clarence C. "Broken Churches, Broken Nation: Regional Religion and North-South Alienation in Antebellum America." *Church History* **52, no. 1 (March 1983): 21–35.**

This article argues that the religious divisions of the Baptists and Methodists in the 1840s presaged and promoted the political crisis between the North and South in the 1850s. The fears, accusations, arguments, and sometimes even the people involved were the same.

Southern religious leaders, like later political figures, expressed a fear of the tyranny of the majority, and the logic of ecclesiological secession proved to be applicable for political division. Northerners, on the other hand, were willing to let the South leave the churches and the nation, believing it could be done peaceably. The key point was the assumption it would be easy. The seemingly successful division of the churches promoted a myth of peaceable secession in general.

Goen stresses that the division of the churches had been deceptively simple because the sense of history and continuity among American religious groups was weak. The primitivism of antebellum sectarians combined easily with an ahistorical outlook of revivalism, and the result was to make the institutional church less important than individual salvation. After breaking their ties with the northern churches, southern Christians had few qualms about political division, and this situation added to the stridency of their views. Northerners and southerners developed distorted images of each other, with religious groups helping to create and maintain them.

Goen concludes that in this era of sectional crisis it became obvious that evangelical Protestantism had been a powerful cultural bonding force, North and South, and proved to be a vital factor in defending regional self-interests.   [C.R.W.]

Gordon, Mary MacDougall. "Patriots and Christians: A Reassessment of Nineteenth-Century School Reformers." *Journal of Social History* **11, no. 4 (Summer 1978): 554–74.**

Gordon's article is an important, revisionist one. On the one hand, she does a detailed examination of the formative years of educational reform in Massachusetts between 1830 and 1837; and on the other, she makes a sweeping survey of American educational philosophy and history. She counters the notion that nineteenth-century American public education grew in and with the nation's major cities and goes on to assert that this popular "urban school reform" theory understates the historic relationship between education, nationalism, and moral and religious sentiments in American culture.

Gordon contends that "the educational awakening was a Protestant crusade to establish a culture that became the dominant system of values in the new nation" (p. 554). Her interpretation does not totally reject the urban school reform thesis but accommodates, corrects, and goes beyond it. Early reformers were motivated by concerns about the progress and character of the entire republican society—urban and rural.

Gordon's article rectifies the short shrift the role of religion has received from leading schools of educational history. She concludes that early school reformers strove to "lay the foundations of a school system that was as much the arm of a Christian republic as the Prussian system of education was the arm of an autocratic state" (p. 567). They redefined and reappropriated the Puritan tradition so that it would be acceptable for all Protestants and applicable to all good citizens. "The common-school crusade" was part of a broad and encompassing "antebellum Protestant crusade to forge a Christian nation" (p. 567). [E.A.W.]

Graebner, Norman A. "Christianity and Democracy: Tocqueville's Views of Religion in America." *The Journal of Religion* 56 (July 1976): 263–73.

On the occasion of America's bicentennial, Graebner reflects on Tocqueville's observation that religion was such a powerful force in American society not just for its own sake but for its apparent contribution to democracy. As Graebner points out, the separation of church and state allows for the new and unexpectedly vital relationship between religion and democracy in America. He states that Tocqueville observed that precisely by avoiding formal connections with the state, American religion was less authoritarian but its influence was more pervasive, and in its own private sphere its authority all the more complete.

Graebner reasons that what allowed for religion's fundamental power in American culture was the recognition of "two distinct realms in the life of a democracy—the spiritual and secular" (p. 266). Authority in religion freed people in secular affairs; and freedom in the secular realm allowed them the integrity and, therefore, authority of convictional religion. It was precisely in this manner that "individual freedom would ultimately benefit the community" (p. 269) by making both religious and democratic principles all the more powerful, effective, and influential. Religion and democracy jointly contribute to the support of a moral that is necessary to the long-range interests of society. However, Graebner concludes that consensus upon which political and religious beliefs were built when Tocqueville observed American life no longer exists. Also, Tocqueville did not question the need for public and private morality; but Graebner sees these issues as pertinent to late twentieth-century America. [E.A.W.]

Gribben, William. "Republican Religion and the American Churches in the Early National Period." *The Historian* 35, no. 1 (November 1972): 61–74.

Fifty years ago historian Gustav Koch examined the political faith underlying the American Revolution and the establishment of the early Republic. Calling it "republican religion," Koch indicated that this phenomenon combined an adherence to republican polity in government with an opposition to orthodox Christianity and its trappings. According to Koch, a state of conflict existed between evangelicals and those who espoused republican creeds, and the true champions of republican religion were deists and rationalists.

In this revisionist essay, William Gribbin calls for a reassessment of Koch's findings. Carefully analyzing the views of churchmen from both mainstream and sectarian religious bodies, Gribbin concludes that the churches not only adopted republican beliefs but that "virtually every denomination in the early Republic claimed that it, more than others, was in accord with republican institutions" (p. 64). The deists, it appears, were not alone in practicing the civic faith. Baptists and Presbyterians, for example, contended that the close resemblance of republican governmental structure to that of their churches clearly demonstrated the divine ordination of both systems. Baptists went a step further, according to Gribbin, "merging denominational identity with the national political ethos" (p. 65). Even Unitarians utilized republicanism by "wrapping their heresy in the flag" (p. 72).

Gribbin's examination of such widely divergent groups as Universalism and Roman Catholicism, and of their common support of republican ways, underscores his plea to historians to "listen sympathetically to the churchmen" (p. 73) in order to discern the total mind of the early Republic. Doing so might constitute a healthy corrective to the standard interpretation of republican religion.   [L.A.H.]

Gustafson, Merlin D. "President Hoover and the National Religion." *Journal of Church and State* **16, no. 1 (Winter 1976): 85–100.**

As high-priest of American patriotic religion, presidents have had to walk a fine line between enthusiasm for a generic public Protestantism and sensitivity to evenhandedness in official dealings with different faith traditions. Gustafson argues that Herbert Hoover was never able to balance these competing religious interests, and this played some part in his loss to Roosevelt in 1932.

Hoover was inconsistent in his responses to religious groups who sought his money, his participation in ceremonies, and his endorsement of public service projects. In a sense this inconsistency created comfortable relations for Hoover with both "liberal" and "conservative" Protestants as evidenced by praise from both *The Christian Century* and *The Moody Bible Institute Monthly.* In spite of this praise earned by Hoover's support of such programs as a shortened work day in the steel mills and Prohibition, his relations with Catholics were poor.

However, Gustafson believes that Hoover was no "religious bigot." Rather, he was, in his presidential role, a high priest who was celebrating an old order that was crumbling, and he did not recognize it. By using President Hoover as a case study, Gustafson addresses the larger issue of the way church-state relations are handled by the White House—an issue of ongoing interest and study. [E.T.L.]

Hadden, Jeffrey K., ed. "The Sociology of Religion of Robert N. Bellah." (review article) *Journal for the Scientific Study of Religion* **14, no. 4 (December 1975): 385–414.**

Robert Bellah is a premier thinker in the sociology of religion and a scholar noted for his integrating approach to religion. Central to Bellah's prophetic mode of sociology is the Durkheimian problem of integrating cultural systems. This issue has been explored most notably in his seminal essay on "Civil Religion in America" (see p. 145) and in his book *The Broken Covenant* (see p. 8).

Of the three essays in this symposium honoring Bellah, Robert Stauffer's article focuses exclusively on the civil religion-broken covenant theme. While sympathetic to Bellah's view, Stauffer believes Bellah too readily assumes that moral and civil religious consensus is attainable and that civil religion is a functional requisite of all societies. Stauffer also criticizes Bellah's tendency to see too much dysfunction in America. William Shepherd shows the continuities in the theoretical development of Bellah's sociology of religion and the relationship between the theoretical and prophetic components of his work. Shepherd emphasizes Bellah's insights into the role of symbols and the meaning of "symbolic realism" in Bellah's theory of religion. The final essay by Dick Anthony and Thomas Robbins proposes a structuralist approach to the study of religion via Bellah's work. Drawing on Chomsky's theory of language, Anthony and Robbins see in Bellah's "symbolic realism" an implicit core unity of all religions. Surface structure is the determination of the particular forms of religion by social and cultural forces. In order to understand variations at the surface level it is essential to understand the uniquely religious dimension of the deep structure. [W.D.D.]

Hammond, John L. "Revivals, Consensus, and American Political Culture." *Journal of the American Academy of Religion* **46, no. 3 (September 1978): 293–314.**

This review essay assesses the role of revivals in American politics before the Civil War. Much of the scholarship over the last thirty years has emphasized how revivalism contributed to an antebellum political consensus. Sociologist John Hammond argues that no such consensus existed and that the deep divisions that did characterize society were caused by revivalism. Based on his empirical study of western New York and Ohio, published as *The Politics of Benevolence,* Hammond suggests that revivalism created "a people committed to the realization of their ideals within the nation, however much they might violate social order and national harmony" (p. 224).

Hammond's critique of three alternative views of antebellum revivalism is penetrating. He suggests that the recent new political history, or "ethnocultural" analysis, offers a static interpretation of the way in which religion influenced politics, because it fails to consider the power of beliefs to motivate unpopular action. Hammond undercuts the idea that revivalism was simply Jacksonian politics in religion by pointing out that evangelical converts did not share many of the laissez-faire attitudes of the Democratic party. He refutes the cultural unity theory on the basis that it relies too heavily on the religious "functionalism" of Emile Durkheim, which assumes that religion always acts to hold society together. Hammond's own position is that all three explanations misinterpret the political consequences of revivalism because they do not understand that religious ideas motivated revival converts to carry out social proscriptions at the expense of national unity during the Civil War era. [L.K.P.]

Hammond, Philip E. "The Sociology of American Civil Religion: A Bibliographic Essay." *Sociological Analysis* **37, no. 2 (Summer 1976): 169–82.**

Even hard-nosed, empirical, pragmatic sociologists need to review the theories and literature behind the subjects about which they do their quantifiable, statistical studies. How far afield from the central topic or issue does one read and range? How much preparatory material does one include? This is what sociologist Philip Hammond takes on as he constructs a significant though brief bibliographical essay on the subject of American civil religion. His analysis is careful, tight, pointed.

Hammond organizes his discussion around five questions (the more ambiguous of which has three subquestions): (1) what is American civil religion?; (2) what has been its course?; (3) what is the relationship of American civil religion and the churches?; (4) what institutions promulgate, transmit, maintain, and modify American civil religion?; and (5) why should this nation or any nation develop a civil religion? The remainder of his article is an economical summary of the major responses to these questions and to the major boundaries of this discussion. A discriminating and select bibliographical list follows the article.

This review and bibliography are important and timely, up to the point of the time of its writing. It must be recognized that a significant number of major articles and books on this subject have been published since that time and will also need to be reviewed to make this bibliographical analysis current.   [E.A.W.]

Handy, Robert T. "A Decisive Turn in the Civil Religion Debate." *Theology Today* **37, no. 3 (October 1980): 342–50.**

This discussion of the merits of John F. Wilson's Public *Religion in American Culture* (see p. 134), views the work as a decisive turn in the civil religion debate due to its questions about Bellah's thesis and its notes regarding methodological assumptions, or lack thereof, in the field.

Noting that the civil religion debate has been focused largely on such basic questions as: (1) its existence; (2) its nature, for example, the various typologies offered by Richey and Jones's volume (see p. 114); and (3) its relative value vis-à-vis denominational religion, Handy affirms Wilson's critique of the subject. He comments on two aspects: Wilson's widening of the discussion to include the *public* aspect of denominational religion and his questioning about Bellah's claim that an institutionalized public religion exists alongside the public aspects of private religion and American public life in general.

Wilson's major contributions arise from his clarification of the generic civil religion "models" and his plea for a self-conscious methodology. Perhaps more importantly, he chooses "public" over "civil" religion as a broadening of the concept to include the neglected area of the public aspects of denominational religion. This suggests that theologians, biblical scholars, and church historians now need to become participants in the civil religion debate, for its origins and dynamism may be laid at the doorstep of institutional religion. Handy says a decisive turn has occurred in the call for methodological strictures and in the broadening of the civil religion concept, calling for participation from the theological community.   [M.L.S.]

Harding, Vincent. "Out of the Cauldron of Struggle: Black Religion and the Search for a New America." In *Religion: North American Style,* **edited by Patrick H. McNamara, pp. 252–64. Belmont, CA: Wadsworth Publishing, 1984.**

Since their emergence in the Revolutionary period, black churches have constituted an impetus toward religious pluralism and a challenge to the inner character of American society. In this essay, Harding traces these threads through American history.

In their fight against slavery, their prayers for freedom and songs of judgment, and their turn toward Africa, black people sought to break the white monolith called America and to participate in creating a new society. During Reconstruction, black leaders lifted up a vision of the common good, but were betrayed by white allies whose vision of expansionism and capitalism prevailed. By World War I, the more radical force of black religion was outside the Afro-Christian institutional framework: the Nation of Islam, the Garvey movement, Father Divine. After World War II, the voice of Malcolm X offered a non-Western base for black religious sensibility. In the 1960s the black struggle exploded in a massive effort for the right to participate in all public institutions. Black religion was central in the campaign. Out of this movement, manifested in Black Power, black studies, black history, arose a new challenge to white American Christianity.

The challenge to create a new America is concerned partly with a vibrant religious pluralism, but more importantly with the formation of a truly humane society given to the public good. Although they are currently exposed to multiple disabling pressures, Harding says black people, particularly, have a central role in the creation of a new America. [D.S.]

Hatch, Nathan O. "The Christian Movement and the Demand for a Theology of the People." *The Journal of American History* **67, no. 3 (December 1980): 545–67.**

In reviewing the history of the Christian movement, Hatch illustrates the impact on religion of the postrevolutionary crisis of authority in American popular culture. In so doing, he clarifies the process by which the traditional idea of the church as organic body with ranks and degrees was virtually replaced with the notion that sovereignty of the people must be the rule in both religious and secular realms. At the same time, Hatch shows how Americans dealt with the "pervasive collapse of certainty" (p. 561) that was the fruit of successful revolution and subsequent separation of church and state, and indicates how culture in the early republic became christianized.

The most obvious move the common people made was their rejection of elites in every sphere. In religion this meant dismantling traditional distinctions between clergy and laity in favor of democratically structured churches. Less obvious, but equally important was the common people's refusal to recognize the authority of intellectual elites. This not only meant rejection of Calvinist theology supporting conceptions of the Christian community as hierarchical, but also rejection of theology itself. In the Protestant fashion, authority was still vested in Scripture, but not as interpreted by learned clerics or trained theologians. By calling for "a populist hermeneutic" the Christian movements' leaders established the New Testament *as read and understood by common people* as the ultimate source of authority in individual Christian lives.

This insightful article contributes much to the understanding of what happened to religion in early nineteenth-century America. [J.S.]

Henry, Patrick. "And I Don't Care What It Is: The Tradition-History of a Civil Religion Proof-Text." *Journal of the American Academy of Religion* **49, no. 1 (March 1981): 35–49.**

The uniqueness of Henry's article resides in its method and approach, not necessarily in its content or conclusions. He raises questions as to why typical methods of critical-historical study of ancient sources and texts have not been focused upon contemporary texts and modern sources. He quickly exhibits an example of what he means by doing the "tradition-history" of a civil religion proof-text, that is, the now famous 1950s remark by President Eisenhower about wanting everybody to have faith and not caring what kind it is. Henry documents the numerous sources he consulted in searching for verification of this remark and for its meaning. From the author's recapitulation of his search, it is clear versions of texts vary and, more important, their meanings are construed differently by different people affecting the ways in which history may be written. As Henry illustrates, such is the case with the Eisenhower remark.

Specifically, Henry's brief "tradition-history" of this Eisenhower text confirms Sidney Mead's linking of Eisenhower's position with that of the Founding Fathers and calls into question the many who have submitted this quotation as evidence of the utter banality of the human mind or of the totally contentless character of American civil "faith." Thus Henry illustrates the value of applying "tradition-history" to contemporary materials to enhance understandings of words spoken and written in certain contexts at specific times. [E.A.W.]

Higham, John. "Hanging Together: Divergent Unities in American History." *Journal of American History* **61, no. 1 (June 1974): 5–28.**

Higham's thesis represents an attempt to bridge the gap between an older school of consensus historians (Hofstadter, Hartz, Boorstin) and the more recent work of community historians (Bushman, Lockridge, McWilliams, etc.). Well aware of divergent patterns among social groups in America, he nonetheless posits three overarching concepts that have played key roles at various stages of United States history. First, there is a primordial unity found among native Americans, regionalists, and ethnic groups best expressed in a feeling of unity based on a set of inherited relationships. This has been gradually replaced by ideological systems of general beliefs that form a common identity, purpose, standard of criticism, and course of action. American ideology has its roots in Puritan culture but quickly graduates into two complementary systems: American Protestantism and American nationalism. By the midnineteenth century, however, a new integrative system—technical unity—entered the scene. Unlike the ideological framework that stressed values as ends, the coming machine age meant a preoccupation with means toward a utilitarian end. More than anything else, it is this third order of ideas that works against the other two, for technology is not dependent upon the voluntary community and is directly antithetical to democratic values. Unless Americans can find some way to infuse their technological society with the intimacy of the primordial group and the conscious convictions of ideology, there is no future possibility of social and intellectual unity in our public life—only debilitating fragmentation.　[S.C.B.]

Hill, Samuel S., Jr. "A Typology of American Restitutionism: From Frontier Revivalism and Mormonism to the Jesus Movement." *Journal of the American Academy of Religion* 44, no. 1 (March 1976): 65–76.

Samuel Hill compares attitudes toward history of Christian groups that understand themselves to be formally linked with the apostolic era through apostolic succession with those whose attitudes reject that linkage. Although the beginning (the primitive era) is normative for all Christians, established churches and historical denominations value their historical ties to Christian beginnings. Thus they regard Christian history either as authoritative or as guide and source of inspiration. The Christian movements that are part of American "Restitutionism" either view Christian history as less important than personal piety or see it as "deviation or impertinence" (p. 74). Those attitudes also affect the role of the church vis à vis the Scriptures as sources of religious authority.

Drawing on these distinctions, Hill presents a typology of American religious movements that see themselves as reinstituting the Christianity of the apostolic era. Latter-day Saints (Mormons), who have created an alternative (restored) institution, are at one extreme, whereas the "new supernaturalists," who have made no effort to institutionalize and virtually ignore Christian history, are at the other extreme. In between are churches whose institutional framework is understood as a re-formed, but not new, Christian church; churches and movements that attempt to recreate the beginnings through "internal realization of the Kingdom of God" (p. 72); and Frontier Revivalism and Pentecostalism whose adherents seek "relational reconciliation" (p. 72) without creating a new formal institution.

Hill considers the cultural significance of these restitutionist forms in an epilogue and concludes they are "eloquent witnesses" to America's "conviction that she holds an authentically fresh position in the history of the world" (p. 76). [J.S.]

Hoge, Dean R. "Theological Views of America Among Protestants." *Sociological Analysis* **37, no. 2 (Summer 1976): 127–39.**

Public theology speaks from particular religious denominations to the national need. In this 1973 study, Dean Hoge surveys Presbyterian ministers and laity to determine (1) what visions of America's mission are prevalent among Protestants; (2) whether Americans have a sense of transcendent universal judgment when viewing the nation; (3) how Protestant theology of America relates to broader theological orientations; and (4) whether there are social-psychological determinants of public theology.

Hoge discovered that both ministers and lay persons felt that America's mission is to improve itself "so that freedom and justice in America will be an example to all nations" (p. 131). Both sets of respondents felt strongly that American Christians must put God's judgement over national loyalty, but there was not a strong correlation between scores on this index and respondents' moral evaluations of America.

Important differences emerged between ministers' and lay persons' theological orientations. The ministers were more oriented to the church's world mission than to nationalism, were more critical in their moral assessments of America, and were less inclined to see America's wealth as a reward for its virtue than were lay persons. These findings, however, may be more reflective of the period in which the study was conducted, coming as it did at the close of the Vietnam War and the beginning of the Watergate controversy.

Hoge concludes that no single statement could be made about public theology's relationship to broader theological orientations, although two "parties" were discerned as theological views of America at the time of the survey—what Hoge calls "internationalism" and "anti-communism." [C.J.]

Hudson, Winthrop S. "The Issue of Church and State: A Historical Perspective." *Religion in Life* **46, no. 3 (Autumn 1977): 278–88.**

Neither the constitutional prohibition against using religious tests for public office nor First Amendment provisions about religion mean that religion is without a proper place in American politics. On the contrary, says Hudson, the First Amendment prescribes only a separation of *institutions,* thereby encouraging a plurality of voluntary religious bodies. This, in turn, spares the United States the bitter religious conflicts of Europe and enhances the inner life of the churches themselves. Moreover, the First Amendment does not detract from the presence of a common religion (variously called civic piety, religion of the republic, civil religion) pervading public life in the United States.

Yet a distinction must be made between public religion and church religion, a distinction drawn from the English Puritans' differentiation between the realm of nature and the realm of grace, both of which are governed by God. Thus to reject the idea of a strictly Christian state is not to adopt that of a strictly secular state. But the common public religion of the new nation was not so much a "natural religion" in the deistic sense, as a public religion in a more Hebraic sense. Hence the prospect and threat of divine judgment should the nation not fulfill its divine mission was preserved. In sum, this author asserts that separation of church and state does not mean separation of religion and politics in the history of the United States. [D.S.]

Hudson, Winthrop S. "This Most Favored Nation: Reflections on the Vocation of America." *Journal of Church and State* **19, no. 2 (Spring 1977): 217–30.**

The United States of America has been widely conceived by its members as "this most favored nation" partly because of its geographical blessings, more significantly because of its presumed divine purpose. Among others, John Adams, Thomas Paine, and Andrew Jackson understood the American people as custodians of a sacred trust. As such, the United States was often equated with ancient Israel. National holidays were originally understood as public expressions of this understanding, although since midtwentieth century these holidays have become wholly privatized and secularized.

In particular, Hudson focuses on national fast days as clear expressions (especially during colonial and Revolutionary days) of the concept of divine favor. They were times for confession of sins and summons to repentence in order to provoke a renewed commitment to divine purpose. Because the idea of America as the "most favored nation" presupposed an Hebraic understanding of history, fast days symbolize a double vision; chosenness and accountability, national vocation and divine judgment. This double vision acted as a restraint on national ambitions through the nineteenth century. However, Hudson says that sense of double vision is now largely lost. Thus Senator Mark Hatfield's effort to declare a national fast day in 1974 failed to strike a responsive chord among contemporary American people.   [D.S.]

Hughes, Richard T. "A Civic Theology for the South: The Case of Benjamin M. Palmer." *Journal of Church and State* **25, no. 3 (Autumn 1983): 447–67.**

As pastor of the prestigious First Presbyterian Church in New Orleans during the Civil War, Benjamin Morgan Palmer was perhaps the leading pulpit voice of the Confederacy. His yoking of the cause of God with that of the fighting forces in gray played a major role in shaping the wartime South's image of itself and its mission. In his sermons, says Richard T. Hughes in this judicious article, Palmer thus "created a mythical South" (p. 467) by weaving together all of the threads of an already well developed southern civic theology.

This theology, according to Hughes, was the synthesis of the biblical faith in Jehovah and the rationalism of Scottish common sense philosophy. Born in their region's defense against the abolitionist onslaught of the 1830s, the new civic faith was an attempt by southerners to find a fresh "primordial frame of reference" (p. 450) in which to understand their experience. The result was a complex group of symbols woven together "to form a coherent pattern of meaning" (p. 450) and expressed best by Benjamin Palmer. In a careful textual analysis of Palmer's rhetoric, Hughes shows how the Louisiana clergyman proclaimed the primary tenets of that faith: the image of the Confederate South as the new Israel, its continuity with the Hebrew patriarchs, and its eventual restoration of primitive Christianity and of the mission of the American Puritans.

Students of southern civil religion will find this article particularly insightful, not only for its picture of Palmer, but also for its revealing glimpses of the structure and content of Dixie's public faith.   [L.A.H.]

Hughes, Richard T. "Civil Religion, the Theology of the Republic, and the Free Church Tradition." *Journal of Church and State* **22, no. 1 (Winter 1980): 75–87.**

Richard Hughes analyzes American civil religion as "a somewhat schizoid blend of Puritanism and the Enlightenment, of coercion and persuasion, of 'Jehovah, god of battles,' and the mild and tolerant god of nature" (p. 77). He inquires into the stance that free churchmen should adopt toward it.

Taking "restoration" as a key theological motif in the free church tradition, Hughes draws a sharp distinction between the European Anabaptist stream of that tradition (e.g., Franklin H. Littell and John Howard Yoder) and the New England Puritan stream. For Anabaptists, restoration of pre-Constantinian Christianity meant confrontation and judgment of a coercive established order, both religious and civil; for Puritans, it served as the ground plan for a new order. At this point, Anabaptists and Thomas Jefferson were in agreement against every form of coercive Constantinianism.

Therefore, Sidney E. Mead's "theology of the republic" in *The Nation With the Soul of a Church* (see p. 88) is not an apology for "civil religion" with which free churchmen should quarrel. In Mead beats the heart of an Anabaptist.

The free church tradition has no legitimate argument with civil religion "so long as that religion is dominated by its persuasive and pluralistic dimensions" (p. 86). The enemy is not persuasive Enlightenment infidels, but coercive Christians.   [L.W.]

Hughes, Richard T. "From Civil Dissent to Civil Religion: And Beyond." *Religion in Life* 49, no. 3 (Autumn 1980): 268–88.

Richard Hughes argues that "primordial theology," in which "the norm for theological reflection is the primordium that is thought to stand outside the dimensions of profane history," has been dominant in much of the American experience (p. 268).

The omnipresence of this method from colonial times through the early nineteenth century accounts for the ease with which the Enlightenment's god of nature displaced the Puritan Jehovah god of battles.

"The primordium" is derived from Mircea Eliade. Hughes extends it to American historical interpretation by deriving a "primordial dimension" in the English Reformation and Puritanism from Christian humanism, the continental Reformed tradition, and William Tyndale's covenant theology. These sources nourished views that church and society were to be reformed into conformity with ancient precedents—Israel, the primitive Christian church, the Constantinian epoch—appropriated as powerful, primordial myths.

Enlightenment rationalists, though their theological content differed from the Puritans, were like them in quest of the primordium; they "simply substituted" the book of nature for the Bible, and primordial Eden for primordial early church, while "the old assumption that truth is to be found in antiquity continued to prevail" (p. 279). Millennial fervor that burst forth around the American Revolution also was a quest for primordium: golden age and present-future millennium were collapsed; intervening profane history was "obscured, ignored, transcended" (p. 286).   [L.W.]

Hughes, Richard T. "From Primitive Church to Civil Religion: The Millennial Odyssey of Alexander Campbell." *Journal of the American Academy of Religion* **44, no. 1 (March 1976): 87–103.**

Shaped both by Puritanism and Enlightenment rationalism, American mythic eschatology never has been quite sure whether hope is best placed in the future of (Protestant) Christianity or the future of the Republic. Richard Hughes portrays Alexander Campbell, patriarch of the Disciples of Christ, as a figure who thought within this uncertainty and moved, in the forty years between 1820 and 1860, from utopian hope for restoration of a primitive New Testament church to utopian expectations for a world liberated by Anglo-Saxon institutions and ingenuity.

In both of his eschatologies, Campbell was an indefatigable millennial optimist, confident that the perfect Lockean social order— united, pluralistic, tolerant, and free—was just around the American corner. In 1830, Campbell pinned his hopes on "the union of Christians, and the destruction of sects," to subject "the world to the government of Jesus" (p. 88). By the 1850s, Campbell argued for establishment and recognition in the United States of a "common Christianity" (p. 96). This nonsectarian public religion would express the "power and magnificence [of] the Anglo-Saxon people, the Anglo-Saxon tongue, sciences, learning, and civilization" and shine into all the world the light and liberty of Jesus (p. 99).   [L.W.]

Hunter, Lloyd. "Mark Twain and the Southern Evangelical Mind." *The Bulletin of the Missouri Historical Society* **33, no. 4 (July 1977): 246–64.**

This article argues that scholars have overlooked the significance of southern evangelical religion to Mark Twain and his writings. Despite Twain's attack on slavery and regional romanticism and despite the influence of the western frontier on him, Hunter demonstrates that growing up in the border South permanently affected Twain's spiritual life. He learned to avoid institutional religion, but he could not escape exposure to the forms and doctrines of southern evangelism, which helped to form Twain's lifelong attitudes toward human nature and God.

Twain's writings deal with key facets of the southern religious mind: the individualistic nature of faith, the emotionalism of revivals, the belief that religion is of the heart, the fear of death and hell, and the importance of personal conversion. His comments, whether satirical or serious, reflected ambivalent feelings toward the religion of his youth. He was often critical of the revivalist tradition, yet the camp meeting is a recurring scene in his fiction. The experience of individual conversion plays a key role in the lives of Twain characters, but he reserves his harshest satire for those selfishly pursuing individual perfection without concern for the needs of others.

Hunter shows that Twain's bitterness late in life partly had religious roots. After a lifetime of experience, he came to affirm the belief in human depravity he had heard from Calvinist preachers in his youth, to reject free will, and to see God as an indifferent, even malevolent being. Twain nonetheless continued to express revulsion at what he regarded as intolerant, repressive southern evangelical religion.   [C.R.W.]

Hutchison, William R. "Americanness of the Social Gospel: An Inquiry in Comparative History." *Church History* 44, no. 3 (September 1975): 367–81.

Professor William Hutchison of Harvard Divinity School is the leading scholar of American liberal Protestantism. In this essay he gives a survey of perspectives on the Americanness of the Social Gospel from 1885 to 1925.

The Social Gospel, a movement within liberal Protestantism, addressed the social problems of modern Western cultures with a prophetic voice and an activist hand. By the 1920s, more than a generation after its inception, Social Christianity was often defined as "Christian Americanism" by both its supporters and its detractors. Hutchison takes issue with this common perception of the movement. By using comparative history, Hutchison finds no basis for an exclusively American claim to the Social Gospel, but instead suggests that Americans offered a distinctive style and set of concerns within a movement that found expression in many Western countries.

The special American contribution to the Social Gospel was part of an optimistic intellectual style that was central to nineteenth-century American culture. American religious liberals felt the dissolving effects of science on religious belief at a less profound level than did their European peers. Americans also tended to express extremely positive evaluations of human nature and the intellectual and social tendencies of the age. From this cheerful context came the strident demands for social justice from America's Social Gospel leaders, and from them was born much of the conscience of twentieth-century American liberalism.

Hutchison's article is not written to assess the American Social Gospel or its contributions, although he is clearly supportive of its liberal tenets. This is, rather, an inquisitive essay that challenges common assumptions about American Social Christianity and points out a mistaken direction of most previous scholarship. [P.J.C.]

Isetti, Ronald E. "The Charter Myth of America: A Study of Political Symbolism in the Inaugural Addresses of the Presidents." *Cithara* **16, no. 1 (November 1976): 3–17.**

The American Revolution and the early years of the Republic have often been regarded as the years in which the American civil religion began to take form. Yet as Robert Isetti argues, the "primary source of the main myths of America's special character and destiny . . . is to be found in the words and acts of . . . the first settlers of many of the thirteen colonies" (p. 3). Their journals, letters, histories, tracts, and sermons, he suggests, make use of typology—a technique of "giving ultimate meaning to a current historical event by viewing it as a fulfillment or reenactment of an episode in the history of ancient Israel, as recorded in the Old Testament" (p. 3). Five elements of the "charter myth" that was forged during the colonial period—the national covenant, the holy experiment, the promised land, the virgin wilderness, and the new Israel—have been drawn upon throughout American history in presidential inauguration speeches.

Isetti examines the colonial sources of each of these motifs and shows how various presidents used them in their inaugurals. The charter myth continues to be a rhetorical resource for presidents, Isetti argues, not simply because Americans still revere the biblical sources from which it is drawn, but because it seems to fit the history of the nation. Although the charter myth has its drawbacks and can lead Americans and their presidents into a false sense of righteousness, Isetti believes that it can also provide a worthy impetus for the nation to achieve its destiny as a "holy experiment." [C.J.]

Johnson, Stephen D., and Joseph B. Tamney. "The Christian Right and the 1980 Presidential Election." *Journal for the Scientific Study of Religion* **21, no. 2 (June 1982): 123–31.**

The emergence of the evangelically informed and politically activist conservative Right led many commentators to believe that the 1980 presidential election would be decided on religious grounds.

After interviewing residents of "Middletown, U.S.A.," however, Stephen Johnson and Joseph Tamney discovered that the Christian Right movement had very little, if any, impact on voting behavior in the 1980 presidential election.

The researchers were able to establish that a "Christian Right," comprised of individuals who hold religiously fundamentalist views, believe in a "civil religion," and urge religious involvement in politics, does exist in the United States. But religious fundamentalism did not exert an independent influence on the presidential vote. Interaction effects suggested that for those of high education, the more they embraced civil religion, the more likely they were to vote for Ronald Reagan; for those of low education, the more they believed in a civil religion, the more likely they were to vote for Jimmy Carter.

In interpreting these findings, Johnson and Tamney suggested that "potential presidents may be judged in terms of their manner of embodying religion . . . the more educated . . . prefer a more rational religious style, which Reagan may have suggested, while the less educated are drawn to a more emotional religion, which Carter exemplified" (p. 130). The only clearcut finding was that those who were committed to religious political involvement were more likely to vote for Carter than for Reagan. The authors conclude by noting that "among those believing that the United States is God's instrument, there is a clear lack of agreement on God's intent" (p. 130). [C.J.]

Jones, O., Jr. "Black Muslim Movement and the American Constitutional System." *Journal of Black Studies* **13, no. 4 (June 1983): 417–37.**

Jones presents the ideology of the Black Muslim movement (mixed as it is with significant political components) as a model for understanding "the current meaning of the First Amendment guarantee of religious freedom in America" (p. 435). The argument falls far short of sustaining its conclusions, however, because of several crucial historical errors and the juxtapositioning of events that occurred during the early years of the movement (in the 1930s), during World War II, and during the 1970s, by which time the nature of the movement's interaction with white power structures had been altered by the numerous incidents of violence connected with the Muslims.

For example, Jones builds much of his case on a discussion of the Muslim's problems with recognition of conscientious objector's status in the 1970s. In the midst of his argument, he notes (incorrectly) that Elijah Muhammad was jailed for his conscientious objection to war. In fact, he was jailed thirty years prior to the time under discussion for sedition (i.e., encouraging others to refuse military service during World War II), a related but completely independent matter. Jones goes on to compare the Muslim problems with draft boards with the Mennonites lack of problem. The more definitive comparison would have been with other, newer, predominantly white religious groups who also have had to run the gauntlet on issues of participation in war. [J.G.M.-n]

Jones, William A. "Freedom of Conscience—The Black Experience in America." *Journal of Ecumenical Studies* **14, no. 4 (Fall 1977): 608–14.**

This sermonlike piece is a contribution to a series of articles on the "Contemporary American Experience of Conscience and Dissent." According to the author, much human history is a catalogue of human sin. In America capitalism, militarism, and racism expressed a trinitarian formula for oppression and established the parameters of power relationships between social groups.

Whereas the pragmatic aspects of racism are not today as overt as they were in the nineteenth century, many of the covert realities of apartheid have not changed. Black people still constitute an oppressed and economically disenfranchised minority.

Racism is anthropological in its overt expression and theological in its covert expression. Christian theology was tailored to fit the sociological realities and exigencies of racism. By capitulating to culture in such a manner, the Christian religion and its institutional structures are deeply implicated in racial oppression.

Black people, however, did not receive the gospel without making their own critical evaluation and analysis. They saw the dichotomy between faith and practice. They demythologized and personalized stories of Scripture, thereby creating a new faith, a new salvation history that drew rich parallels between the experiences of the Israelites in Egypt and black experience in America. Slaves intuitively knew "where God stood" and developed a religious vision that was antithetical to white religion.

The black church has served as a vital connecting rod between black history and black hope by presenting as an institution a vision of emancipation and a more noble life. [W.D.D.]

Jung, L. Shannon. "The Shape of American Space." *Religion in Life* **44, no. 1 (Spring 1975): 36–46.**

Americans living behind chain link fences in walled suburbs reveal how we perceive our cultural space, despite the fact that we have lost our sensitivity to the transformative effects of space. Jung states that theology and ethics must attend to how we do and should design our space.

The distinction between personal space and our national place indicates the difference in the number of people with whom we share terrain. Shared space turns space to place.

A person chooses a home out of desire for security; but once that particular home is chosen, the resident begins to internalize the spatial contingencies chosen and is unconsciously affected by them. For example, protective walls and electronic surveillance might intensify fear and might produce a provinciality resulting in shallow intimacy.

Ironically, search for a place of one's own has co-opted search for shared space. Home is the space where we expect to control our lives, but public housing residents have exchanged any sense of control for low rent.

Homogenization of national place acts as a deterrent to appreciation of one's space. If every place is similar to every other place, there can be no sense of place because the experience of place depends on the distinctiveness of particular places.

The author concludes that medical ethicists must ask whether hospital design makes patients feel powerless, and social ethicists must ask how spatial configurations contribute to violence.   [M.K.T.]

Kazin, Alfred. "The Drama of Good and Evil in American Writing." *Review of Politics* **38, no. 3 (July 1976): 343–58.**

"The Drama of Good and Evil in American Writing," according to Alfred Kazin, has been played out in relation to the drama of America itself. In the beginning, as it were, America was good, or at least was ripe with redemptive possibilities, even if the men and women who settled here in those first Puritan migrations knew they were not. But the land, the wilderness, the New World subsumed Calvinist self-doubt, like Enlightenment skepticism, in a baptism of hope that was to continue long into the nineteenth century and to find a kind of culminating expression in Emerson.

The earliest major critics of this New World optimism were writers like Poe and Melville who realized that evil is not merely privative, as Emerson contended, but also possibly cosmic. Yet it was not until after the Civil War that writers responsive to the burgeoning development of capitalism redefined evil, first, as in Dickinson, Crane, and Dreiser, as the insignificance, the "nullity," of humanity in a world no longer constructed for the benefit of all, and then, second, in the early years of the twentieth century, as the excesses of the profit system. In either case, evil has come to be associated with a kind of power inimical to humanity but sovereign over it, a power that for later twentieth-century writers, goodness can question but can no longer entirely resist or overcome.   [G.G.]

LaFontaine, Charles V. "God and Nation in Selected U.S. Presidential Inaugural Addresses, 1879–1945." *Journal of Church and State* **18, no. 1 (Winter 1976): 39–60 and no. 3 (Autumn 1976): 503–21.**

LaFontaine asserts that the inaugural address of an American president is an essentially religious statement because it is comprised of those norms, values, and beliefs of American society that have transcendent reference. In this article, LaFontaine examines six significant addresses, from George Washington to Franklin D. Roosevelt, that give expression to common American beliefs and reveal careful attention to a deity or divine force as contained in *all* inaugural addresses.

George Washington's address introduced a theme that was expanded upon and modified by subsequent presidents. He asserted the existence of a deity mainly interested in law and order within the universe, but having special concern for the American people and their government. This special concern was earned through proper moral behavior and public policy based in goodness and truth. From Washington to Buchanan, the addresses reveal a definite fixed canon of ideas concerning God, the nation, and their relationship. But with Abraham Lincoln the deity no longer merely blesses, fosters, guides, and protects. It also shows wrath, punishes, purges, and prohibits. LaFontaine points out that Lincoln was the first major revisionist of the American tradition in its classical form. Since Lincoln, presidents have reflected their concern and have pointed out that even with God's help the United States has often failed by the measure of its own high ideals.

Though limited to six addresses, this study is useful in helping the student to discern common threads of thought for American beliefs held by all, at all times, and everywhere.   [V.T.A.]

Lincoln, C. Eric, and Lawrence H. Mamiya. "Daddy Jones and Father Divine: The Cult as Political Religion." *Religion in Life* **49, no. 1 (Spring 1980): 6–23.**

In this helpful and illuminating essay, black religious scholars Lincoln and Mamiya combine insights in an attempt to understand the attractiveness for black people of Jim Jones and the Peoples Temple. The Peoples Temple is placed within the context of the "black cult," and Jones is compared to Father Divine, the epitome of the black cult leader, whom Jones consciously tried to imitate. Both are seen as effective organizers dedicated to goals of integration (rather than black separatism) who enjoyed their greatest success in time of social upheaval (a highly debatable point).

The most helpful insight enlarging our comprehension of the Peoples Temple tragedy, however, is the discussion of "political religions," movements in which a person or secular institution are transformed into a sacred reality that finds expression in the movement's symbols and rituals. In such movements, politics and religion intertwine into a total world view and program to which ultimate allegiance is given and for which one is willing to die. Ultimately, Jonestown was the fulfillment of a political-religious vision that ended in a political-religious word-deed, like that pronounced at Masada and by Kamikaze pilots. [J.G.M.-n]

Linenthal, Edward T. "From Hero to Anti-Hero: The Transformation of the Warrior in Modern America." *Soundings* 63, no. 1 (Spring 1980): 79–93.

Relying on conceptual categories from the history of religions to interpret American attitudes toward war, Edward Linenthal argues that Americans have viewed war as a ritual process essential to the progress of history. Beginning with the American Revolution, which shaped perceptions of subsequent wars, Americans have understood warfare as a symbolic struggle in which history is advanced through the triumph of good over evil. Americans have viewed their soldiers as warriors for the force of goodness who vanquish evil to save their people and who sacrifice their own lives for the progress of history.

Linenthal argues that warfare has degenerated in the twentieth century because the warrior and his symbolic universe have disappeared. The advanced technology of modern warfare, in which victories are unrelated to individual feats of heroism, makes the mythic idealization of the warrior absurd. But without a warrior ideal, the association between warfare and goodness is lost, and warfare degenerates to an activity in which wholesale violence is accepted as an ordinary state of affairs. With the Vietnam War, the warrior's heroism had not only disappeared but was turned on its head; in the absence of both victory and a credible moral cause, the U.S. solider became a victim at best and at worst a murderer.

This essay demonstrates the usefulness of history of religions methodology for analysis of the role of warfare in American perceptions of history. Moreover, Linenthal's appreciation of the symbolic role that warfare has traditionally played in the American imagination has led him to an analysis of the peculiar dilemmas of contemporary warfare that is a sophisticated alternative to analyses based in political or moral ideologies.　[A.P.]

Littell, Franklin H. "Foundations and Traditions of Religious Liberty." *Journal of Ecumenical Studies* **14, no. 4 (Fall 1977): 572–87.**

Littell contends movingly that religious liberty is a matter of high religion as well as sound government, that the free exercise of religion is both historically and theoretically prior to the prohibition of any establishment of religion, that affirming "soul liberty" in religion requires also affirming the dignity and integrity of everyone's individual and collective experience, and that present-day religious liberty continues to depend upon action on behalf of those who are not free. Drawing upon an ecumenical range of historical quotations and several Supreme Court opinions, Littell argues that religious liberty is not merely a matter of passive "separation of church and state." Thus totalitarian regimes never actually guarantee the freedom of religion, which instead is always derived from the high ground of moral religious thought.

Since "high religion" involves voluntary, honest conviction about religious truth, Littell asserts that the substantial case against coercion and repression is not simply that they do not work or make bad politics but that they point toward hypocrisy, dissimulation, and death. Therefore, Littell argues, not only must we stand together against any establishment of religion, but we must also support the free expression of religion in America and throughout the world—for the most fundamental argument for religious liberty is not pragmatic but theological, indeed eschatological.

While Littell's essay is neither a critical analysis of "church/state" arguments nor a comprehensive review of resources, it conveys effectively the "reasons of the heart" that make religious liberty vitally important in America and throughout the world.　[J.G.M.-y]

Little, D. "Max Weber Revisited: The Protestant Ethic and the Puritan Experience of Order." *Harvard Theological Review* **59, no. 4 (October 1966): 415–28.**

Was Weber wrong about Puritanism with respect to its causes, content, and implications? Was Calvin more of a politician, sociologist, or theologian? How does one reconcile Calvin's teaching that we are to be self-initiating agents of social change with the rigorous disciplines imposed by his theology?

Little reminds us that Calvin was, of course, preeminently a theologian, that Puritanism was derived from his conception of God, and that the social implications that emerge from this emphasis are dialectical rather than contradictory. The marks of the Calvinistic (Puritanic) social order are voluntarism, consensualism, private initiative, and toleration.

At the same time that God is free of creation, God remains sovereign over it. People find their best fulfillment in a voluntary submission or obedience to God. The church is a distinctive community where discipline is institutionalized. It is characterized by "an independent style of life in which self-initiated achievement-oriented and consensual conduct is the ideal" (p. 423).

Little contends that in Puritanism there is an inclination in both directions—towards regimentation and towards a voluntary self-determination. The paradox of modernism is that it requires a degree of social control and self-discipline that places restraints on participants. What is needed, then, is a new form of discipline, that can make sense of these opposing inclinations.

But Little believes that Weber was right with respect to Puritanism. He regards it as an experiment that resulted from a twofold commitment: (1) to an order founded on voluntary choice, and (2) to the use of involuntary means to extend that order. Maybe so, but it seems to create a kind of schizophrenic character that in the long run seems to be destructive. [W.C.O.]

Marty, Martin E. "The Church in the World: Civil Religion and the Churches Behaving Civilly." *Theology Today* 32, no. 2 (July 1975): 175–82.

Marty describes the adversarial relationship that many scholars posit between the churches and civil religion (implicitly defined here as a value-and meaning-laden system that has at least a quasi-metaphysical claim and that enacts its myths and symbols through rite and ceremony). He reviews the positions of the debate's major discussants—Robert Bellah (see pp. 8, 145–47), J. Paul William, Will Herberg (see p. 61), and Sidney Mead (see pp. 88, 192)—by presenting concise descriptions of their work. But rather than simply acceding to what he presents as a sort of consensus regarding antagonism between "the common faith" implied by the phrase civil religion and the "particular religions of divided ecclesiastical communities" (p. 176) Marty points out two neglected factors bearing on this issue.

One of these is the "denominationalism" of civil religion itself. Women have described it as a male concept. Vincent Harding and other blacks regard it as "white sectarianism," whereas British observer D. W. Brogan pictured it as Protestant. The other factor is that "virtually all the denominational religions share the national consensus that calls for religious support of civil society and the state" (p. 170). Rather than deviating from this national consensus, most Catholics, Lutherans, and Evangelicals apparently embrace the tenets of civil religion. Marty concludes that if these two factors are taken into consideration, reflections on the relationship between the spheres of civil and church religion will be less adversarial. In the resulting atmosphere of civility, "fresh thinking, marked by clarity and charity, can emerge" (p. 182).   [J.S.]

Marty, Martin E. "Ethnicity: The Skeleton of Religion in America." *Church History* **41, no. 1 (March 1972): 5–21.**

This paper, delivered as the presidential address at the meeting of the American Society of Church History in 1971, is addressed to the failure of the assimilationist theories to explain the American religious experience.

Marty discusses five models of religion in America, all of which operate with the assumption that American religious self-understanding is characterized by a spiritual "sameness." This "sameness" is expressed as an affirmation of religious nationalism, civil religion, or the religion of the "triple melting pot."

Defenders of a generalized American religion consistently overlooked ethnic and racial factors because they accepted a prime article of the American creed: the New World would transform and homogenize human nature. As a consequence, students of religion in America became committed to theories of interpretation that led them to neglect, gloss over, or obscure the durable sense of peoplehood in the larger American community.

The heightened racial and ethnic self-consciousness among "minority groups" in the 1960s caught many Americans off guard. During this decade the issues of ethnicity and racism served as new occasions for reexamination of the assumptions and biases of the "sameness" school. Only after the racial upheavals and new ethnic consciousness of the 1960s did scholars begin to perceive again that ethnicity has been the supporting framework ("skeleton") of American religion. The traditional models for interpreting American religious experience apply appropriately only to the white and largely generalized Protestant academic circles where they originated. Ethnic and racial themes now must be reintegrated into questions about the role of religion in American life. [W.D.D.]

Marty, Martin E. "Experiment in Environment: Foreign Perceptions of Religious America." *The Journal of Religion* **56, (July 1976): 291–315.**

If there is to be "American religion" that is a larger category and a more indigenous reality than just "religion in America," then one must look to the environment as a significant part of the nation's identity, a part that has put "some sort of stamp" on the varied religious forces and expressions of American life and culture. "Experiment" and "experimentalism" have often been suggested as the unifying thrust or theme, and Marty holds them to be "fundamental for understanding the whole of American spirituality" (p. 291).

Marty admits that he is neither the "inventor or discoverer of the motif" (p. 292). He cites church historians Robert Baird and Philip Schaff as pointing to America as the locus of "experiments" and developments in church history. But without a doubt the most compelling data to persuade Marty's thinking that there is in fact a new and distinctive set of American religious phenomena are the countless testimonies from diverse foreign observers of American life. Marty says that if the observations of these persons are taken seriously it is possible to speak with confidence of more than "religion in America," and to recognize the presence of "American religion" (p. 315). These observations, which have an eye on experiment in environment, are given attention in this article through the inclusions of samples of remarks of foreign observers. Based on these observations, Marty says one can speak with hope of American religion. [E.A.W.]

Marty, Martin E. "Religion in America Since Mid-Century." *Daedalus* **111, no. 1 (Winter 1982): 149–63.**

Marty's central point is that religion in America, while showing changes that are continuous and on occasion dramatic, is best described by a model that includes both "all-pervasive religiousness and persistent secularity" (p. 151). He documents convincingly that the widespread "secularization paradigm" (p. 154) that prevailed through the midsixties and foretold the demise of religion *and* the "pervasive religiousness in the broad culture" (p. 154) paradigm that followed it were too one-dimensional to be accurate. Neither has come to pass in the eighties.

Both paradigms, as Professor Marty understands them, were developed by social scientists and reinforced by theologians. Thus, in the first instance, social theorists postulated that industrial societies would become more secularized. Theologians clambered aboard the secularization bandwagon and wrote about "religionless Christianity" (p. 153), proclaiming a new gospel of "Christian atheism" (p. 153). In their turn, later theorists proposed a view of "modernity" that featured "diffused religiousness" (p. 159). Culture was inherently religious, and religion thus became inescapable. Theologically, religion became "ultimate concern."

Using as a case in point what he calls resurgent antimodern religion, especially Protestant fundamentalism, Marty demonstrates the greater adequacy of his proposed "religio-secular model of indeterminacy" (p. 157). The fundamentalist resurgence clearly shows the inadequacy of the secularization paradigm; it is clearly religious. But it is also anything but diffuse, being well institutionalized.

Marty concludes that religion and secularity are both aspects of "the viscous aspects of American cultural life" (p. 161), and they will doubtless remain so. The writing is vintage Martin Marty—both eloquent and elegant. [J.G.M.-y]

Marx, Leo. " 'Noble Shit': The Uncivil Response of American Writers to Civil Religion in America." *Massachusetts Review* **14, no. 4 (Autumn 1973): 709–39.**

This essay constitutes an exploration of the strategy American writers have employed, since the time of Emerson and Melville, to combat the rhetorical pomposities associated with turning patriotic nationalism, of the sort often heard in the inaugural addresses of American presidents, into a de facto public religion. The spectre of such a faith was evoked again in Robert Bellah's controversial essay of 1967 on "Civil Religion in America" (see p. 145), and Marx wishes to challenge it by examining what might be construed as its counter-tradition in American literary culture.

Perceiving the essence of this tradition to consist in the "reductive philosophy" Norman Mailer has discerned in the vernacular tendency to use obscenity for the sake of returning the hard edge of proportion to overblown values, Marx traces this philosophy from Santayana's critique of the Genteel tradition to Emerson's theory of language. He then proceeds to show how the desire to deflate the rhetorical pretensions of cultural religiosity with language drawn from the vulgate of experience has been carried from Emerson to Whitman and Mark Twain and beyond to Hemingway and a host of other writers who share a commitment to a democratic religious faith that stands in marked contrast to Bellah's civil religion. Bellah means by civil religion something scarcely different than a theological veneration of America. America's vernacular writers propose a counter-religious tradition that is radically egalitarian, socially and experientially inclusive, and theologically immanentist.   [G.G.]

Matthews, Donald G. "The Second Great Awakening as an Organizing Process, 1780–1830: An Hypothesis." *American Quarterly* 21, no. 1 (Spring 1969): 23–43.

This essay is an imaginative exploration into the Second Great Awakening and its impact on American society between 1780 and 1830. Donald Matthews argues that revivalism and theological changes by themselves do not explain the religious revitalization of the period. He suggests instead that the Second Great Awakening was an important social movement that can best be understood as the American Revolution "at work in religion" (p. 35). After the War of Independence, the new ideals of participatory democracy, nationalism, and social mobility were at risk because of a changing economy, untried political structures, and a population on the move. According to Matthews, the Second Great Awakening helped to organize national unity by forging a religious coalition that cut across disparate elements of the American population.

With this essay, Matthews also became one of the first to apply the new social history to the study of religion. Borrowing concepts from the social sciences, especially anthropology, sociology, and psychology, and integrating them into traditional explanations of the Second Great Awakening, Matthews developed a wide-ranging, speculative analysis of the interaction between religion and society in the early nineteenth century. Particularly valuable is his characterization of religious change during this period as a process initiated by revivals, but sustained only through the successful institutionalization of evangelical rituals and theology. This essay continues to be a major source of ideas about the origins and impact of the Second Great Awakening.   [L.K.P.]

May, Henry F. "The Recovery of American Religious History." *The American Historical Review* 70, no. 1 (October 1964): 79–92.

Studies in American religion reached a nadir during the 1920s and 1930s, when deterministic relativists belittled its importance. A decade later, however, secular scholars found it too big to be ignored, and neo-orthodox theologians helped by defining religion as a prophetic vision capable of self-renewal, not completely tied to institutions that became moribund over time. May chronicles these changes and notes additional influences such as greater appreciation for ideas in intellectual history, a search for identity in postwar conformism, and renewed evangelism in the 1950s. He observes that historians came to see revivalism as the keynote of American religion, rejecting Calvinist covenants as the interpretive template. He also finds a renewed sensitivity to theology as counterweight to positivistic preference for organizational structures. Through this resurgence May recognizes a new balance between secular and religious-minded historians, a new dialogue between secular and religious thought that denotes fruitful variety, not sterile dominance by either perspective.   [H.W.B.]

McLoughlin, William G. " 'Enthusiasm for Liberty': The Great Awakening as the Key to the Revolution." *Proceedings of the American Antiquarian Society* **87, no. 1 (April 20, 1977): 69–95.**

McLoughlin notes two ways for historians to face the challenging question of religion and the Revolution. One may, like Gordon Wood, describe the Revolution itself as a quasi-religious movement; or one may, like McLoughlin, demonstrate that the political movement of the Revolution was rooted in the profound, widespread religious movement of the Great Awakening. Calvinist pietism was at work a generation before the Revolution, producing new conceptions of God's power, plans of church organization, perceptions of the role of the clergy, views of God's plan for America in the design of the world's salvation, definitions of relations between church and state, and understandings of true virtue and its place in social life. Widespread enthusiasm thus initiated a sense of intercolonial unity, egalitarianism, a republican ideal of government by consent, a postmillennial theology, an optimistic activism, a system of mass communication, and a source of energy for cultural transformation. Hence McLoughlin concludes that the Revolution was the political revitalization of a people whose religious regeneration began in the Great Awakening.

McLoughlin constructs his argument carefully upon the work of such other historians as Alan Heimert, Clarence Goen, Gorden Wood, Sidney Mead, David Lovejoy, Richard Bushman, Philip Greven, and Kenneth Lockridge. McLoughlin makes a strong case for the interaction of religious and political movements in American history, an argument made even more interesting by Jon Butler's sweeping denials (see p. 151). These two articles show the lively conflict of interpretation at work today regarding even the most central claims and fundamental assumptions about American religious history. [J.G.M.-y]

Mead, Sidney E. "Abraham Lincoln's 'Last Best Hope of Earth': The American Dream of Destiny and Democracy." *Church History* **23, no. 1 (March 1954): 3–16.**

Lincoln expressed the spiritual center of America when he spoke of a nation "conceived in liberty, and dedicated to the proposition that all men are created equal" and of "government of the people, by the people, and for the people." This essay, which was Professor Mead's 1953 presidential address for the American Society of Church History, explores implicit components of these themes. Among those components are belief in God, faith in the voice of the people as the voice of God, the importance of free and open debate, and the belief that truth will emerge in conflict. Through all of this, the will of the majority must prevail. But democratic faith is not faith in the majority; it is faith in God. This is what finally protects the views of the minority, which, after all, might be right. All of this means that democracy is essentially a way of faith and that through study, debate, dialogue, and attention to the unfolding events of history, the truth will emerge— a faith, according to Mead, well expressed by Lincoln.   [R.T.H.]

Mead, Sidney E. "The Theology of the Republic and the Orthodox Mind." *Journal of the American Academy of Religion* **44, no. 1 (March 1976): 105–13.**

As is often the case in Mead's articles, this exercise has many facets, intriguing sidebars, and memorable one-liners. The main feature is an exposition of two frames of mind or different premises. One— called variously orthodoxy, sectarianism, and Christian loyalty—is characterized as parochial, exclusivist, and inclined to coercion because of concern about confessional precision. The other—called deism, rationalism, and enlightenment—is characterized as cosmopolitan, inclusivist, and inclined to persuasion because of concern about free inquiry.

Mead expounds on these alternatives and clarifies what was at stake in the debate between rational philosophy and biblical supernaturalism at the founding of the Republic. He also helps explain contrary strains throughout American history: one pressing for open toleration and another equating good citizenship with churchly beliefs and morals. This thorny, sometimes convoluted commentary is as relevant to today as it is to eighteenth-century conditions. It illuminates every contest between religious use of coercive power and civil neutrality toward pluralistic nonconformity.   [H.W.B.]

Meyer, Donald H. "American Intellectuals and the Victorian Crisis of Faith." *American Quarterly* **27, no. 5 (December 1975): 585–603.**

Desiring unity but no longer able to find it in the universe around them, the late Victorians were perhaps the last generation among English-speaking intellectuals able to believe that man was capable of understanding his universe, just as they were the first generation collectively to suspect that he never would. Given the rise of science and the spread of technology, in the Victorian period doubt was more unsettling and thoroughgoing than ever before. American Victorians found their culture's distinctively internalized and secular religiosity rather well suited to withstand intellectual challenges, at least on the popular level. Meyer shows how American Victorians coped intellectually with the psychological need for cosmic comfort, the moral demand for a sense of cosmic momentousness, and the aesthetic quest for cosmic unity. They longed, he writes, for a universe that was not just intelligible, reassuring, and morally challenging, but symphonic as well.

Because they were vigorous, serious people, American Victorians created many of their own problems. Yet their concerns remain prominent in the history of twentieth-century culture and thought. As Meyer concludes, lacking their self-confidence and hopefulness, we are nevertheless still Victorians in our moral searchings and cosmic homesickness.

Thus Meyer brilliantly analyzes a complex period, relating religious thinking to general intellectual problems, showing what ingredients were distinctively American and what were more generally modern and European, and demonstrating how this set of religious intellectual problems was unique to the particular period he studies and how it is also undeniably connected to our own.   [J.G.M.-y]

Meyer, Donald H. "Secular Transcendence: The American Religious Humanists." *American Quarterly* **34, no. 5 (Winter 1982): 524–42.**

In the 1970s, the religious right in America identified "secular humanism" as the author of all the evils in America since the 1950s. A group, identifying themselves as religious humanists in the 1920s, emerged as a reaction, along with liberalism and fundamentalism, to modern thought in American Protestantism. Meyer presents material to distinguish the two "humanist" movements and illustrates the misunderstandings that have surrounded the humanist movement and the reasons for its lessened appeal in the 1920s and 1930s.

The religious humanists of the 1920s shared some common beliefs: (1) nontheism; (2) natural world is the only real world; and (3) science is the only proper method to describe the universe. The 1920s movement sought to transcend life's circumstances (which religion should do) by affirming human worth in the face of cosmic purposelessness. However, this movement failed to capture the American thought as the rise of neo-orthodoxy with its stress on the transcendence of God presented a palatable alternative for the intellectuals.

In contrast to the religious humanism of the 1920s, contemporary secular humanism derives some thought from its predecessor, but lacks the earlier concern for the nature of reality itself and, as referred to by the fundamentalists, is a much more vague notion. [V.T.A.]

Meyer, Donald H. "The Uniqueness of the American Enlightenment." *American Quarterly* **28, no. 2 (Summer 1976): 165–86.**

The American Enlightenment was part of the eighteenth-century movement inaugurating the West's intellectual and cultural assimilation of the scientific revolution. Its philosophical basis was epistemological; criticism and an experimental attitude were its chief ingredients. Intellectual life during the American Revolution combined religious commitment with a sense of public responsibility, so the American Enlightenment was at once religious and political. By grouping its peculiarities under the headings of provincialism, democracy, and nationalism, Meyer shows how the movement's embodiment of humanitarian and liberal ideas involved more than political thought and extended beyond the revolutionary years.

The Enlightenment in America began with British ideas in the early eighteenth century, climaxed with more radical French thinking during the revolutionary years, and concluded by taming radical ideas (in response to the French Revolution) and accommodating enlightened thinking to traditional moral and religious values. By the early nineteenth century, Americans had joined science and faith in an intellectual synthesis that lasted until the First World War. In a new republic, ideas did the work of institutions in giving the people a sense of common purpose and direction, and developing an enlightened public philosophy enabled Americans to use ideas in new, creative ways. As the *Federalist Papers* show, Americans assimilated the Enlightenment pragmatically and employed its ideas to overcome provincialism, bolster democracy, and serve the new national interest. Consequently, radical Enlightenment thought was blurred, mellowed, and made safe for American democracy. By illuminating this process,

Meyer adds to and provides a model for American intellectual history. [J.G.M.-y]

Michaelsen, Robert S. "Americanization: Sacred or Profane Phenomenon?" In *New Theology* 9, edited by Martin E. Marty and Dean G. Peerman, pp. 91–106. New York: Macmillan, 1972.

First appearing in a 1971 issue of the *Reconstructionist*, this article examines the process of Americanization through the categories of Eliade's sacred and profane. Transforming ethnic peoples into "one nation" is a unique process of inculcating a "sacred sense" of American identity and history. Evidence of this process can be found within the modern, secularized consciousness of Americans, in the private and public existential realms.

The concept of the "new world" has an eschatological element in that it promises a new epoch, a new human nature, a fulfillment of aspirations, a new Eden. Pilgrimage to this new world involves a separation from the old and refashioning a new identity through appropriating a new "past." In this process, the second generation may become "Yankeeized" as rational, secular citizens as old identities are discarded and the *novus homo seclorum* emerges. Finally, through education, the ethnic past is replaced by an American past in which the historical characters and events of normative American history are appropriated as one's own.

Utilizing Durkheim's concept of society as "the idea which it forms of itself" (p. 101), Michaelson points to the pressure toward sacred peoplehood ushered in by World War I as being critical in shaping a tribal national consciousness. Americanization became a sacred phenomenon excluding ethnic diversity and minorities as unpatriotic divergences. Michaelsen says this monolithic imposition is unhealthy and needs to be replaced by a desacralized and pluralistic view of the nation in which "orthodox Americanism" is left undefined and unimposed in the interests of true democracy. [M.L.S.]

Michaelson, Robert. "Red Man's Religion/White Man's Religious History." *Journal of the American Academy of Religion* 60, no. 4 (December 1983): 667–84.

Robert Michaelsen wrote an article that needed to be written. He surveys the history of writing histories of American religion and demonstrates that most writers of such histories have dealt with the religions of the native American peoples from the perspective of (usually Protestant) Christianity. The native Americans appear chiefly as the object of missionary endeavors and thus are not seen in their own light. He proposes as a thesis that "just as treatment of Native Americans by the Republic is a major litmus test of the American proposition, so attention to Native American religions is one significant test of the adequacy of a comprehensive history of religions in that Republic" (p. 667).

Michaelsen examines history from Robert Baird (1844) (see p. 6) to Sidney Ahlstrom (1972) (see p. 3) and then looks beyond that era to more recent and, in his view, somewhat better works. From Baird to Ahlstrom, Michaelsen's judgment is the same: these treatments of native American religions fail to do them even minimal justice. He then acknowledges those interpreters of American religion who *have* come closer to an adequate treatment: Clebsch (see p. 26), Marty (see pp. 82, 187), Albanese (see p. 4), Bowden (see p. 15), and Gaustad (see pp. 41, 43).

As more data become available, we need an adequate framework for them. The current situation is one of "data in search of a perspective" (p. 676). Michaelsen suggests the concept of *Respublica* as a framework: the notion of pluralism in which diversity is protected and encouraged, while also recognizing the very real commonality that exists. Michaelsen's article should serve as a guide for all interested in the religions of the earliest Americans. [J.M.C.]

Moore, Leroy. "Sidney E. Mead's Understanding of America." *Journal of the American Academy of Religion* **44, no. 1 (March 1976): 133–53.**

This statement presented by Leroy Moore in December 1972 at a joint session of the American Historical Association and the American Society of Church History on the occasion of Professor Mead's forthcoming retirement is the best single summary and analysis of Mead's mind and work anywhere.

Moore expertly summarizes and interrelates Mead's thoughts and work. Always one with an impeccable concern for accuracy and soundness of detail, Mead's writings are given comparable and flattering scrutiny by Moore. In examining Mead's writings, Moore offers not only flattery but also criticism of some omissions from those works resulting in telling an inadequate story that exacerbated tensions between the real and the ideal.

Beyond his concern for historical content and conclusions, Mead was always one to attend to methodological considerations. Moore offers the conclusion that, among Mead's total output of articles, probably one in five is devoted to methodology with its three essential elements: conditionedness, vulnerability, and concern for identity.

Being the consummate historian, beyond both content and methodology, Mead had a flare and taste for style. Befitting Mead's stylishness, Moore selects a metaphor of his own—that of the serpent—to symbolize this trait. Moore concludes by combining this metaphor with the Hindu Nataraja, leaving Mead "with one foot planted on the terra firma of 'deist ideology' and the other poised in midair as it is about to dance humorously over the whirling, whirring world of the late twentieth century" (p. 153). This piece is a substantial and stylish tribute to a brilliant and artistic historian!   [E.A.W.]

Moore, R. Laurence. "Insiders and Outsiders in American Historical Narrative and American History." (AHR Forum) *The American Historical Review* **87, no. 2 (April 1982): 390–423.**

The boundaries of a particular religious mainstream may be broad and fluid but historians distinguish between the people in its central currents and those in side channels and backwaters. By locating the mainstream according to their conceptions of majority and minority groups, historians conceal a multitude of judgments about American socioeconomic structure. In some historians' views, a tiny governing class created the mainstream and the mainstream won by splintering the center viewpoints in ways that nullified threats to the status quo. However, Moore argues that in American religious history, insider and outsider identities are rarely unmixed and the assertion that one is an outsider often implies the opposite and vice versa. Sometimes to be an outsider can really mean, both objectively and figuratively, to stand at the center of American experience.

Noticing outsiders only as agents of change often leads to neglect of such groups, leading to a muddling of the line between historical insiders and outsiders. Moore suggests that perhaps American historians should drop these perspectives in constructing narrative. He asserts that differences between ostensibly antagonistic groups have often been more apparent than real and remain important only if someone affirms their existence and takes them seriously. Moore insists that the study of religion not constrict itself by arbitrary divisions. This thesis, which struck the preliminary note for the author's recently published book *Religious Outsiders and the Making of Americans* (see afterword, p. 223), presents a challenge to those who will be writing religious history.   [V.T.A.]

Moseley, James G. "Culture, Religion and Theology." *Theology Today* **37, no. 3 (October 1980): 315–22.**

One of the current topics of conversation in almost all political, religious, and cultural circles is the alleged crisis of authority, particularly as it affects the place of organized or established religion in the lives of people. The crisis is said to be a spiritual one, in many instances, because of the great difficulty there is in speaking with any ease of the traditional God. Whereas nearly everyone agrees that religion is a necessary factor, those religions that we have among us are suspect for their shallow theologies, political agendas, or ambitious greed. Truth in the ultimate sense is forever elusive.

Moseley reviews some earlier writers, such as Walter Lippman, Daniel Bell, and Arthur Schlesinger, who addressed religion's inability to deliver itself of its contradictions. What Moseley finds is that every age has had its crisis of authority, finding itself in a state of disjunction and in need of a more conscious awareness of its plight. The question is rightly asked, then, if religion is both the answer and the problem, as it has always been, why the quest for a "new" one? The proper course for theology is not to seek for "new" answers or new religions, but rather to inquire how to make the need for religion more compatible with its functions and expressions. Moseley is convinced that the crisis in authority is as much, if not more, a cultural crisis as it is a spiritual one, and one about which religion can do little.   [W.C.O.]

Neuhaus, Richard John. "The War, the Churches and Civil Religion." *The Annals of the American Academy of Political and Social Science* **387 (January 1970): 128–40.**

In this article written during the height of the Vietnam War, Neuhaus discusses the sources of protest and silence within the American churches. A vocal minority of liberal clergy and laypersons succeeded in making the war an unpopular issue among the majority of church members. This occurred, in part, because of published accounts of atrocities that made support unrespectable but was reinforced by the stance of larger denominations (Lutherans and Southern Baptists) that politics and religion should remain separate. For the majority of churches, denominational harmony remained intact because of the creed of political disengagement.

The liberal element that saw the war as an issue was, as in the civil rights movement, bound together more by their cause than by denominational or creedal ties. In Neuhaus's opinion, the result was a distancing of these liberals from the mainstream of church activity.

For Neuhaus the debate over Vietnam is not a conflict between Christianity and government but a function of the dispute between proponents of American civil religion and the Johnson/Nixon administrations that violated its principles. While the power of civil religion in its emphasis upon civil justice is drawn from analogies with the Gospel, liberals neglected the wellsprings of the Christian faith as the source for their indignation. Abandoning traditional ties they failed to engage the consciences and commitment of their denominations in the effort to end the war. [S.C.B.]

Parkinson, Thomas. "When Lilacs Last in the Door-Yard Bloom'd and the American Civil Religion." *The Southern Review* **19, no. 1 (January 1983): 1–16.**

Traditionally, Walt Whitman's renowned poem, "When Lilacs Last in the Door-Yard Bloom'd," has been seen as the poet's elegy to the martyred Lincoln. In this engaging essay, however, Thomas Parkinson argues that the poem is not an elegy—a lament for a fallen individual—but rather "a nocturne for the nation" (p. 3), a song to what Whitman himself described as the "composite, electric, *Democratic Nationality*" (p. 15). As such, Parkinson asserts, it rightly belongs in the canon of the American civil religion along with its other sacred documents, including Lincoln's second inaugural and Jefferson's Declaration of Independence.

By examining the first printed version of "Lilacs" and carefully explicating each section of the poem, the author develops a strong case for his contention that the "self or personality" of which Whitman writes is "a primarily social reality" (p. 6). The poet's intention, therefore, was to give expression to the aggregate democratic nation, not to one man alone; the person lamented is collective, a representation of the land as a whole. Lincoln himself, in fact, is never identified, and the poem's symbols suggest participation in composite, not individual, action.

While Parkinson presents a convincing argument for the collective focus of Whitman's famous poem and clearly demonstrates that his interpretation squares with the poet's overall goal of singing paeans to the democratic land, it is not clear just how "Lilacs" reveals the various doctrinal elements of the civil religion. Still, this intriguing article gives Whitman proper recognition as a prominent formulator of America's public faith. [L.A.H.]

Parsons, Talcott. "Religion in Postindustrial America: The Problem of Secularization." *Social Research* **41, no. 2 (Summer 1974): 193–225.**

Parsons's schematic paradigm of medieval Christianity clarifies connections between alterations in the social and economic structure of society and religious change. The Reformation revolutionized the religious constitution of Europe, preparing the ground for religious pluralism and secularization. Because Protestantism diminished the significance of the sacraments, clerical mediation with divinity was no longer indispensable and the traditional two-tiered religious class structure (clergy-laity) was no longer a given. Participation in corporate Christianity became voluntary, which encouraged both the development of religious pluralism and the privatization of religion. (Parsons suggests that, if Robert Bellah's work is used, American civil religion can be compared to civil religion in post-Revolutionary France.) Post-Reformation European revolutions were as anticlerical, antiaristocratic, and antimonarchical. Marxism presented Europeans with a secular religious option.

As opposed to Marxism, the American commune movement is described as "nontheistic" (p. 211), yet essentially religious. Parsons enumerates problems that make institutionalization of these communes unlikely, but indicates that the commune movement was part of an "expressive revolution" (p. 221) in which Americans seemed to be placing less stress on self interest and more on "affective solidarity" (p. 222).

The primary significance of this discussion for students of American religion is Parsons's suggestion about the process of religious change and his speculation about religious movements of the 1960s and 1970s foreshadowing new forms of American religion.   [J.S.]

Pearson, Samuel C., Jr. "Nature's God: A Reassessment of the Religion of the Founding Fathers." *Religion in Life* 46, no. 2 (Summer 1977): 152–65.

The rational religion of the Founding Fathers needs to be understood in its own terms and in relation to the thought of the Revolutionary era, argues Pearson, rather than in terms of subsequent religious and philosophical movements. The eighteenth-century English thought of Locke, Clarke, and Wollaston—instead of the nineteenth-century American pietism of Dwight and Finney—is the proper context for interpreting the deism of Franklin, Jefferson, and Adams. Pearson argues that the religious rationalism of these three founders of the republic was of a piece with that of the moderate English Enlightenment and with that of liberal Boston Congregationalism and latitudinarian Anglicanism. Ambivalence rather than rejection characterized the views toward Christianity propounded by these cosmopolitan, tolerant thinkers. They helped achieve the separation of church and state, a formidable accomplishment at the end of the eighteenth century. Although their theological contributions were soon muted, their ideas continued to echo in the configuration of beliefs broadly shared by the nation's people and recently interpreted by Robert Bellah and others as America's civil religion. While delivering nothing new or surprising, Pearson's brief essay is a sound starting place for students of the religious history of Revolutionary America. [J.G.M.-y]

Piediscalzi, Nicholas. "Studying Religion in the Public Schools." *Church and State* **34, no. 10 (November 1981): 14–16.**

This brief, yet substantive discussion reviews the "unique history" of the American public school system in relation to religious institutions, paying particular attention to the Jeffersonian idea about the public schools' task of inculcating students in a national democratic faith and morality. Supreme Court decisions dealing with religion and public education are described, and their impact on the curriculum is considered. Also, an approach to the study of religion designed to give students a broad, balanced understanding of the nature and functions of religions in their personal, social and historical lives, and the lives of others is presented.

The reality of genuine religious pluralism led to the midtwentieth-century Supreme Court decisions that declared devotional readings from the Bible and required recitations of prayer unconstitutional, while holding "dismissed-time" programs for religious instruction constitutional. Taken together, *dicta* in these decisions clarify the distinction between (1) indoctrination in specific religions and inculcation of particular moralities, and (2) teaching about religion as a significant dimension of human history. Piediscalzi believes these decisions provide "flexible legal parameters" (p. 15) that make possible effective religious studies programs in public education.

An approach that should help students understand that "pluralism does not necessarily imply relativism" (p. 16) is recommended. Piediscalzi articulates this new approach's goals, which involve analyzing religious phenomena according to canons of empirical investigation while at the same time developing "an empathetic grasp of the world view of the group being studied" (p. 15). [J.S.]

Porterfield, Amanda. "The Religious Roots of American Feminism." *Conversations: A Journal of Women and Religion* **1, no. 3 (Spring 1983): 21–34.**

Describing feminism as "commitment to women's freedom of expression and empowerment" (p. 21), Amanda Porterfield persuasively argues that the American brand of that phenomenon originated in religion. Specifically, she contends that the great wave of feminist activity from the 1830s through the 1850s grew out of the religious enthusiasm of the Second Great Awakening. During that revival, the majority of the most enthusiastic participants were women, who found in their evangelical zeal a chance to express themselves freely, find oneness with their sisters in the faith, and engage in social action.

Religion thus provided American women with a social and theoretical framework for the expression of feminist concerns. Not only did the Awakening offer women "opportunities for life fulfillment" (p. 24), but it also laid the foundations for the development of female community and encouraged freedom of speech—two crucial elements of nineteenth-century feminism. Out of the prayer meetings and benevolent societies generated by the revival evolved the Protestant and Catholic sisterhoods, which empowered women to commit themselves to educational and social involvement. Likewise, according to Porterfield, the women's new freedom to express themselves led to their support of black emancipation, which in turn was a catalyst for ideas about their own lack of freedom.

Porterfield's interpretation provides an interesting glimpse into the reasons why women found empowerment in their religion, and her explanation of the decentralization of feminism after the Civil War is especially compelling. In short, this essay is an important foray into new territory in feminist historiography. [L.A.H.]

Pritchard, Linda K. "The Burned-over District Reconsidered: A Portent of Evolving Religious Pluralism in the United States." *Social Science History* **8, no. 3 (Summer 1984): 243–65.**

Ever since Whitney Cross published *The Burned-over District* in 1950 (see p. 32), historians have viewed the area of western New York of which he wrote as being a unique region. There the fires of the Second Great Awakening apparently burned hotter and had more dramatic results than elsewhere in the nation. Linda K. Pritchard has now reconsidered that renowned area, however, and found reason to question Cross's interpretation. Agreeing that the Burned-over District clearly exhibited "unusual religiosity" (p. 253), Pritchard nonetheless argues against Cross's contention that its religious enthusiasm was unique.

Because Cross traced the cause of western New York's spiritual fervor to "the distinctive combination of Yankee cultural predisposition and new economic imperatives" (p. 244) that prevailed in that area, Pritchard logically examines those particular aspects of the section's experience from a regional and national perspective. Using quantitative techniques, she compares the development of organized religion in the Burned-over District with that in other sections of the country and determines that the scorched counties "had somewhat less, rather than more, organized religion than elsewhere" (p. 246). Likewise in her analysis of the economic aspects of the region, Pritchard finds that the "high level of economic development" (p. 261) in the district heightened its religious trends, a pattern that paralleled the experience of neighboring Ohio River valley counties.

In addition to viewing the Burned-over District from a fresh perspective, this important article demonstrates the value of investigating religious changes in light of larger social transformations, including economic shifts. It also exhibits a successful use of quantification in doing religious history.   [L.A.H.]

Pritchard, Linda K. "Religious Change in Nineteenth-Century America." In *The New Religious Consciousness*, edited by Charles Y. Glock and Robert N. Bellah, pp. 297–330. Berkeley: University of California Press, 1976.

Pritchard seeks to illustrate, through this case study, how the "interaction of religion and society must be analyzed in order to understand the rise of new religious consciousness during any particular time period" (p. 297). She presents demographic data of changes in the larger society and relates that data to the dramatic changes in church membership, during the Second Great Awakening, that were precipitated by challenges to orthodox Calvinist theology and alterations in religious practice and church organization.

Pritchard looks at four stages of religious transformation: (1) a crisis in "established religion" (Pritchard's term) generated by societal changes; (2) the appearance of new theologies and new religious practices precipitating change in existing denominations; (3) new sect development; and (4) the development of "a new established religion which realigned religion and society" (p. 299). In her study, the author classifies the new sectarian movements as regenerative, schismatic, cultic, and quasi-religious. Following an in-depth discussion of the stages of transformation that led to the various sectarian movements, Pritchard examines the similarities between those changes in the nation's religious life with the "contemporary religious upheaval" of the 1970s. As the author states, it was too early at the time of the writing of the article to draw any conclusions about the 1970s, but she asserts that the four stages of religious tranformation can help focus ongoing discussions about religious change. However, based upon her case study and analysis, Pritchard does speculate that "it seems more likely that we are witnessing a new phase in the history of American religion than its demise" (p. 330).   [J.S.]

Reynolds, David S. "The Feminization Controversy: Sexual Stereotypes and the Paradoxes of Piety in Nineteenth Century America." *The New England Quarterly* **53, no. 1 (March 1980): 96–106.**

This essay reviews the argument advanced by Ann Douglas that nineteenth-century fiction and theology celebrated a tenderminded femininity that weakened the vigorous intellectuality associated with Calvinism. Professor Reynolds points to the conflict between this argument and the view held by earlier researchers that nineteenth-century fiction encouraged feminism. He also examines the charge leveled by David Schuyler that Douglas has "invent(ed) a feminine past." Reynolds settles the controversy by defining each of these views as partial truths and by incorporating them within his own view of nineteenth-century American culture. In that view, an ideal of "masculine" willfulness coexisted with an ideal of "feminine" sensitivity in the imaginations of nineteenth-century Americans. Reynolds points out that evangelicals encouraged heroic acts of Christian willfulness and liberal theologians celebrated manliness as well as esthetic receptivity. Even the heroines of sentimental literature combine Arminian vigor with an all-permeating emotional sensitivity. Reynolds concludes that masculine stereotypes were as influential as feminine ones and suggests that these opposing stereotypes balanced and strengthened one another.

Although his thesis is more sketched than definitively presented, it is a compelling one and suggestive for other eras of American culture. An amplified version of Reynolds's thesis might resolve the latent conflict about Puritan culture as to whether it was a bracing, patriarchal form of this-worldly asceticism or a debilitating, feminizing mechanism from which nineteenth-century Arminians were proud to escape, in favor of a view of Puritanism as a combination of opposing stereotypes of masculinity and femininity. [A.P.]

Roth, John K. "Free at Last?: The Pragmatism and Predicament of Black Religious Experience." *American Journal of Theology and Philosophy* **1, no. 1 (1980): 29–36.**

Exploring the question of how black theology can inform contemporary religious consciousness, John Roth examines recent works of William Jones, C. Eric Lincoln, Benjamin Mays, Henry Mitchell, and

J. Deotis Roberts in ways that focus on the pragmatism of black religion and the predicament of black theology. The pragmatism of black religion has allowed blacks to identify their deepest needs and find reassurance, hope, and courage in the face of massive evil. The predicament facing black theology arises from the pragmatic leanings of black religion. Black philosophers of religion "imply that the validity of religious life depends on particular historical outcomes" (p. 33). Confronted with the reality of a history that has yet to be transformed, black theology finds itself encountering the predicament of theodicity. How it resolves this predicament promises to be of great significance in enabling black religion to contribute to the spiritual life of the nation. [C.J.]

Roth, John K., ed. "American Theology After Auschwitz." *American Journal of Theology and Philosophy* **2, no. 3 (September 1981): 81–129.**

As guest editor of this journal issue, John K. Roth argues that American theology now confronts a world in which individuals can imagine themselves in the situation of Adam Czerniakow, the chairman of the Warsaw Jewish Council who negotiated with Nazi officials to obtain food for his people while at the same time following orders to deliver them up to the gas chambers. In various ways, each of the contributors to this journal issue respond to the new modes of human destruction realized in the Holocaust. The diversity of these responses represents the wide-ranging impact of the Holocaust on both Jewish and Christian theologians.

Michael Berenbaum argues that comparing the genocide of the Jews with the extermination of Poles, Gypsies, and Armenians will not dejudaize the Holocaust, as some fear, but will establish the uniqueness of the Jewish experience on solid historical grounds. S. Daniel Breslauer argues that Jews today are faced with the difficult problem of reimagining the covenant at Sinai. He imagines them as survivors who stand in relation to a God who needs their humanity.

Two other essays discuss the meaning of Jewish history for Christians. Paul M. van Buren argues that Christians should understand their apostolic writings as part of Jewish history. Furthermore, the Holocaust has essential significance for Christian theology because Jewish history is the ongoing locus of God's revelation. Stephen T. Davis argues that Christianity is not inherently anti-Semitic, that the Nazis were not Christians, and that Christians and Jews should stand together against institutions that violate human rights and justice. [A.P.]

Sarna, Jonathan. "The American Jewish Response to Nineteenth Century Christian Missions." *The Journal of American History* **68, no. 1 (June 1981): 35–51.**

This article reflects the growing sophistication of research into the relationship between American Protestantism and the new immigrant religions of the nineteenth century. Jonathan Sarna traces the response of Jewish leaders to the aggressive proselytizing campaign of Christian missionaries in the nineteenth century. Organized Protestant efforts to convert the Jews began with the founding of the American Society for Meliorating the Conditions of the Jews in 1820. Sarna discusses three major types of Jewish responses. The first was polemical, with theological defenses of the Hebrew Bible and tributes to the historical Jewish culture and its successful adaptation to the modern American society. The second type of response was passive resistance, whereby Jewish community members expressed their outrage, mostly in the Jewish press, at the attempted Protestant subversion of their religion and culture.

Sarna makes his biggest contribution to American religious history with his discussion of the third type of Jewish response. He suggests that active resistance occurred when Jews organized new structures within their own communities, often using characteristic Protestant methods and tactics, which made Christian alternatives unnecessary. Sarna describes the subsequent scores of Jewish religious schools, hospitals, newspapers, synagogues, and social service agencies in terms of "functional alternatives" to Protestant missionary activities. The result was a Jewish community organized around the same social institutions as the dominant Protestant community, but one which fostered a distinctive Jewish identity.   [L.K.P.]

Sarna, Jonathan D. "Anti-Semitism and American History." *Commentary* **71, no. 3 (March 1981): 42–47.**

The historiography of anti-Semitism makes clear that idyllic portraits of tolerance and acceptance of Jews in America omitted much ugliness and violence. In this essay, Sarna traces this tendency by reviewing some literature from the late 1800s and then reflects on changes in presenting Jewish history in the 1960s and 1970s.

Those early "cheery" portrayals of the American situation for Jews were part of a larger, generally accepted portrait of American exceptionalism. Such studies demonstrated the success and degree of prominence attained by American Jews and pictured late nineteenth- and early twentieth-century anti-Semitism as a passing aberration, not characteristic of American culture.

That this was an erroneous reading of Jewish history in America became clear in the 1960s and 1970s when theories of American exceptionalism were challenged. The search for the nation's "underside" revealed that anti-Semitism was present in American culture from the beginning. Positive comparisons between Europe and America that made this nation a place where Jews were welcomed were questioned. Emphasis on the Holocaust generated works asking whether "it" could happen here. As a result, the idyllic picture of Jewish experience in America has been replaced with a bleak one. Sarna calls for more balanced treatment, pointing out that in America Jews fought anti-Semitism freely; that anti-Semitism is foreign to American ideals, if not practice; and that American politics works against anti-Semitism. [J.S.]

Sarna, Jonathan D. "The Great American Jewish Awakening." *Midstream* **28, no. 8 (October 1982): 30–34.**

Turning his attention to the current scene, historian Jonathan Sarna places the revival of interest in tradition and ritual in American Judaism in historical context. He notes that emphasis on Jewish education, stress on religious ceremonies, and celebrations of Jewish culture extend across all major forms of Judaism in America, signaling a revitalization of the tradition. Although this essay provides enough description to suggest the movement's intensity, its main purpose is to explore the causes for this *teshuva* movement.

The "most visible component" of Jewish revival are the *baale teshuva*, who exemplify the Jewish turn away from secularism. Like "born-again Christians," some of these Jews seem to be returning to the tradition as a refuge from the complexities of modern life, while others are on a spiritual quest leading to wholehearted commitment and a full-scale embracing of Judaism from the dual perspectives of belief and behavior. At times, as in the instance of the Lubavitch movement, the depth of commitment leads to soliciting like levels of commitment from other Jews.

Sarna recognizes that identifying reasons for this complicated development is not easy, but he suggests two primary lines of inquiry: the renewal movement as a "a reaction to liberalism" (p. 32) and as "a search for meaning, direction, and truth" (p. 33). Finally, the author places this movement within the context of the "assimilationism/traditionalism" (p. 33) cycle, which he believes has characterized the Jewish experience in America. If this interpretation is correct, this revitalization of the Jewish tradition may give way in a reasonably short period to a new turn toward secularism. [J.S.]

Sarna, Jonathan D. "Jews, the Moral Majority, and American Tradition." *Journal of Reform Judaism* **29, no. 2 (Spring 1982): 1–9.**

This valuable little article places perspective not only on the concerns of its title, but also on the whole matter of sectarianism of any stripe as it confronts opposing views in the pluralistic national political and social scene. The ways in which Sarna suggests Jews deal with the Moral Majority are, in essence, principles by which any minority group can confront challenges, making this article useful far beyond its intended scope.

Within its context and purposes, the article is succinct, rational, and historically interesting and helpful. One is struck by the advantage Jews have by their very antiquity. "Moral Majorities" come and go in many guises, and Jews have outlasted them all. Sarna offers techniques for coping with the Moral Majority that are applicable to other challenges.

In particular, Sarna suggests these appropriate Jewish responses: (1) "when rights conflict we must search for balance; absolutist claims on any side violate justice and engender hatred"; (2) "we ought to reexamine our policies on church-state issues . . . believers and nonbelievers both deserve fairhanded treatment"; (3) "we must carefully separate issues of broad Jewish concern from issues that narrowly concern Jewish liberals"; and (4) "we must be governed by the fact that it [the Moral Majority] is . . . a legitimate political undertaking" (p. 7). Sarna concludes that "viewed in this context, the Moral Majority becomes considerably less frightening" (p. 8).

Sarna has given persons from all religious stances some notion of ways to come to grips with questions of diversity, pluralism, and interfaith relations that arise from time to time.   [W.C.O.]

Schlesinger, Arthur M., Jr. "America: Experiment or Destiny." *The American Historical Review* **82, no. 3 (June 1977): 505–522.**

Invited to participate in bicentennial reflections, Schlesinger juxtaposed basic American traits with his usual erudition and conceptual power. He discussed two broad perceptions of the nation, two divergent outlooks that have characterized much of American culture. One theme was that of experimentation. Whether derived from a Calvinist emphasis that every epoch is under God's judgment or from a Classicist knowledge that republics can be corrupted, this viewpoint knew that American life was fraught with risk and problematic in outcome.

Alongside and developing from this rather unpretentious attitude were optimistic convictions about a glorious destiny for God's elect, a sacred mission for the redeemer nation. Schlesinger explains these latter convictions as a narcissistic withdrawal from historical consciousness and the result of political and economic isolation. In contemporary times, he sees less room for such delusions and hopes that a return to the first attitude will correct the excesses of overweening self-congratulation. [H.W.B.]

Schneider, Mary L. "A Catholic Perspective on American Civil Religion." In *America in Theological Perspective*, edited by Thomas McFadden, pp. 123–39. New York: Seabury Press, 1976.

The typologies of American civil religion have a decidedly Protestant content. Schneider argues that the emphasis by Bellah, Ahlstrom, Marty, and others on America as the new Israel needs to be balanced by a consideration of the Catholic tradition concerning the role of nationhood within the faith. A Protestant interpretation of American civil religion easily overlooks nativism, imperialism, racism, and genocide in its focus upon biblical covenant as national destiny. Catholics too often retreat into defense upon the same grounds when charged with double loyalties to the nation and a foreign church.

Schneider contends that an appraisal of Aquinas's hierarchy of political and spiritual institutions and Catholic natural theology can help illuminate civil religion in its more universal meaning. Unfortunately, her discussion of Aquinas's use of *religio* and *pietas* is too brief to be more than suggestive. But her delineation of natural theology as a function of will could be of much use in the debate. Yet natural theology brings into the discussion the limits of reason in the eyes of faith.

Schneider is not the first Catholic to bring this source to our attention. John Courtney Murray's *We Hold These Truths* (see p. 100) is still relevant, and in the nineteenth century, the journalist Orestes Brownson constantly advocated the tenets of natural theology to a readership caught in the fever of Protestant majoritarianism and nativist inclinations. [S.C.B.]

Scott, Nathan A., Jr. "New Heav'ns, New Earth—The Landscape of Contemporary Apocalypse." *Journal of Religion* 53, no. 1 (January 1973): 1–35.

Unlike the skepticism, irony, flexibility, and modulation of the 1950s, the recent American scene has witnessed, beneath shrillness and bedlam, a hope for release from the contingent duties of historical life. Our era, Scott argues, is inebriated by apocalyptic dreams—deep desires to view actual existence in the light of some great final transformation. By analyzing early extracanonical Jewish apocalypticism, Scott shows the logic in secular apocalyptic hopes for removal from the dehumanized, hyperorganized society of contemporary America. Yet by contrasting ancient apocalyptic with the historical realism of the prophetic tradition, Scott also demonstrates that our time requires the renewal of the critical work begun by thinkers such as Reinhold Niebuhr, Lionel Trilling, and Paul Tillich.

Scott analyzes the unbridled optimism of such current apocalypticists as Charles Reich, R. D. Laing, Norman Brown, and Marshal McLuhan and the subjectivity and antinomianism presaged by Phillip Rieff. Scott's range of argument is as vast as his insight is trenchant. After reviewing the work of such writers as Heller, Barth, Pynchon, Baldwin, and Burroughs—and referring with instructive accuracy to the creative and critical work of hosts of others—Scott reappraises Blakes's judgment that "the tygers of wrath are wiser than the horses of instruction" (p. 31), concluding that theology today must seek grounds for the courage and strength of endurance at the heart of the Christian tradition. Although the 1980s may require more ballast from the other side of the cultural scale, Scott's sure sense of balance shows brilliantly how cultural analysis can empower a theological revision of America.   [J.G.M.-y]

Sittler, J. "Space and Time in American Religious Experience." *Interpretation* 30, no. 1 (January 1976): 44–51.

In this article Sittler addresses the question of how an American theology and culture historically shaped by openness of movement in space can reformulate its self-understanding to include an historical or temporal sensitivity. No longer can issues be resolved simply by moving to a different place. The American "spirit" has never until recently had to come to terms with boundaries, limits, and ending; space constituted the field of pragmatic operations. Now the questions of time—tragedy, historical consciousness, death, mutability, limitation—have come to the fore.

The theologian and other Americans are called on to confront new tasks, to deal with political, environmental, and justice issues in a setting where the old answers will not wash. One resource that Sittler identifies is the thought of Reinhold Niebuhr who "fused a way of witnessing to the power of the reality of grace, given and received within historical actuality" (p. 51). Attention to the formulation of a theology of grace and order is needed. In the opinion of many, dealing with grace and order in strictly temporal terms would only lead to different mistakes; any adequate American theology and ethics must comprehend both the temporal and spatial dimensions of human experience.   [L.S.J.]

Smith, Timothy L. "Religion and Ethnicity in America." *The American Historical Review* **83, no. 5 (December 1978): 1155–85.**

This essay originated as one of six addresses on "The American Experience" delivered at the annual meeting of the American Historial Association in Washington, D. C., during the 1976 bicentennial.

Historians long believed that ethnicity was a synonym for nationality and that religious and ethnic sentiments of immigrant minorities were anachronisms that had to give way to modernization and the formation of political associations by individuals of "similar market orientation." In the late 1960s, the resurgence of interest in ethnicity in a flood of new sociological, anthropological, and social history studies and in the reconstruction of Jewish and Christian theology challenged this assumption. However, much of the new ethnic studies literature focused on "racial" minorities whose ethno-religious system has been interpreted as a mechanism for sustaining sociopolitical objectives. Religious institutions of Jews, Catholics, and immigrant Protestants are treated as dysfunctional or arcane.

This essay redresses this imbalance by focusing on the role of religion among "white ethnics." In the United States, European immigrants regrouped into larger aggregations that preserved and revised inherited patterns of language, religion, and culture. Migration and resettlement altered the relationship between faith and ethnicity. Uprooting, migration, resettlement, and community building became a theologizing experience rather than the secularizing process some historians have pictured. We are now at a point where anthropological, sociological, psychological, and historical perspectives can coalesce into a more fruitful discussion of the complex relationship between religion and ethnicity.   [W.D.D.]

Smith, Timothy L. "Righteousness and Hope: Christian Holiness and the Millennial Vision in America, 1800–1900." *American Quarterly* **31, no. 1 (Spring 1979): 21–45.**

American history has been marked by hopes for an inauguration of Christ's rule on earth. In the nineteenth century the spread of religious awakenings convinced many that the Spirit of the Lord was ushering in the millennium through the hallowing of America. Biblical ideals of righteousness and sanctification became pervasive in Jacksonian America and remained normative to the end of the century. The conviction that grace alone purified the inner spirit and made possible the creation of the righteous society, and not simply popular or romantic idealism, sparked movements for foreign and home missions and for a variety of moral crusades. Millennialism and perfectionism combined to make social radicals out of Christians by compelling them to recognize that the triumph of God's justice and love in society required the sanctification of individuals.

Smith argues that the civil religion operative in American culture came to rest not primarily on the faith awakened by the Enlightenment in one's moral powers, but on revivalistic, reform-minded, millennialistic Christianity. The law of holiness and freedom called citizens to moral action to rid the nation of injustice, while perfectionism preserved the faith from prostitution to the political and economic interests. Unlike the contemporary Charismatic movement, the emergence of nineteenth-century Pentecostalism did not diminish social concern. The sense of divine and human cooperation in determination of moral destiny of persons and society held Judaism and Christianity back from the path of esoteric mysticism on one side and that of pragmatic humanism on the other. [W.D.D.]

Smylie, James H. "The President as Republican Prophet and King: Clerical Reflections on the Death of Washington." *Journal of Church and State* **18, no. 2 (Spring 1976): 233–52.**

Although the framers of the Constitution delineated the formal and legal structure of the American presidential office, in actuality a host of American clergy informally shaped the office by casting over George Washington "a religious, historical, and moral aura" (p. 234) that fixed a significant and lasting ideal image of the American presidency in the popular mind. At the occasion of the first president's death, clergy affirmed Americans' confidence in the new constitutional system and commended the fallen leader's contribution as a worthy model and heroic ideal for the guidance of his successors in that calling.

The above are conclusions drawn from Smylie's study based on a careful analysis of fifty sermons, selected from among the 440 extant eulogies delivered at the time of the first president's death in 1799. Washington was eulogized in Greek and Roman contexts, but more often in biblical archetypes such as Moses, David, and Joshua. In the process of eulogizing Washington, these clergy used the Bible to legitimate the presidential office.

Smylie asserts that the nation's clergy turned Washington into an "ideal type" but not an "idol," and this in turn allowed for Washington's image to be a light by which his successors, even to the present, might be examined rather than escape public scrutiny.   [E.A.W.]

Smylie, James H. "Testing the Spirit in the American Context: Great Awakenings, Pentecostalism and the Charismatic Movement." *Interpretation* **33, no. 1 (January 1979): 32–46.**

This article represents an expression of the mildly supportive appraisal by mainline Christian spokespersons of the Charismatic movement, which took "holy-roller" religion, complete with speaking-in-unknown-tongues, into the older Protestant and Roman Catholic churches and spread to become a worldwide revival. In this piece, Smylie assesses the potential assets and problems in the revival that so concerned Christians in the 1970s. Based upon knowledge of previous large-scale revival movements, which were largely devoid of charismatic phenomena, he advocates the common standard of confirming personal spiritual experience as a true movement of the Holy Spirit by its resultant expression through public acts of love and service. He is most fearful of the revival becoming just another expression of American individualism and being forgetful of the corporate context of Christian faith. He is encouraged by the element of transcendence of denominational barriers among Charismatics and an increasing appreciation of new and different religious experiences among the great body of church members.   [J.G.M.-n]

Sontag, Frederick. "The Religious Origins of the American Dream." *American Journal of Theology and Philosophy* **2, no. 2 (May 1981): 67–78.**

Vestiges from a uniquely religious past still influence contemporary America. Because their religious origins have largely been forgotten, Sontag argues, these residual forces confuse modern Americans. So he prescribes "a national religious psychoanalysis" in order to "reconstruct a forgotten but still significant past experience" (p. 67) and outlines the first steps of cultural reexamination.

The dream began with transplanted Reformation Protestantism and a special sense of mission, acquired a distinctive balance of tolerance and repression, and was individualized in the revivals that patterned American expectations for repentance, reform, and renewal. Education at home and missionary activity abroad promulgated religious idealism. Then material goals joined religious motivation; "and the nation only suffers when one outbalances the other" (p. 73).

When the religious component of the dream is lost, "Americans wander aimlessly" (p. 73), continuing an "essentially religious ritual of confessing their guilt" (p. 74). Alexander Solzhenitsyn's view of the West suggests to Sontag that "the core problem today may be that evil has returned to the heart of human affairs, but the humanistic and optimistic outlook we sustained for Christianity does not know how to cope with this" (p. 75). Yet Sontag hopes that the strong American religious-utopian drive will draw new forms of religion from the demise of traditional faith, contending that "a critical reappraisal of our national goals involves becoming clear about the religious roots of this dream and our primal drive toward it" (p. 78) and showing how vital an understanding of American religious history is for a satisfying present and a promising American future.   [J.G.M.-y]

Stout, Harry S. "Religion, Communication, and the Ideological Origins of the American Revolution." *William and Mary Quarterly* **34, no. 4 (October 1977): 519–41.**

This short but densely written and synthetic essay sheds as much light on twentieth-century historiography of the Great Awakening and the American Revolution as on eighteenth-century culture itself.

Stout begins with an argument for viewing religion as a prime force in the coming of the American Revolution and defends his position against secular interpreters who emphasize political ideologies and Enlightenment culture. Stout argues that religious ideas and sentiments that came out of the Great Awakening, such as the emphasis on individual conversion and the distrust of authority, were as important for the style of their presentation as for their content. This religious revolution was spread to a largely illiterate public through a "rhetoric of sensation" (p. 528) that was distinctively oral rather than written. Paradoxically, Stout offers a sophisticated argument for the power of simplicity: revivalist preachers shunned classical learning and refinement and spoke rather than wrote to the religiously minded masses in colonial America, yet the egalitarian appeal of their rhetoric had a greater and more widespread influence than any articulate essay every could.

Stout concludes with the sound and comprehensive theory that "two ideological explosions"—one religious and one secular, one oral and unsophisticated and one written and polished—"propelled the colonies into a new nation" (p. 538). These two styles both contributed to the revolutionary rebellion for independence from England and to the social revolution in democratic America. A large part of the success of the American Revolution lay in its demonstration that the two ideologies "could work in concert" (p. 538); and the success of Stout's essay lies in his ability to synthesize two schools of interpretation. Stout provides an important explanation of how the ideas of the revolution gained wide popular appeal through the rhetorical revolutions of religious revivalism. [P.J.C.]

Sturm, Douglas. "A Critique of American Protestant Social and Political Thought." *The Journal of Politics* **26, no. 4 (November 1964): 896–913.**

The "Protestant principle" holds that the only absolutes are God as divine being and the proposition that God is the sole absolute. Sturm directs attention to the work of Paul Tillich, Reinhold Niebuhr, H. Richard Niebuhr, and Joseph Sittler in which this principle leads to social and political philosophies that are pragmatic, relativist, and contextualist. He then outlines the major questions with which an adequate social and political philosophy must be concerned. Presented here as framed by Aristotle, these questions are treated as the basis for a typology that sets forth the four possible types of social and political philosophies. Sturm labels them finalistic, pragmatic, formalistic, and situational. In a third section, Sturm shows that all four types are represented in the history of Christian social and political thought. He asserts that "the pragmatic and the situationalist types prevail in contemporary American Protestantism" (p. 911).

A summary of the fundamental affirmations of Christian theology (God is creator, man *(sic)* is made in the image of God, but is fallen; and God is redeemer) lead to Sturm's conclusion that since the doctrine of redemption deals with "the proper destiny" (p. 913) of persons and of their "ultimate end and final purpose" (p. 912), it is the doctrine of central concern. From this he argues that pragmatic, formalistic, and situationalist political and social philosophies are deficient or inadequate. Only the finalistic type can take account of the concern of Christian theology with the proper destiny of humanity and the fulfillment of the essential nature of people. [J.S.]

Sturm, Douglas. "American Legal Realism and the Covenantal Myth: World Views in the Practice of Law." *Mercer Law Review* **31, no. 2 (Winter 1980): 487–508.**

Sturm challenges the understanding of the world that characterizes "legal realism" in America by confronting it with that "relational" conception of life founded in Western culture in the covenant-myth of Judeo-Christian traditions. American legal realism, articulated for Sturm mainly by Karl Llewellyn, is pragmatic in theory, behaviorist in practice, utilitarian in effect. Faced with its own "situational" character, it reaches the limits of its adequacy in the question of the relationship of law and morality.

The covenant-myth proposes another reality, in which the work of law is dialectical in theory, associational in practice, communitarian in effect; it drives out of lived experience toward the common good. In jurisprudence, modern America unfortunately neglects the world view implicit in this form of religious sensibility, perhaps because it seems anachronistic. But in contemporary religious inquiry like that of Bernard Meland, Sturm argues, one finds the critical means for restoring modern access to the covenant idea, both as it illumines a deeper "realism" and as it might open to the law a keener sense of the context of *praxis* and the meaning of justice. [R.A.S.]

Sturm, Douglas. "Politics and Divinity: Three Approaches in American Political Science." *Thought: A Journal of Culture and Idea* **52, no. 207 (December 1977): 333–65.**

Douglas Sturm argues that insights of various schools of political science could be more acute if they would take into account the "divine alternative." Religious reflection on human experience needs to be factored into any systematic account of political life. Sturm details the perspectives, procedures, political orientations, and implications for viewing the "divine alternative" of three dominant views: behavioralism, traditionalism, and post-behavioralism. Each weighs differently the value of taking religion seriously, and each corresponds to a particular type of philosophy of religion.

Behavioralism values "explanation without evaluation and prediction without prescription" (p. 340) and factors out religious bases of human behavior that weaken analytic accuracy. Traditionalism, which traces political life to classical Western cultural roots, is sensitive to the individual search for God; but it does not factor out the political significance of this search. Post-behavioralism prizes relevance and action.

According to Sturm, the study of political science is part of the process of identifying and correcting social injustice with the implicit theological concern being the nature of the self interacting with the world. God is not the First Cause or the ground of being but is met in worldly struggles. Politics and religion are ways of interacting with the world, and Sturm argues that each school should take account of the "divine alternative." However, only religion seems ready to do so. [E.T.L.]

Suderman, Elmer F. "The Mennonite Community and the Pacifist Character in American Literature." *Mennonite Life* **34, no. 1 (March 1979): 8–15.**

Peter Epp's novel *Erloesung;* Rudy Wiebe's novel *Peace Shall Destroy Many;* Ken Reed's novel *Mennonite Soldier;* James Juhnke's and Harold Moyer's musical play *The Blowing and the Bending;* Warren Kliewer's play *The Beserkers;* and Lee Brackett's novel *The Long Tomorrow* are all about Mennonite communities. All except Brackett's are by birthright Mennonites. Suderman examines the novels for the ways war and its violent mentality affect the characters and the communities in which they live.

In general, the author concludes, the Mennonite communities are unable to escape the devastating and tragic effects of war. Pacifist convictions are of little help in holding the community together. Evil lies as much in the hearts of Mennonites as in the world they seek to escape.

In these works, the characters as well as the communities are flawed. Suderman laments the weak depiction of peace and calls for a vision of peace in which life is lived not only in contentment but with vigor, compassion, and conflict.

This article, written by a Mennonite scholar, reflects the Mennonite communities belief structures and contributes to our understanding of a part of the American society that has always been at odds with certain national practices. Even though this article covers a small segment of American society and examines a rather narrow field of interest, it points to aspects of that society that should be understood by all and to ways in which literature is utilized to present those understandings.   [M.K.T.]

Suderman, Elmer F. "Religion in the Popular American Novel 1870–1900." *Journal of Popular Culture* **9, no. 4 (Spring 1976): 1003–9.**

After reading 150 novels from this period for his Ph.D. thesis, the author concludes that popular religious novels are optimistic, sentimental, and dull—reflecting the society for which they were written.

Prominent examples, cited by the author, are Eggleston's *Hoosier School Master,* Wallace's *Ben Hur,* and Sheldon's *In His Steps.* All reflect optimism about the United States, the possibility of progress, world order, God, and humankind.

To these novelists, the United States is a Christian nation, and any Christian ought to be proud to be alive in it. Seeing only hope, the novelists naturally turned their back on despair. With emphasis on the goodness of humankind and the generosity of God, the novels were naturally sentimental. Feeling, not reason, was stressed.

The author concludes that the novels were dull because they lacked craft and depended on a traditional plot formula of love triumphant. Though presumably religious, the novels showed religion only incidental to plot and theme, and there were not great religious characters. This article provides an example of a way to understand society at a certain period as manifested in its literature and points to ways in which other periods of literature might be examined.   [M.K.T.]

"Tocqueville's Religion: An Exchange." *Political Theory* **8, no. 1 (February 1980): 9–38.**

If Tocqueville's "fifth dimension" is the religious one, then Cushing Strout's article on "Tocqueville and Republican Religion: Revisiting the Visitor" (pp. 9–26) and Peter Dennis Bathory's "Tocqueville on Citizenship: A Response to Strout" (pp. 27–37) are a dialogue on American civil religion.

Strout proposes a "fifth dimension" for Tocqueville's classic *Democracy in America* (see p. 127) be added to the four different images that he has presented to Americans of different eras, according to Robert Nisbet. He asserts that views of Tocqueville have evolved from that of "herald of American progress" to "prophet of totalitarianism," to "anatomist of affluence and alientation," to "ambivalent analyst of equality as boon and bane of modernity" (p. 9). To these four, Strout adds that of religious commentator and apologist. After all, says Strout, it was the country's religious atmosphere that was not only the "first thing" that struck him on his arrival in America but was the most novel ingredient in the new nation. That dimension allied with republicanism contributed to Tocqueville's vision of how nations are guided toward a stable, liberal form of constitutional democracy.

Bathory agrees with Strout's idea of making religion Tocqueville's "fifth dimension" and that it is fundamental to the health of republican institutions and for public morality. He raises provocative thoughts about Strout's thinking on Tocqueville as it relates to contemporary life and presents his own ideas about those things which are necessary for civil and moral freedom. The juxtaposition of these two articles provides a forum for readers to launch into their own dialogues on the importance of religion in American life.   [E.A.W.]

Whitfield, Stephen J. "One Nation Under God: The Rise of the Religious Right." *The Virginia Quarterly Review* **58, no. 4 (Autumn 1982): 557–74.**

In this sprightly essay, Stephen J. Whitfield traces the historical roots of the new religious right to the anti-Catholic Nativism of the nineteenth century. In Whitfield's view, Nativist-born religious conservatism has been a defensive and divided movement since its inception and even in its heyday in the 1920s. It has been increasingly beleaguered since the Roosevelt era, when Supreme Court justices reinterpreted the Constitution according to liberal views of human rights. Although in our own day the religious right has abandoned its original anti-Catholicism and enlarged its fold to include conservative Catholics, Whitfield believes it is still a minority protest movement working against the liberal principles of toleration and pluralism that are deeply and happily entrenched in American culture.

In Whitfield's view, religious conservatives have every right to change social institutions by persuasion. For example, they would act in accord with the Constitution if they succeeded in changing the popularity ratings on which television programming are based by urging Americans not to watch certain programs. But they work against the American philosophy of government when they seek to impose their morality on others, as in their efforts to remove certain books from public libraries or to deny abortion or equal rights to women.

This essay is a paragon of a liberal answer to the new religious Right. But its strengths as a liberal essay prevent it from being a definitive discussion of American religious conservatism. Such discussion would explore why conservatives themselves are more likely to associate the origin of their movement with Puritanism than with Nativism and more likely to find the truest articulation of American values in eras other than the Roosevelt one.   [A.P.]

Wilson, Charles Reagan. "American Heavens: Apollo and the Civil Religion." *Journal of Church and State* **26, no. 2 (Spring 1984): 209–26.**

Science and technology have been of fundamental importance in Americans' conceptions of identity and mission, yet discussions of American civil religion have not paid attention to this relationship. Elements of the civil religious tradition were at work, indeed often in tension, in the official rhetoric and public perceptions of the American space program of the 1960s. "Prophetic" critics of the space program questioned its expense, but more popular "priestly" figures celebrated a rebirth of American destiny "achieved through science and technology" (p. 212). Nationalistic tendencies existed in tension with internationalist impulses.

New scientific-technocratic heroes celebrated the American-led "new age of Enlightenment." Astronauts were celebrated as potential (and occasionally actual) martyrs, heroes who were products of the American system but whose work was universal in its implications. The astronauts used religious language to convey their universalistic message of hope for a renewed earth. Artifacts from both the United States and other countries were taken to the moon, and religious leaders on earth praised the "millennial event." Wilson suggests that a scientific-technocratic civil religion may inevitably broaden the narrowness of national religion, and eventually prove to be the basis of the universal civil religious tradition for which Robert Bellah hoped.   [E.T.L.]

Wilson, Charles Reagan. "The Religion of the Lost Cause: Ritual and the Organization of the Southern Civil Religion, 1865–1920." *Journal of Southern History* **46, no. 2 (May 1980): 219–38.**

Charles Wilson's study of the religion of the Lost Cause in the American South points out the plurality of civil religious traditions in the nation. Wilson argues that southern defeat in the Civil War (a holy cause) confronted southerners with a crisis of identity, and this crisis was managed through the mythologies, rituals, and institutions of a distinct civil religious tradition born out of Confererate defeat.

Canonization of Confederate heroes, iconography, sacred relics, and hymnody all contributed to the tragic heroism of Lost Cause memories. Ritual activity (fast days, Confederate Memorial Day, funerals of wartime heroes, and dedication of monuments) celebrated and commemorated the continuing righteousness of the cause, despite the failure of arms. Institutions such as veterans groups, Christian churches, and public schools also enshrined the righteousness of the Confederate cause. Several colleges ("institutional shrines") and in particular private military academies added to the institutional strength of this civil religious tradition.

Wilson carefully articulates the existence and power of a distinct religious tradition that has shaped the identity of the postwar South.   [E.T.L.]

Witheridge, David E. "No Freedom of Religion for American Indians." *Journal of Church and State* **18, no. 1 (Winter 1976): 5–19.**

From the arrival of whites in America to 1976, the author documents that native Americans have never had freedom of worship. The author chose the American bicentennial as a time to reflect on this conclusion because this was a time to celebrate freedoms, such as that of freedom to worship.

Witheridge traces this oppression from colonial days, when he asserts the colonists never intended to allow religious freedom, to later periods, when partnerships between government and religious bodies established Christian schools joined lay Christians to policy-making groups and, generally, made those religious bodies representatives of the government.

The author states that the removal of subsidies for Christian schools did not bring about religious freedom for the native Americans. He contends that ambiguity about freedom of religion to native Americans is exacerbated by the interpretation of the Fourteenth Amendment, which grants freedom of religion specifically to the states—reservations are not states.

Even though this article was written with an eye to the American bicentennial celebration, its material is relevant for study at any time as the article provides some insight into the interaction between church and state and the ways in which policy was formed from that special relationship that affected a people. [M.K.T.]

Afterword

Several books have been published in the period between the compilation of the analysis in this volume and the actual publication date. Representative examples of works that have appeared during this period are highlighted here.

The Brookings Institution has published a volume entitled *Religion in American Public Life* by A. James Reichley, which focuses largely on the currents of religious and social-political-economic thought in the United States from the seventeenth century to the present. Another publication with the title *Religion in America Today*, edited by Wade Clark Roof, was published in late 1985 by Sage Publications. This work concentrates on major American religious trends in the mid-1980s. Professor Roof has edited a collection of essays in which he attempts to put into perspective the continuities and changes within institutional religious traditions, as well as in the public faith. One more general book that is an appropriate addition to this bibliography is *Religion and American Public Life: Interpretations and Explorations* edited by Robin M. Lovin. This collection of essays looks at religion in America's past and its place in the future of American life.

Professor Roof and a colleague, William McKinney, produced a book entitled *American Mainline Religion: Its Changing Shape and Future*, which examines the changes in America's social and cultural life since the 1960s and the influences those changes have had on the religious "landscape." Although this book does not talk specifically about religion outside the institutional structures, it does present insights into the forces that will shape those institutions and in turn will have an impact on the larger social and cultural forces in American life.

Another publication that examines the various components of the American religious community and the tensions that have manifested themselves between Jews and Christians, Protestants and Catholics, liberals and conservatives is an edited work by Robert N. Bellah and Frederick E. Greenspahn called *Uncivil Religion: Interreligious Hostility in America.* The underlying thesis for this volume of essays is that "uncivil religion" breaks the boundaries that have maintained the religious order in American society and culture. In examining the many ways in which boundaries and identities between and among religious groups have been muddied, the authors present insights into larger cultural and social questions related to life in America.

Charles Mabee's *Reimagining America: A Theological Critique of the American Mythos and Biblical Hermeneutics* is the first of a series to be published by Mercer University Press called "Studies in American Biblical Hermeneutics." As the author states in his introduction, this first book serves to introduce the series and to "inaugurate an explicitly public reading of the Bible by addressing it in the context of the common American cultural experience." Professor Mabee seeks to promote interdisciplinary conversations "with the Bible as the formative text of the American experience" (p. xi). He examines the dialogue, as he sees it, between the Bible and the American self by juxtaposing discussion of biblical themes with those in various secular works such as *Moby Dick, Poor Richard's Almanack,* and many others. A related piece looking at questions of the religious roots of American cultural experiences is *Wilderness Lost: The Religious Origins of the American Mind* by David R. Williams. As a reviewer said, Williams "shows how a wilderness mentality is persistently at the edge of American consciousness" (*The Christian Century,* 14 October 1987). Marcus Singer has edited a volume called *American Philosophy,* which includes a collection of essays from philosophers and historians who are seeking to pinpoint exactly what was American about American philosophy. In addition to essays examining specific philosophers, others look at legal and constitutional philosophy in America

Other new works address the church/state theme. One book that has received a great deal of attention is William Lee Miller's *First Liberty: Religion and the American Republic.* Miller examines the deliberations the Founding Fathers, particularly James Madison, engaged in when drafting various documents concerning the relation of the church and the state leading up to the formulation of the Constitution. Specific questions about church/state issues in America are examined in a volume called *Religion and the State: Essays in Honor of Leo Pfeffer,* edited by James Wood, Jr. The essays include scholarly and historical ones as well as those addressing policy questions with the views of all essayists reflecting the thought of Pfeffer, who was a "strict separationist." Another related volume is *The Bible in American Law, Politics and Religion* edited by James Turner Johnson, which contains essays looking at the relationship between the Bible and politics and political rhetoric in America. This volume, which is one of the volumes in the Society of Biblical Literature series on "The Bible in American Culture," presents not only the historical view of the Bible's role in the democratic process, but also illustrates the continuing evolution of that role. A thematically related work is a collection of essays in *Civil Religion and Political Theology* edited by Leroy S. Rouner. Some of the works address the theme of American religion and politics, whereas others look at specific "minority" theologies within the context of the general theme. Others deal with civil religion and the concept of "home" and the idea of a "common religion."

A new volume that leads to deeper understandings of an important theological viewpoint and geographical region is Harry S. Stout's *New England Soul.* Stout examines the sermons of numerous New England preachers and illustrates the powerful reach of the pulpit during the Puritan era. Other recent works that look at early American religious life are *Visionary Republic: Millennial Themes in American Thought, 1756–1800* by Ruth Bloch and *The Puritans in America: A Narrative Anthology* edited by Alan Heimert and Andrew Delbanco. The first appraises the ways in which preachers and others dealt with the idea of America as a redeemer nation-to-be by looking not only at clerical literature, but also at secular literature of the time. The second, an anthology, is compiled in such a way as to reflect shifting scenes and issues from the 1620s to the early eighteenth century.

Martin Marty has produced two more books that are relevant to the interests reflected in the selections in this volume. *Religion and Republic: The American Circumstance* explores this society's religious pluralism. The other pertinent publication by Professor Marty is the first in his projected four-volume work called Modern American Religion. This first piece, *The Irony of It All: 1893–1919,* documents what he feels was the beginning of the gradual decline of the white, Anglo-Saxon Protestants' dominance.

R. Laurence Moore has written a book that was preceded by an essay that is discussed in the body of this bibliography (see p. 196). *Religious Outsiders and the Making of Americans* sets out to challenge many of the assumptions upon which American religious history has been written—that includes a challenge to the premises upon which many of the books in this bibliography are based. Professor Moore contends that American religious diversity has been subordinated to themes of Protestant unity and dominance, and that in actuality, religious "outsiders" have played important roles in shaping American identities around religious identities. To back up his claims, the author looks at Mormons, Catholics, Jews, Christian Scientists, Millennialists, twentieth-century Protestant fundamentalists, and black churches as well as the role of religious persecution in American history. Alternative religion receives attention in *The Dark Lord: Cult Images and the Hare Krishnas in America* by Larry D. Shinn. While examining one movement in particular, the author presents general notions about the true nature of such movements.

Other books look at specific regions or people. One such contribution, *Broken Churches, Broken Nations: Denominational Schisms and the Coming of the American Civil War* by C. C. Goen, explores denominational schisms and how they contributed to the break-up of the Union in 1861.

Soul Theology: The Heart of American Black Culture by Henry H. Mitchell and Nicholas Cooper Lewter focuses on the beliefs that are at the core of black culture in America. *A Testament of Hope: The Essential Writings of Martin Luther King, Jr.,* edited by James M. Washington, presents some of the multitude of Dr. King's works. Another recent publication focusing on the black heritage is *Afro-American Religious History: A Documentary Witness,* edited by Milton C. Sernett. This volume contains a collection of documents illustrating black religious history in the United States. As this work is billed as the first comprehensive collection of the above-mentioned documents, it should prove to be a very useful tool for researchers delving into studies to enhance understandings of the black religious community's place in American religious history.

One book selected for inclusion in this collection is not in the final listing. *Significations: Experience and Images in Black American Religion* by Charles H. Long was originally scheduled for publication in 1985; however, business complications prevented this from happening. This work was described as a cross-disciplinary work studying the phenomenon of religion in general, the black religion in the American context, and the methodology and practice of hermeneutical retrieval. Professor Long's book was made available to students in 1987 through Fortress Press—too late to receive adequate attention in this bibliography.

Dynamic Judaism: The Essential Writing of Mordecai M. Kaplan edited by Emanuel S. Goldsmith and Mel Scult; *The Utopian Dilemma: American Judaism and Public Policy* by Murray Friedman; *A Certain People:*

American Jews and Their Lives Today by Charles F. Silberman; and *And Dawn in the West* by Allan Tarshish and edited by Sefton D. Temkin present valuable information about the various strands of thought and slighted historical materials important for understanding the place of Jews in American culture through time. Joseph R. Washington, Jr., has edited a book of essays that address the tensions between Jews and blacks in America called *Jews in Black Perspective: A Dialogue*. These essays, which were originally presented at a conference in 1982, represent diverse scholarly fields ranging from ethics, to history, to philosophy, to religion.

Books cited

Bellah, Robert H., and Frederick E. Greenspahn, eds. *Uncivil Religion: Interreligious Hostility in America*. New York: Crossroad Publishing, 1987.

Bloch, Ruth. *Visionary Republic: Millennial Themes in American Thought, 1756–1800*. New York: Cambridge University Press, 1985.

Friedman, Murray. *The Utopian Dilemma: American Judaism and Public Policy*. Washington, DC: Ethics and Public Policy Center, 1985.

Goen, C. C. *Broken Churches, Broken Nations: Denominational Schisms and the Coming of the American Civil War*. Macon: Mercer University Press, 1986.

Goldsmith, Emanuel S., and Mel Scult, eds. *Dynamic Judaism: The Essential Writings of Mordecai M. Kaplan*. New York: Schocken Books/The Reconstructionist Press, 1985.

Heimert, Alan, and Andrew Delbanco. *The Puritans in America: A Narrative Anthology*. Cambridge: Harvard University Press, 1985.

Johnson, James Turner, ed. *The Bible in American Law, Politics and Religion*. Philadelphia: Fortress Press, and Chico: Scholars Press, 1986.

Long, Charles H. *Significations: Experience and Images in Black American Religion*. Philadelphia: Fortress Press, 1987.

Lovin, Robin M., ed. *Religion and American Public Life: Interpretations and Explorations*. Mahwah, NJ: Paulist Press, 1986.

Mabee, Charles. *Reimagining America: A Theological Critique of the American Mythos and Biblical Hermeneutics*. Macon: Mercer University, 1985.

Marty, Martin E. *The Irony of It All: 1893–1900*. Chicago: University of Chicago Press, 1986.

———. *Religion and Republic: The American Circumstance*. Boston: Beacon Press, 1987.

Miller, William Lee. *The First Liberty: Religion and the American Republic*. New York: Alfred A. Knopf, 1986.

Mitchell, Henry H., and Nicholas Cooper Lewter. *Soul Theology: The Heart of American Black Culture*. New York: Harper and Row, 1986.

Moore, R. Laurence. *Religious Outsiders and the Making of Americans*. New York: Oxford University Press, 1986.

Reichley, A. James. *Religion in American Public Life*. Washington, DC: The Brookings Institution, 1986.

Roof, Wade Clark. *Religion in America Today*. Beverly Hills: Sage Publications, 1985.

————, and William McKinney. *American Mainline Religion: Its Changing Shape and Future*. New Brunswick: Rutgers University Press, 1987.

Rouner, Leroy S., ed. *Civil Religion and Political Theology*. Notre Dame: University of Notre Dame Press, 1986.

Sernett, Milton C., ed. *Afro-American Religious History: A Documentary Witness*. Durham: Duke University Press, 1986.

Shinn, Larry D. *The Dark Lord: Cult Images and the Hare Krishnas in America*. Philadelphia: The Westminster Press, 1987.

Silberman, Charles E. *A Certain People: American Jews and Their Lives Today*. Boston: Summit, 1986.

Singer, Marcus, G., ed. *American Philosophy*. New York: Cambridge University Press, 1985.

Stout, Harry S. *The New England Soul: Preaching and Religious Culture in Colonial New England*. New York: Oxford University Press, 1986.

Tarshish, Allan. Edited by Sefton D. Temkin. *And Dawn in the West*. Lanham: University Press of America, 1985.

Turner, James. *Without God, Without Creed: The Origins of Unbelief in America*. Baltimore: The Johns Hopkins University Press, 1985.

Washington, James M., ed. *A Testament of Hope: The Essential Writings of Martin Luther King, Jr.* San Francisco: Harper and Row, 1986.

Washington, Joseph R., Jr., ed. *Jews in Black Perspective: A Dialogue*. Rutherford, NJ: Fairleigh Dickinson Press, 1984.

Williams, David R. *Wilderness Lost: The Religious Origins of the American Mind*. Selinsgrove: Susquehanna University Press, and London: Associated University Presses, 1987.

Wood, James, Jr., ed. *Religion and the State: Essays in Honor of Leo Pfeffer*. Waco: Baylor University Press, 1985.

Index of Authors

Index of Titles